Globalizing Family Values

The Christian Right in International Politics

Doris Buss and Didi Herman

University of Minnesota Press
Minneapolis / London

Parts of chapter 2 were previously published as "Globalism's Siren Song: The United Nations and International Law in Christian Right Thought and Prophecy," by Didi Herman, in *Sociological Review* 49, no. 1 (2001): 56–77.

Published by the University of Minnesota Press
111 Third Avenue South, Suite 290
Minneapolis, MN 55401-2520
http://www.upress.umn.edu

Library of Congress Cataloging-in-Publication Data

Buss, Doris.
   Globalizing family values : the Christian right in international politics / Doris Buss and Didi Herman.
      p.   cm.
   Includes bibliographical references and index.
   ISBN 0-8166-4207-9 (alk. paper) — ISBN 0-8166-4208-7 (pbk. : alk. paper)
   1. Christianity and international affairs—History.   2. Conservatism—Religious aspects—Christianity—History.   3. Fundamentalism—Political aspects—History.   I. Herman, Didi.   II. Title.
BR115.I7 B87 2003
327.1—dc21

                                          2002153273

Printed in the United States of America on acid-free paper

The University of Minnesota is an equal-opportunity educator and employer.

12 11 10 09 08 07 06 05 04 03   10 9 8 7 6 5 4 3 2 1

To our mothers

Betty Maria Buss and Nina Klowden Herman

Contents

Acknowledgments

This project owes much to the generosity of many people who took the time to listen to our ideas, read drafts of chapters, forward information of interest, and express general but invaluable support. In particular, and at the risk of forgetting some names, we would like to thank Jim Beckford, Jutta Brunnée, Susan Boyd, Jennifer Butler, Davina Cooper (who read draft after draft at a moment's notice), Shelagh Day, Brian Dottery, Martin Durham, John Harrington, Karen Knop, Ambreena Manji, David Maxwell, Daniel Monk, Kelly Prince, Sally Sheldon, Carl Stychin, Ken Wald, Clyde Wilcox, Jutta Zalud, and our colleagues in the Gender, Sexuality, and Law Research Group. Thanks also to Carrie Mullen, our editor at the University of Minnesota Press, for her help and encouragement.

We thank the activists who gave their time for interviews and, in some cases, opened their libraries to us.

Research for this book could not have been undertaken without the support of Keele University and our colleagues in the Department of Law. Both provided us with the intellectual stimulation and room to develop this project. We gratefully recognize the financial assistance of the Junior Research Award scheme of Keele University, the Leverhulme Trust, and the Nuffield Foundation.

No acknowledgment would be complete without recognizing the warmth and support we receive from our friends and families. Davina and Jo are, of course, central to it all and to whom we owe the biggest thanks. Whether it's proofreading drafts, providing suggestions and encouragement, or giving rock scrambling tips, your help is essential and invaluable. An additional nod goes to Polly and Dotty and their unfailing willingness to walk the hills in whatever the weather.

While we were writing this book, a close friend and academic colleague, Marlee Kline, died of cancer. To say that Marlee was inspirational, personally and professionally, does not really capture what we would like to acknowledge. Marlee has been, and will remain, a part of us.

Abbreviations

CCA	Catholic Campaign for America
CDF	Congregation for the Doctrine of the Faith
CEDAW	Convention on the Elimination of All Forms of Discrimination Against Women
C-Fam	Catholic Family and Human Rights Institute
CR	Christian Right
CR UN	Christian Right at the United Nations
CWA	Concerned Women for America
FRC	Family Research Council
HLI	Human Life International
ICCPD	The 1994 Cairo Conference on Population and Development
ILGA	International Lesbian and Gay Association
NGO	nongovernmental organization
NWO	new world order
PRI	Population Research Institute
RI	Rockford Institute
UDHR	Universal Declaration of Human Rights
UN	United Nations
UNFPA	United Nations Population Fund
UNHCR	United Nations High Commissioner for Refugees
WCFII	World Congress of Families II
WFPC	World Family Policy Center
WHO	World Health Organization

Introduction

Imperatives for the future include:
To take energetic action within the NGO process to blunt or prevent new assaults on family integrity; to identify, protect, and help advance existing "friends of the family" within the U.N. Secretariat; to "place" such friends in positions of current or potential influence within the U.N. Secretariat; and to build an international movement of "religiously grounded family morality systems" that can influence and eventually shape social policy at the United Nations.

Allan Carlson, *The New Agrarian Mind*

In the final days of the twentieth century, a remarkable conference took place in Geneva, Switzerland. The opening event, a plenary gathering in the imposing United Nations Palais, was addressed by, among others, Raymonde Martineau, the United Nations Head of Non-Governmental Organization Relations; Jehan Sadat, the wife of assassinated Egyptian president Anwar Sadat; and George Haley, the American ambassador to Gambia. Among the conference's sessions were "A Life-long Covenant of Marriage," "The Needs of Children," and "The Family at the UN." This conference, World Congress of Families II (WCFII), brought together conservative religious activists representing the three monotheistic faiths from around the world, and it was only one step in an unfolding effort to build a global alliance of orthodox faiths to counter the perceived liberal dominance of the international legal and political arena. The objective of WCFII and similar events has been to form a global, orthodox community of political actors, ostensibly bringing conservative Jewish and Muslim interests into what is primarily a Christian Right (CR) movement.

Such an alliance clearly represents faiths that are, on several levels, opposed theologically. As competing monotheisms, each belief system has a long history of mutual antagonism. Nevertheless, the WCFII is an example of the curious global alliance, arguably pragmatic, expedient, temporary, and inherently unstable, between conservative Christians, Muslims, and, to a lesser extent, Jews, that emerged around a "natural family" agenda at the end of the twentieth century. In the words of the Howard Center, one of the leading CR actors in our text:

> The World Congress of Families coalition model represents the final option for an effective pro-family movement worldwide. All coalition members, usually orthodox religious believers, are asked to set aside their own personal theological and cultural differences and agree on one simple, unifying concept: the natural family is the fundamental unit of society. If coalition members can agree on this concept, then all of their other disagreements take a back seat.[1]

The WCFII represented a new sophistication on the part of American activists: the recognition that conservative social change, at the global level, requires a networked alliance of orthodoxies. Yet, despite attempts to diversify participation at the WCFII, American conservative Christians predominated among delegates, speakers, and organizers. Thus, the WCFII heralded, perhaps more than anything else, the arrival of the U.S. Christian Right on the United Nations scene. This book is an analysis of the American Christian Right's contribution to the upsurge in conservative religious activism in international forums.

We have narrowed the focus of our study to examine, most closely, the CR's global activism to defend and promote what it calls the "natural family." In terms of international activism, it is through the deployment of "natural family" discourse that the CR has had the most success in forging global alliances with other conservative religious movements. Spatially, our concern is with developments in international legal arenas, most specifically at the United Nations. In terms of temporality, we high-light the 1990s and the early twenty-first century, a period of CR emergence and consolidation on the international scene. Our intention in this book is to examine the CR sectors involved in UN activism and to assess to what extent the CR has been successful in achieving its ambitions for international law and policy. Perhaps most important, we seek to explore the CR's "global vision"—to understand how and why the CR constructs international space and politics in the ways that it does.

An understanding of the CR's international vision in the area of family-oriented activism is important for several reasons. In addition to their involvement in intensive international missionary work (see Brouwer, Gifford, and Rose 1996), the CR is a powerful movement with the ability and talent to influence international policy making; indeed, it has already done so. Some examples of successful CR impact include providing significant leadership to the anti-UN movement in the United States; injecting an antiabortion ethos into international population policy and aid; maintaining pressure on the U.S. government to remain a nonsignatory to international human rights conventions; influencing the content of final drafts of documents, such as the 1995 Platform for Action of the Fourth World Conference on Women in Beijing; monitoring the activities of UN-sponsored bodies such as UNESCO and the World Health Organization; and providing an extensive critique of the perceived "global liberal agenda."

As well as assessing the impact of CR international politics, we argue that a comprehensive analysis of the CR's domestic agenda is not possible without understanding how that agenda is intimately locked into a global program of action. The American CR is not simply interested in combating "secular liberalism" on American soil; rather, the CR is intent on both internationalizing its domestic concerns and shaping its domestic activism in light of CR global understandings. Another motivation for our study is that international orthodox alliances, for example between conservative Christianity and conservative Islam, are proving to be significant actors in global politics. This was the case at both the 1994 Cairo Conference on Population and Development and its five-year review (Cairo +5), and, more recently, at the five-year review of the Beijing Women's Conference, where a relatively united international religious orthodoxy proved a formidable opponent to feminist activists.

Despite the CR's level of global activism, and, to a certain degree, success, academic analysis of the CR's international politics has been thin at best. Within the social sciences, for example, work on conservative religious forces has tended to focus on the political agenda and cultural life of various orthodoxies in a national or domestic context, the most comprehensive treatment of which can be found in Marty and Appleby's five-volume "Fundamentalism" series (1991; 1993b; 1993c; 1994; 1995; see also Caplan 1987b; Misztal and Shupe 1992b; Smidt and Penning 1997; Smith 1996). Even studies that discuss "religion and global politics" ignore the international political sphere represented by the United Nations (e.g., Haynes 1998; Rudolph and Piscatori 1997; Turner 1991, chapter 9). And while the American CR itself has been subject to a wide range of scholarly interest (Bromley and Shupe 1984; Bruce 1990; Diamond 1989, 1995, 1998; Durham 2000; Liebman and Wuthnow 1983; Moen 1992; Smidt and Penning 1997; Wilcox 1992, 1996), almost all of this work focuses exclusively on developments within U.S. national space (see, however, Lienesch 1993, chapter 5; Martin 1999). Similarly, Brouwer, Gifford, and Rose's (1996) global study of American "fundamentalism" concentrates on missionary activities in specific locales, rather than CR international political mobilization. In the United States, CR organizations, such as the Family Research Council or Concerned Women for America, may be household names, but their international activities are far less well known. While there are CR "monitoring" sites throughout the Web,[2] very few progressive organizations have begun to compile information on the international CR presence (but see Butler 2000; Druelle 2000). Sara Diamond goes so far as to say that the CR has no intention of fundamentally remaking society, and, additionally, that "there has been little movement focus on international affairs" (1998, 7). We disagree with both these statements. One of our aims here, then, is to begin to uncover these neglected aspects of CR politics.

A similar lacuna exists in the vast literature on globalization and transnational social movements. Peter Beyer, for example, author of the influential *Religion and Globalization,* tends to underplay the international significance of a CR he describes as "waning" (1994, 132). Roland Robertson, an acknowledged "guru" of globalization theory, including in the context of religion, generally appears to overlook the importance of United Nations–type forums (1991a). Equally, other accounts, for example of international law reform and social movement struggle, have tended to neglect religious actors. Although critical work on the women's movement

(Buss 1998, 2000b; Charlesworth 1996; Chen 1996; Higer 1999; Joachim 1999; Miller 1999; Stienstra 1995; Tinker 1999; West 1999) and the lesbian and gay movement (Morgan 2000; Sanders 1996) in international human rights law has emerged in recent years, few scholars have turned their attention to the considerable inroads being made in international law and policy by conservative religious alliances (but see Buss 1998, 2000a). For example, Keck and Sikkink (1998a), in their important analysis of international advocacy networks, give the CR virtually no attention at all.[3] Arguably, although there has been some study of "transnational religion" (i.e., Rudolph and Piscatori 1997), the dimensions of CR politics in international legal arenas have been significantly overlooked in the social science literature.[4]

We argue that the emergence of CR global activism, and, more broadly, a conservative religious alliance at the UN, are both part of, and a response to, a developing international political landscape in which social justice issues—from human rights to international trade—are the subject of discussion and negotiation by a diversity of actors. We do not herald CR international activism as contributing to a democratization of the international sphere that is sometimes said to accompany globalization (Falk 1987; Thiele 1993), nor do we bemoan it as an example "of a totalitarian or proto-totalitarian solution offered to all those who find the burden of individual freedom excessive and unbearable" (Bauman 1998, 74). Rather, we explore changing CR politics and theology in the context of an emerging global consciousness, in which the world is conceived and theorized, to use a now trite phrase, as "a single place" (see Held et al. 1999; R. Robertson 1992b; Waters 1995).

Whether it is around "theories of globalization" or about the activities of anarchic protestors against global capitalism, much has been written and spoken of concerning the impact of new technologies, dissolving borders, rootless capital, and a host of other developments. Partly as a result of the very international developments that concern the CR, a number of issues have become key sites of debate at both the local and global levels. Environmental concerns are clearly part of this evolution, as are debates about human rights, world trade, and debt relief. Though few of these issues are entirely "new," they have taken on new forms and significance in the context of increasingly networked global forums (see also Keck and Sikkink 1998a; O'Brien et al. 2000) and an invigorated international public sphere. The ascendancy of CR politics at the

United Nations is both a response to and a product of these developments. Our project, then, constitutes a contribution to filling these two lacunae: the neglect of the CR's international activism in studies of the CR itself, and the overlooking of the CR as an international actor in the literature on globalization and social movements.

Terminology and Definitions

Christian Right

The first and probably most important term we need to define is "Christian Right." There is no "correct" way to define this phrase; it is used by a range of scholars to mean similar but different things. Others might prefer the term "fundamentalist" to describe the movement that is the focus of our inquiry (Lawrence 1989, 1998); however, for various reasons, we have chosen not to use that term.[5] Thus, in our view, what is important is making clear why we use the term "Christian Right" (CR) and what we mean by it. We use the term CR to refer to a broad range of American organizations that have tended to form coalitions, both domestic and international, around an orthodox Christian vision and a defense of the traditional nuclear family formation, referred to by the CR as the "natural family."[6] Although domestically CR political activism often focuses on issues such as gay rights and school vouchers, internationally the CR's main concerns are United Nations population policy, women's rights, and children's rights. The "natural family" agenda also encompasses a range of related issues, such as the welfare state, environmentalism, and development and foreign aid, on which CR organizations take different and sometimes conflicting positions. We thus do not see the CR as a monolithic movement speaking in unison (even if our terminology at times suggests this), or even one that necessarily shares a unified normative vision in relation to a range of sociopolitical issues.

Perhaps controversially, we include neoconservative Catholics (Weigel 1995) in our definition of the CR (see generally Cuneo 1997a; Weaver and Appleby 1995). Although the relationship between the Protestant and Catholic Right is an uneasy one *within* the United States (Appleby 1997; Bendyna et al. 2000), in terms of global activism, particularly at UN venues, the organizations and individuals we discuss act as a unified bloc. Further, as we discuss below and elaborate on in chapter 1, there is reason to think that American conservative Protestants and Catholics are, in recent years, sharing more ground theologically. This observation also resonates with studies that show a growing political rapprochement between different conservative Christian denominations within the United States (Wilcox, Rozell, and Gunn 1996; see also Wuthnow 1988).

This development also underlies why we include conservative Mormons in our definition of the CR (Butler 2000, 6–8; White 1986). We do not consider ultraconservative Mormon splinter groups as part of the CR (see Introvigne 1997, 39–42), but rather those individuals and organizations associated with the Church of Latter Day Saints (see generally Mauss 1994). American Mormon organizations have taken a leading role in constructing a global, conservative, religious network, and, we argue, are legitimately characterized as CR activists.[7] Our decision to include them in our definition has resonances with scholarly work on Mormon "retrenchment," which argues that late twentieth-century mainstream Mormonism became increasingly conservative and "fundamentalist" in outlook (Mauss 1994, chapter 12; Mauss and Barlow 1991).

Although the different ideologies informing the various CR groups can result in theoretical and strategic difficulties, both for them and for interested academics, we would argue that the term "Christian Right" remains a useful category for describing and explaining the loose and diverse coalition with which we are concerned. The organizations we discuss under the umbrella term "CR" are united in a shared opposition to a perceived "global liberal agenda," and, in particular, to "international feminism" and "secular humanism." The CR shares a belief in a divinely ordered set of relations within the family, the nation, and the church, with each essential to the other. Most fundamentally, the CR groups we discuss cohere around a shared conviction that conservative Christians must form a bulwark against encroaching liberalism and the chaos it represents. Thus, the term "Christian Right" is essential in characterizing the very particular relationship between theology and politics that informs the international activism of this movement. Notwithstanding what we have just said, there are points in our text where we believe it is important to distinguish between different CR sectors, and so, where appropriate, we refer to the Protestant, Catholic, or Mormon Right specifically.

A question that could be asked is, why do we not use the term "religious right"? We have deliberately avoided that phrase because, we argue, it obscures and occludes the real religious basis to the movement, namely, a belief in Jesus as the son of God and Savior, the "truth" of the

New Testament (of particular relevance to our themes, the words of Revelation), and, importantly, a denial to non-Christian faiths of legitimate authenticity and value. While conservative American Jewish and Islamic organizations have, on occasion, made alliances with the CR (see, e.g., Redman 1993), it is, in our view, wholly inaccurate to speak of a unified "religious right" in relation to the issues we discuss in this book. Indeed, one of the key themes of our project is to explore to what extent the CR has been successful in building an international orthodox alliance, both for its own internal politics and coherence and in terms of wider questions of sustainability and impact (see, in particular, chapter 5).

We should also note that not included in our definition of the CR are survivalist, militia, and race-based organizations (see Aho 1990, 1996; Barkun 1994; Coates 1987; Lamy 1997). In fact, we are particularly interested in the ways in which the CR has distanced itself from these organizations and their inward-looking, separatist politics. We do not argue that the CR, as we have defined it, has a race-based theology or politics, although as a social movement it is overwhelmingly white at both leadership and constituency levels, despite attempts by some CR organizations to build more racial diversity (Calhoun-Brown 1997, 1998; Diamond 1998, chapter 11; Durham 2000, chapter 2). Similarly, our CR does not operate outside the rule of law. On the contrary, this book is concerned with the CR's activities in international legal forums. Thus, the global network of "Christian extremists" does not concern us here.[8]

Christian Right at the United Nations

Having said all this, we nevertheless have further refined our terminology to reflect the very particular conjunction of CR groups active at the United Nations. We refer to this grouping as CR UN. Our rationale for distinguishing the CR UN from the CR as a whole is threefold. At a spatial level, the operation of the CR UN is different from that of the domestic CR. This contrast is evident, for example, when analyzing the relationship between the CR UN, the state, and civil society. The CR UN's ideology reflects its engagement in the international sphere and is noticeably divergent, in certain areas, from that of the domestic CR. Second, there are conflicting agendas between the CR UN and the domestic CR, most particularly, for our purposes, around the very fact of UN activism itself. Third, the alliances the CR UN is prepared to make, for example with so-called Islamic "pariah" states (particularly in the aftermath of the September 11 attacks), are a very visible parting of company with the CR as a whole.

So, although the CR UN conforms to our definition of "CR" above, there are additional factors that justify a further refinement. We are not suggesting a clear division between the CR and the CR UN, however; indeed, many of the CR UN organizations, for example the Family Research Council and Concerned Women for America, are leading domestic CR actors. We thus discuss the difficulties CR UN groups have reconciling their domestic politics with their strategic pragmatism in international legal arenas. We would not, therefore, argue that the CR UN is a "global" or "transnational" social movement in itself (see, generally, Colàs 2002, 76; O'Brien et al. 2000; Smith 1997); rather, we would say that CR groups active at the UN are a particular subset of the U.S. Christian Right as a whole. As we go on to discuss in chapter 6, the CR UN's efforts to establish a single alliance of orthodox believers at the UN has the makings of a global social movement. But as we demonstrate, that alliance remains uncertain at this stage.

Finally, a word about the Vatican (see also Hanson 1987; Keely 1994; Reese 1996). In this book, we explore the role of the Vatican at the UN in terms of how it is providing informal leadership and continuity to the sometimes fledgling international "natural family" movement. However, the Vatican's unique status as a Permanent Observer at the UN, together with its arguably more welfarist economic ideology, sets it apart, in our view, from other CR actors. Its centrality to CR politics at the UN, however, means that the Vatican's own policies and actions are an essential aspect to any work on this emerging orthodox alliance. Thus, although we do not "count" the Vatican as a "CR UN actor," we devote a chapter to exploring its role and politics vis-à-vis the CR UN.

Globalization

Another important term we need to define is "globalization." A perhaps overused word, the topic of globalization has spawned a vast body of literature and academic debate, not all of which is relevant to this text. For our purposes, "globalization" refers to a "deepening internationalization" (Camilleri 1995, 211) of issues, structures, and consciousness brought about by a growing interconnectedness in economic, political, and cultural spheres. Our interest in this book is less on the (disputed) aspects of global structural change (Colàs 2002, 149) and more on the cultural consequences of this growing sense of interconnectedness (Eschle 2001, 77). In particular, we tend to use "globalization" to refer to the circumstances yielding a changing consciousness in which issues relating to such things as the environment, human rights, and economics are seen as having global, rather than just national, significance. The "internationalization" of these issues is a product, among other things, of a deepening interdependence of global economic structures and the emergence of a global "mindset," referred to by Roland Robertson as "globality": the "extensive awareness of the world as a whole" (1992b, 78). One of the by-products of these developments is a rethinking of the ways in which self and community are conceived and reconceived in a changing world order (R. Robertson 1991b, 72; 1992b, 27; Stevenson 1997, 51). We agree with Robertson's argument that part of "global consciousness" is a definition of "the world as an 'imagined community'" (1992b, 183). Our analysis of the CR UN, in the context of globalization, is thus a consideration, not just of its conceptions of the "global," but of a worldview in which definitions of self, community, and "other" are subject to renegotiation.

Central to much of the academic work on globalization in political science, international relations, and law is an exploration of the diminished or reconfigured nation-state. While a review of this literature is beyond the scope of the book, we are interested in the "flip side" of this issue—the resulting redefinition of political space in the context of changing conceptions of the local, the global, self, and community. The mechanisms of globalization—capital and labor mobility, technological compression of time and space, the emergence of a "global culture" (Camilleri 1995, 224)—have, in various ways, redefined the role of the nation-state. While the sovereign state remains the central international actor, its authority has been reconstituted (Held and McGrew 1998, 236–37) and, in some cases, superseded by global processes and institutions. At the end of the twentieth century, this reconstitution is manifest in the growing number of spaces in which law and policy can be contested by nonstate actors. We focus here on political spaces that are both separate from, and reconstitutive of, the domestic realm of the state and the sphere of "international relations," defined in terms of interactions between states (see Camilleri 1995, 217; Clark 1999; Deacon 1997; Falk 1987; Jarvis and Paolini 1995).

These international political spaces have become, for good or bad, a "central terrain for social movements" (Waterman 2000, 135). The growth in the number of groups that operate at the international level to promote social change—sometimes referred to as "international civil society"[9]—has impacted both the process and the substance of international policy making (Keck and Sikkink 1998a, 19–28, 203; O'Brien et al. 2000). The formalized inclusion of nongovernmental organizations in UN operations, including treaty negotiations, has raised the profile of the NGO sector, giving NGOs unprecedented access to international decision makers (Clark, Friedman, and Hochstetler 1998, 6, 22–23). Nowhere is this more apparent than in the growing practice of including NGO representatives on state delegations to UN meetings and conferences.

The growth of international civil society parallels developments to strengthen and expand international regimes in a number of areas, including human rights, environmental law, and international trade. This increasing regulation of affairs between and among states is symptomatic—and constitutive—of the processes of globalization and global social change (Scholte 1993, 75–77; see also Held and McGrew 1998). Regime building has, in some areas such as human rights and the environment, been conducted largely through interstate conferences at which NGOs are present and have limited rights of access. NGOs have seized on regime building in these areas as a "focal point for a number of strivings for social transformation" (Scholte 1993, 77; see also Lipschutz 1996). Thus, under the broad rubric of the "environment" or "human rights," NGOs have succeeded in extending the spheres of international discourse (Keck and Sikkink 1998a, 203), placing on the agenda topics ranging from gender equality and sexual orientation to global structural inequality.

This expanding political activity is both a product of, and a contributor to, an emerging global political culture at the heart of which is a discourse on international human rights. This "global political culture," in our understanding, refers to neither a homogenization nor a hybridization of culture (Holton 2000; see generally Featherstone 1990). Rather, it is intimately tied to Robertson's definition of globality: the conception of issues as having global or transnational significance. This global consciousness, together with emerging political spaces, has enabled a global political engagement around social justice issues. That engagement, we argue, mobilizes and further entrenches a global political practice predicated upon certain "keywords" (Appadurai 1990, 300), of which human rights and democracy are central. These key words may be used in support of very different worldviews, but their use signals a shared "sense of the structure of the entire world in its modern (or postmodern) form" (Robertson 1992a, 403). International human rights, and its institutionalization as a legal regime, has become a dominant framework within which to argue for, contest, and evaluate social justice standards (Simpson 1992, 21). While rights discourse may reflect a particular western bias, it has become, for good or bad, a global language of empowerment and a key means by which various social movements have advanced their global agendas. As we go on to show, the human rights of women (to control their own fertility) and increasingly of lesbians and gays to equality, is the central topic/terrain on which CR UN politics is situated.

The emergence of an international civil society and the apparent radicalization of international debate is seen by some as heralding a new democratic world order (Held 1995; Lipschultz 1996): a form of world community and global citizenship (see, for example, Falk 2000; Linklater 1998). In this view, the infusion of nonstate actors is viewed as helping to move the world "community" toward some kind of a "cosmopolitan" democracy (Archibugi and Held 1995; Held and McGrew 1998, 241–42). The common thread to these arguments is a celebration of global change as heralding the possibility of transformative politics.

CR mobilization at the international level needs to be seen as a response and commitment to this emerging political landscape. An invigorated international civil society has placed issues like women's rights and sexual equality on the international agenda, which alarms the CR. Thus, on one level, CR UN politics is a form of "antiglobalism"; an opposition to this perceived globalization of social relations. We agree with Roland Robertson that the CR's "antiglobalism" is itself an outcome of global consciousness. While at one level rejecting the idea of "globality," CR UN activism is "held to a significant degree in 'subliminal thrall' by that which they oppose" (Robertson 1992b, 80). But, crucially, this study demonstrates that the CR UN is not simply reacting *against* globalization, it also embraces the international realm as a space for conservative social change. We thus concur with Vásquez and Marquardt, who argue that contemporary religious activism, in the context of globalization, should not be understood "in negative terms, as a lack, anomie or any other social pathology" (2000, 139; see also Harding 1991). In our analysis, conservative religious actors, such as the CR UN, are both "antimodern and distinctively modern" (Robertson 1992b, 170); they are "antisystemic and prosystemic at the same time" (Beyer 1994, 3), opposed to globalization while advancing it. In an important comment on some of these themes, Lechner has put it thus:

> [Fundamentalism] actively strives to reorder society; it reasserts the validity of a tradition and uses it in new ways; it operates in a context that sets nontraditional standards; where it does not take decisive control, it reproduces the dilemmas it sets out to resolve; as one active force among others, it affirms the depth of modern pluralism; it takes on the tensions produced by the clash between a universalizing global culture and particular local conditions; it expresses fundamental uncertainty in a crisis setting, not traditional confidence about taken-for-granted truths; by defending God, who formerly needed no defense, it creates and recreates difference as part of a global cultural struggle. So compromised, fundamentalism becomes part of the fabric of modernity. (1993, 30)

International Legal Arenas

The final term we wish to outline at this stage concerns a key terrain on which the CR UN and globalization encounter each other: the international legal arena. While the CR UN is intimately involved with the domestic politics of many states (Brouwer, Gifford, and Rose 1996), our text is about the supranational spaces where the CR is currently engaged in fighting battles over what, and whose, ideology will prevail globally. The terrain of international law and policy, particularly human rights, is an obvious and important point of focus.

For the most part, the CR UN's global activities in international legal forums take place at the United Nations and at UN-sponsored events. Starting with the 1992 UN Conference on the Environment and Development in Rio de Janeiro, the 1990s emerged as the decade of the UN-hosted international conference. These conferences are, formally, meetings of state representatives to negotiate consensual agreements governing international and domestic action in a variety of areas, from the environment to human rights to housing. Despite this rather dry sounding description, informally the UN conference has become a large, loud, and dynamic forum attracting a panoply of nongovernmental organizations. In addition to the main conference, at which state delegates meet and negotiate complex language for inclusion in a final agreement, NGOs often hold parallel meetings where more controversial proposals and ideas are discussed. NGO representatives are then given limited rights of attendance at the main conference, where they meet with and lobby state representatives (Charlesworth 1996; Clark, Friedman, and Hochstetler 1998, 15).

The final agreements are often lengthy, technical documents setting out basic principles, objectives, and recommended state action. Although the consensual agreements are not binding in the same way as treaties, these plans of action are subject to intense negotiation where individual wording is scrutinized and hotly debated. Reflecting, in part, the influence of a diverse range of participants, the final agreements have often moved international law and policy into new and sometimes controversial directions. The final agreements resulting from the 1994 International Conference on Population and Development in Cairo, and the 1995 UN World Conference on Women in Beijing are two such examples.

In the early years of the twenty-first century, UN conferences continue to be important sites for negotiating and formulating international consensus. International conferences on racism (Durban 2001), HIV/AIDS (2001), and children (2002) maintained the tradition of the large, loud, and high profile UN-conference phenomena. Starting in 1999, the UN began conducting five-year reviews of previous agreements. Intended as a process to monitor the implementation of, and progress on, earlier commitments, these meetings, of which Cairo +5 and Beijing +5 are examples, have become controversial sessions at which the terms of the original agreements are discussed and what were once seen as settled issues are reopened (see Buss 2000a). As we discuss in chapters 3, 4, and 6, the CR UN has a significant presence and impact at these review meetings. In some respects, the CR UN's particular interest in the "+5" process is a reflection of its more recent organizational drive, as well as the impression that it "missed out" on influencing the original documents.

CR UN groups have also become increasingly interested in the more day-to-day functioning of the UN. Individual UN agencies and departments, such as the World Health Organization, UNICEF, and the UN Population Fund, are subject to intense scrutiny by the CR UN for their involvement in reproductive rights, abortion, and the rights of children. In addition, CR UN representatives attend the annual meetings of UN monitoring committees, such as the one overseeing the Convention on the Elimination of All Forms of Discrimination Against Women (CEDAW). International human rights conventions, such as CEDAW or the Convention on the Rights of the Child, establish these monitoring committees to receive state reports on compliance with the terms of the convention, and, in some limited cases, to hear complaints of human rights violations (Hannum 1992).

Some CR UN organizations attend UN forums as "ECOSOC-accredited NGOs," meaning they have been granted special NGO status through the UN's Economic and Social Council.[10] This process is more vigorous than that used at UN conferences, where a broader range of NGOs are authorized to attend and participate. A growing number of CR UN organizations have been granted ECOSOC accreditation, including the Concerned Women for America, the Couple to Couple League, the David M. Kennedy Center (sponsor of the World Family Policy Center), the Eagle Forum, the Real Women of Canada, and the Worldwide Organization of Women.

Actors and Activists

Our research for this book involved analyzing a mix of CR books, organizational publications, and Web site material. We also conducted interviews with several members of the CR active in UN forums (these interviews are included in the references list). We incorporate this interview material throughout our text. In addition, we attended the World Congress of Families II Conference in Geneva in 1999, and this experience informs the analysis in chapter 5. Our focus is partly on actors sometimes referred to in social science literature as "elite cadres"; in other words, we analyze the texts and discourses of individual and organizational CR UN leaders. To use another related phrase, our concern is with CR and CR UN "official discourse." Although this focus obviously limits and constrains our approach, the United Nations is an inherently "elite" forum; it is a place where social movement leaderships meet to engage politically with friends and enemies. In that sense, "street-level" or "rank-and-file" ideologies (e.g., Williams and Blackburn 1996) are less relevant. However, we have also interviewed several individuals who are, in fact, "street-level" actors, in the sense that they are the individuals actively promoting a CR "natural family" politics at the UN. Whether defined as elites or as street-level actors, they have become the front line in CR global politics. In this capacity, they are instrumental in building alliances, articulating CR positions on emerging international developments, writing press reports and activist briefings, and feeding back to the grassroots membership. As such, they have become "policy entrepreneurs" whose impact is not fairly captured by an "elite/street-level" distinction.

Catholic Family and Human Rights Institute

The main Catholic organization we discuss is the Catholic Family and Human Rights Institute (C-Fam), founded in 1997 by Human Life International. With its headquarters in New York City, C-Fam's mission is to monitor and lobby the UN "within the framework of the family as the fundamental unit of society."[11] Austin Ruse, C-Fam's president, is an active public speaker and prolific journalist. In addition to covering news items for Newsmax, an online conservative news service, Ruse, through C-Fam, distributes the "Friday Fax," a weekly e-mail bulletin detailing developments at the UN and mobilizing supporters to action.

Concerned Women for America and the Beverly LaHaye Institute

Concerned Women for America (CWA), and its partner, the Beverly LaHaye Institute, are important members of the Protestant Right (although they do claim a large Catholic membership). CWA, set up by Beverly LaHaye[12] in the 1980s, leads, together with the Eagle Forum (Phyllis Schlafly's flagship organization), the CR antifeminist movement in the United States. During the 1990s, CWA became a savvy participant in global politics; activists regularly attend UN/NGO conferences and other international venues and have had a great deal of success influencing agendas. The Beverly LaHaye Institute was inaugurated in 1999 as a CWA think tank—part of an explosion of CR social science research initiatives we focus on in chapter 1. The institute "recognizes the power of good data" and promises to "stand strong in defense of the family and biblical values" (CWA, "Description," n.d.).

The Family Research Council

Another key actor is the Family Research Council (FRC). Originally the more overtly political arm of Focus on the Family, James Dobson's Protestant Right, multimedia conglomeration, the FRC is now nominally separate.[13] FRC activists are vocal participants in international legal forums, and FRC publications, such as the *Insight* series, function as valuable position papers for the CR movement as a whole. The FRC is an active participant in the CR's global movement and has been instrumental in formulating "natural family" positions. For example, Thomas

Atwood of the FRC headed the drafting committee responsible for the WCFII's "Geneva Declaration."

The Howard Center

The Howard Center for Family, Religion, and Society, located in Rockford, Illinois, is another CR research center dedicated to affirming the "family and religion as the foundation of a virtuous and free society."[14] Although the Howard Center functions as a research think tank rather than an advocacy group per se, it provides a base for CR global activists (it is, for example, the headquarters of the World Congress of Families) and produces material that gives the movement its intellectual sustenance. Under the Howard Center umbrella are two specialized research units: the Family in America Studies Center and the Religion and Society Studies Center, which both publish monthly newsletters (*The Family in America* and *The Religion and Society Report*). Each publication reports on and analyzes sociopolitical change from a conservative Christian context. The Family in America Studies Center defends "the natural family as the source of social order" and its monthly report analyzes related issues and summarizes recent social science research, using a relatively secular-sounding discourse. The Religion and Society Studies Center assumes a more explicitly religious mantle, explaining and "celebrating the spiritual motivations and dimensions of current events" within an explicit "Christian framework."[15] Supplementing these two centers is the Swan Library, with a mission to "provide a clearinghouse of truthful and effective information" in support of "the natural family."[16]

The Howard Center has past connections to another nearby research center, the Rockford Institute (RI). Two of the Howard Center's most senior figures, Allan Carlson (1988; 1999a, b; 2000a, b, c) and Bryce Christensen (1990, 1991), are past senior officers of the Rockford Institute. Researchers there take a more nativist interest in global issues and produce a variety of materials, including the controversial journal *Chronicles*. The Rockford Institute proclaims itself to be "the authentic voice of the American Heartland," striving to "contribute to the renewal of Christendom in this time and place."[17]

Human Life International/The Population Research Institute

Human Life International (HLI), founded in 1972, operates worldwide and is an important force in uniting conservative Catholics. The HLI network, for example, played an important role in boosting participation from Catholics in developing countries at the WCFII in Geneva. HLI, like other antiabortion organizations, has long been critical of the UN Population Fund's policy of reducing population growth in the "developing world" (see chapter 4). HLI's monthly newsletter, *HLI Reports,* regularly includes stories on UN activity. An HLI affiliate, the Population Research Institute, founded in 1989 and located in Virginia, focuses exclusively on international population policy, defining its mandate as telling "the truth about population-related issues" while documenting "abuses of human rights in the name of population control."[18] In chapter 4, we examine the activities of the Population Research Institute and Stephen Mosher, its controversial president.

The Vatican

Although not included in our definition of the CR UN, for reasons outlined above, the Vatican is nonetheless one of the most important international conservative voices in the areas of gender, sexuality, and the family.[19] The Vatican, through the Holy See, has "Permanent Observer" status at the United Nations. As a Permanent Observer, the Holy See is entitled to rights of attendance and representation at the UN that are somewhat less than those given to a full state member, but more than those awarded to organizations with NGO status (see, generally, Kunz 1952). Because of this unusual status, the Vatican plays a key role in advancing *some* aspects of the CR agenda in forums to which CR UN organizations would otherwise not have access.

Indeed, the Vatican's status at the UN, together with its interventionist politics around women's rights issues, has prompted an outcry from feminist and women's groups, who argue that, as a religious body, the Vatican should not be given a special, statelike status at the UN. In 1998, women's groups, together with religious and reproductive rights organizations, formalized their objections into the "See Change" campaign, an initiative designed "to challenge the Vatican's power at the U.N. and to downgrade its status from a nonmember state to a traditional NGO" (Flanders 1999).[20]

World Family Policy Center, United Families International, Worldwide Organization for Women

We noted in our discussion of terminology that we were including conservative Mormons within our definition of the CR. There is no question that Mormons are playing an increasingly significant role in CR UN politics. Several organizations associated with Brigham Young University in Utah, most notably for our purposes the World Family Policy Center (formerly NGO Family Voice), have made important alliances with the Protestant and Catholic Right. The World Family Policy Center (WFPC) describes its mission "to provide worldwide democratic input and effectively educate the United Nations System on pro-family and other value-based issues" (World Family Policy Center n.d.). Richard Wilkins, the WFPC's managing director, was, along with Allan Carlson of the Howard Center, the driving force behind the development of the World Congress of Families. Former WFPC director Kathryn Balmforth is a leading figure on the CR UN, particularly in terms of antifeminist politics.[21] The international political effectivity of the WFPC is enhanced by its association with the ECOSOC-accredited David M. Kennedy Center for International Studies, also at Brigham Young University. Two other, still fairly fledgling Mormon organizations are also active internationally: United Families International and the Worldwide Organization for Women, which received ECOSOC accreditation in 1999.

Other Organizations

While the above organizations constitute the key "mainstream" CR UN bodies upon whose work we draw, there are other significant ones, some of them arguably more "fringe" (though not "extreme" as defined above). Thus, we also refer to publications produced by the John Birch Society, the Eagle Forum, and Real Women, a Canadian CR organization with ECOSOC accreditation. Real Women has been a fixture on the Canadian political scene for over a decade, where it defines its work as upholding "the Judeo-Christian understanding of marriage and family life."[22] Along with its American counterparts, Concerned Women for America and the Eagle Forum, Real Women has been very active internationally, sending delegates to the Beijing World Conference on Women and the Rome Conference on the International Criminal Court, among others. Their monthly online newsletter, *REALity*, includes regular reporting on international developments at the UN and elsewhere.

In addition to C-Fam and Human Life International, a growing number of smaller Catholic organizations are emerging on the international stage, such as the Couple to Couple League, the World Movement of Mothers, and the C-Fam offspring, World Youth Alliance, established to provide a conservative Christian "youth voice" at UN meetings. There are also a number of "right-to-life" groups active in UN fora, for example the International Right to Life Federation (accredited in 1987), the American Life League (accredited in 2000), and Campaign Life International Coalition (accredited in 1999).

The above, arguably disparate, organizations display an impressive ability to work together in the international realm. That they do so relatively well confirms the success of several "new" CR strategies identified by Rozell and Wilcox (1996), including rhetorical downsizing, coalition building, and political compromise. Recently, this fledgling alliance has found a new ally in the George W. Bush administration. The international policies of this presidency on issues such as abortion, funding for population policy (see chapter 5), and children's rights closely align with those of the CR UN. In addition, this administration is pursuing an active policy of building alliances at UN meetings with other like-minded states, including Iran and Sudan (see chapter 8). It is unclear at this early stage what effect the Bush presidency will have on the politics and strategies of the CR UN. As will become evident in the following chapters, some of the tactics and positions taken by the CR UN reflect its perception that, at least until recently, it was the only hope for the "natural" family globally. Its push for a unified opposition to feminist and globalist forces (chapters 4 and 6) and its attempt to build a global orthodox alliance (chapter 6) are, in many respects, predicated on the belief that the official sources of power—from individual state governments to the United Nations itself—are aligned against the "natural" family. The impact of George Bush on the global politics of the Christian Right is an unanswerable question at this stage but is a development worth watching.

Themes and Arguments

Understanding the "International"

A recurrent theme throughout the book is the way the CR UN understands the purpose and role of international institutions and events, in particular, the United Nations (chapters 2, 3, 4). We also examine how the CR UN constructs its international friends and enemies. We argue that the CR UN views global space as controlled by a number of anti-Christian forces, all working in concert to undermine the "natural family" and, even more fundamentally, religious belief itself. Despite this relatively coherent vision, however, the CR UN faces a series of obstacles, both philosophical and pragmatic, in combating what they call "the forces of globalism."

Politics and Theology

Another of the book's themes is the way the CR UN's understanding of "the global" is shaped by a theological foundation. We explore the relationship between politics and theology most directly in chapters 1 and 2, where we consider how the CR, and the CR UN in particular, envisions "the natural family," the relevance of the Second Coming, and the role of prophecy in helping to constitute the CR's political ideologies. Although theology is not the sole motivator or inspiration for CR UN global activism (see Hopson and Smith 1999), we argue that it cannot be fully understood without acknowledging the role played by theological belief systems. We also highlight the importance of taking theology seriously by tracing the links between the CR UN's secular discourse and its religious roots.

Christian Right Social Science

The CR UN does not rely on theology alone to inform its political activism. As we noted above, driving much of the CR UN's intellectual energy are organizations such as the Howard Center, modeled as think tanks. The "intellectualization" of the CR, particularly CR UN organizations, is therefore another theme we explore. The CR UN's constructions of "the global," while having a theological foundation, are reinforced and produced anew through a proliferation of studies offering scientific and academic authority for the CR's "natural family" politics, domestically and internationally. Interestingly, a great deal of this material relies on the expertise of Mormon lawyers and social scientists, as well as "ex" feminists (see chapter 1). We argue that the CR, in response to the perceived ideological and political successes of its feminist and gay rights opponents, has developed a powerful counterdiscourse. A potent mix of religious doctrine and social science, the CR's "new family theology" is anchoring its "natural family" politics, domestically and internationally.

Ideological Shifts and Transformations

CR ideology, whether theological or social science–based, is not static, unchanging, or uniform. We trace several ways that CR thought has shifted, often in response to external pressures and challenges. One example, discussed in chapters 1 and 6, is how the notion of "women's rights," once completely derided by the CR, has been reconceived, particularly among CR global actors. This transformation has resulted in the rehabilitation, in some CR circles, of even the word "feminist." Another example, analyzed in chapters 3 and 4 and traced throughout this volume, is how CR conceptions of "friends" and "enemies" have changed over time and in different contexts. With the end of the cold war, many scholars assumed that the CR would replace their archvillain communism with a new enemy, Islam (see, for example, Brouwer, Gifford, and Rose 1996, 18–19). CR UN attempts to build alliances with Islam have shown this assumption to be limited. Rather than look to Islam, the CR UN finds the threat to "nation, church, family," even in a post–September 11 world, in actors and institutions at the global level (see chapters 2, 3).

While the threat to the "natural family" may shift over time, what is clear is that in its relationship to the UN and in its courting of international allies, the CR UN is not attempting to simply exert "power over" others; CR UN politics are *not* about the CR simply trying to "export" its product abroad. Rather, the pattern of CR UN engagement with UN forums and international partners is a dynamic process involving the ongoing reconstitution of priorities, practicalities, and politics.

Domestic and International Tensions

Although a few of the CR organizations we discuss have been involved in global politics since the 1980s, for the most part the CR's international activism, particularly at the UN, is a new development. The decision to participate in UN forums has, for the CR, entailed compromise and pragmatic shifts in outlook. As a result, a continuing uncertainty is evident within CR UN organizations concerning their level of commitment and long-term objectives, with the needs and aspirations of the global activists conflicting with, or posing a challenge to, domestic politics and expectations. This is particularly noticeable, for example, in tensions over the UN's continued existence. Many CR organizations active on the U.S. domestic front, such as Concerned Women for America or the Eagle Forum, are committed to an isolationist politics opposed to any role for the United States in international organizations such as the UN. In chapter 3, we explore how this isolationist stance may conflict with the CR's international activism, ostensibly directed at a "Christian reformation" of the UN. Another example, discussed in chapter 5, involves the CR's pragmatic alliance with orthodox Islamic states; within CR domestic discourse, these same states exemplify satanic force and anti-Christian persecution.

These tensions are also reflected within the CR global alliance, as we explore in chapter 5. The attempt to create an international, unified lobbying—and hopefully voting—bloc of religious conservatives is still very much in its infancy but suggests a host of potential problems. The difficulties of sustaining a conservative, global religious alliance are traced throughout the book, as are the problems involved in "packaging" such a coalition for CR domestic constituencies. As we argue, the attempt to build a conservative religious network has required both compromise and, to a certain extent, a more flexible political mandate. The result, at this stage, is a certain degree of incoherence in the alliance's identity. Sometimes an orthodox Christian movement, other times a conservative religious movement, the alliance appears to be pulled in different directions as it struggles to include various agendas under the broad "natural family" banner.

Globalization

As discussed earlier, we consider globalization to result in structural and conceptual reconfigurations of the local and global, self and community. Our analysis of CR UN activism explores conceptions of both "the global" and "globalization" within CR politics, but also the importance of CR UN activism to an understanding of the scope and impact of globalization. We examine CR UN activism, therefore, as both resulting from, and constitutive of, a "global mindset." In our analysis, the increasingly vocal international debates around issues like women's rights, population policy, and world trade are a (not unproblematic) struggle over the meaning of social relations in an increasingly global world. In the case of the CR UN, recognizing this global mindset is important in orienting its international politics within a worldview that is neither solely a rejection of global change, nor a "backlash" against social change. It is both these things *and* a commitment to engaging with global processes. Thus, an important theme in this book is the ways in which globalization both threatens and facilitates CR international politics.

The Plan of the Book

The first chapter examines the theological foundation of CR global activism. Two concepts are of particular relevance to later analysis: the "natural family" and the "Second Coming." Our exploration considers how the CR conception of the "natural family" is anchored in both divine texts, and, more recently, in social science data. Our discussion of Second Coming scenarios focuses on Protestant millennialism; however, we also examine Catholic approaches and conclude by considering whether a kind of "endtimes rapprochement" is occurring among conservative Christian denominations in the United States.

In chapters 2 and 3, we focus on CR constructions of the United Nations. We particularly explore the CR's objection to the UN as an institution dominated by radical feminists, gay activists, and anti-Christian forces generally. Chapter 2 focuses on how the UN and its agenda are conceptualized in Protestant Right literature, while chapter 3 takes a close look at the details of the CR/UN engagement. For many CR actors, the UN and its increasing prominence in world politics represent the undermining of the "natural family" and the destruction of Christian values and ways of life. It is, in effect, the culmination of a "world government" that only Christ's Second Coming can usher in with authority. With the advent of an orthodox alliance at the UN, CR UN groups are now looking anew at the UN as an important arena for CR "natural family" politics. In chapter 3, we explore the possibilities for and tensions within this new CR engagement at the UN.

In chapter 4, we explore the CR's engagement with international population and reproductive policy, examining CR tactics, thought, and effectivity around a specific issue on the international stage. Population policy, as one of the original motivators for CR UN politics, provides a rich context within which to explore, first, some of the key issues for the CR UN, namely abortion and contraception; and second, the sometimes uneven evolution of CR international engagements.

Chapters 5 and 6 move away from a focus on the U.S. Christian Right itself to concentrate, instead, on CR UN international allies. In chapter 5, we take the World Congress of Families II conference as a case study. We consider, in particular, the problems and potential of the CR UN's attempt to build an international orthodox alliance. In chapter 6, our focus is on the Vatican, perhaps the leading "natural family" voice in international legal arenas. We explore the role of the Vatican in international forums, particularly in terms of Vatican politics on the issue of women's rights. In its self-proclaimed role as the international "voice of conscience," the Vatican has become something of an official leader of the "natural family" contingent at the UN, focusing its efforts on opposing a "gender ideology" that is seen as promoting both abortion and homosexuality. In our discussion, we consider how the topic of women's rights, for both the Vatican and the CR UN, has come to symbolize the very essence of "natural family" politics, increasingly defined in antiabortion and antigay terms.

In chapter 7, and by way of conclusion, we draw together two themes traced throughout this study of the global politics of the CR UN: global political spaces and social movements, and the relationship between globalization and religion. In this chapter, we sketch out some of the implications of our study for understanding the nature of global political space as a terrain of struggle, and the complex relationship between globalization and religion, particularly in a post–September 11 world.

1.

Divinity, Data, Destruction: Theological Foundations to Christian Right International Activism

This chapter assesses the role of religious belief in CR global politics. While much of the material we refer to in subsequent chapters is secular in tone, the CR's secular-sounding analysis and rhetoric has only limited meaning without an understanding of its theological foundations and raison d'être. We use the word *theology* to mean, simply, a set of religious beliefs. We see theology as the religious form of *ideology* or worldview, containing a set of both ontological and epistemological foundational "truths" premised on a notion of the divine. While it is possible to explore CR theology on any number of levels, and in relation to a huge range of doctrine, we have chosen to narrow the focus considerably. We examine two key concepts that CR activists and intellectuals interpret in terms of their religious vision: "the family" and the (more overtly theological) "Second Coming."

A relatively coherent and consensual understanding of the family forms the primary basis of unity for both the different CR denominations and the international orthodox alliance that we discuss throughout the book. Although biblical references to the family are indirect to say the least, the CR has nonetheless constructed "new family theology" as a way to anchor its family politics in a Christian foundation. In contrast, CR perspectives on the Second Coming have a clear biblical source; however, interpretations are diverse and, at times, in conflict. At the same time, prophecy belief is one of the key animating roots giving life and politics to the international CR movement, particularly, though not exclusively, to its conservative Protestant members (see also Martin 1999).

In considering the CR's understanding of the family, we examine the authorities cited in defense of their definition. We argue that conservative Protestants in particular have, in a sense, been left biblically bereft when it comes to substantiating their family claims. We suggest that, in response to this lacuna, the CR has constructed a new, orthodox doctrine to fill this gap. This new family theology embodies a mixture of divinity and data; in other words, it is the product of both authoritative "original sources" and contemporary, conservative social science. In the second part of the chapter, our analysis of Second Coming beliefs explores Protestant millennialism—both its "pre" and "post" varieties. We also consider Catholic perspectives on the Second Coming and suggest that a new mix of pre- and postmillennialism may be fueling CR UN activism. The chapter concludes by bringing together the discourses underlying the "family" and the "Second Coming," asking the question: whither the family in Christ's world order?

The Natural Family

When the CR refers to "family" and advocates a "pro-family" politics domestically and internationally, it is a very particular form of family: mother, father, and their (preferably biological) offspring. The CR has taken to calling this unit the "natural family," distinguishing it from family forms they believe to be unnatural, both socially and religiously. The phrase "natural family" has especially been taken up by CR UN activists, who like to claim that it is derived from the United Nations Declaration of Human Rights, although the actual phrase is not used there. This concept of the natural family constitutes one of the pillars of CR global politics. The natural family is what the CR believes is threatened by international law and policy development, and the "defense" of the natural family lies at the heart of the CR's international alliance building (see chapter 5).

Original Sources

What is of initial interest is that there is very little biblical authority underpinning conservative Christianity's defense of the natural family. Unlike homosexuality, about which some, albeit contested, biblical injunctions exist, the idea of the natural family as the basic cornerstone of society is not something easily identified in biblical texts. For example, Richard Wilkins, a speaker at the 1999 World Congress of Families II conference in Geneva, offered only the following quote from Genesis 2:18: "And the Lord God said, it is not good that the man should be alone" (Wilkins 1999). Others in the CR also cite biblical authority for their statements on the family, but these passages provide scant evidence for their claims. Allan Carlson, a leading CR intellectual light, uses the biblical injunction "be fruitful and multiply" (Genesis 1) to support his argument that "any significant departure from the family rooted in stable marriage . . . makes us in a way less 'human'" (1999a, 5–6).

In another attempt, Grant and Horne give ten biblical references to buttress the following argument:

> The fact is, the family is the primary agent of stability in a society. It is the family that is charged with the responsibility of infusing children with the principles of God's law (Deuteronomy 6:6–7). It is the family that is charged with the responsibility of upbraiding, restraining, and rebuking unrighteous behavior (Proverbs 23:13–14). It is the family that is charged with the responsibility of balancing liberty with justice, freedom with responsibility, and license with restriction (Deuteronomy 11: 18–21). It is the family that is charged with the responsibility of being culture's basic building block (Genesis 9:1–7).
>
> The family is central to virtually every societal endeavor under God: from education (Proverbs 22:6) to charity (1 Timothy 5:8), from economics (Deuteronomy 21:17) to spirituality (Ephesians 6:1–4), from the care of the aged (1 Timothy 5:3–13) to the subduing of the earth (Genesis 1:26–28). (1993, 234)

Not one of these references, however, says anything resembling authority for Grant and Horne's statements about the family.[1] In fact, the words of Jesus himself could be read as demonstrating a disdain for the traditional family form:

> He was still speaking to the crowd when his mother and brothers appeared; they stood outside, wanting to speak to him. Someone said, "Your mother and your brothers are here outside; they want to speak to you." Jesus turned to the man who brought the message, and said, "Who is my mother? Who are my brothers?" and pointing to the

disciples, he said, "Here are my mother and my brothers. Whoever does the will of my heavenly Father is my brother, my sister, my mother." (Matthew 12:46–50) [2]

As Reuther has shown, the New Testament is in fact anti-family; it constructs the Jesus movement as an alternative community that leaves biological family behind (2001, 25–35, 223). Yet, despite the biblical failure to justify the "natural family" and its purposes, and indeed Jesus's words, which appear to condemn it, conservative Christians continue to refer to it as "God-given," time and time again. The Catholic Right can perhaps do this with some authority, as there is at least a clear statement on the role and purpose of the family in the Catechism (2202–11): "A man and a woman united in marriage, together with their children, form a family. This institution is prior to any recognition by public authority, which has an obligation to recognize it" (2202; see also discussion in chapter 6).[3] But perhaps our search for biblical authority is somewhat unfair. For most of the last century, the very idea that the family needed justifying, theologically or otherwise, was unheard of. Conservative Christians (and many others) simply took its "naturalness" for granted.

The CR's late twentieth-century justification for the "natural family" thus emerged partly as a counterdiscourse and must be placed in that context.[4] In the latter half of the twentieth century, restrictive notions of "the" family began to be challenged by new social movements, particularly those motivated by ideologies of feminism and gay rights. CR activists and writers grew increasingly alarmed: "the fundamental concepts of 'faith,' 'life,' 'motherhood,' 'parents' and 'family' have become contentious battlefields"; "the re-definition of an old word—homosexuality—and the creation of a new word—homophobia—is not a minor event or a mere curiosity. Through these semantic changes, normalcy is put on the defensive" (Wilkins 1999; Dobson and Bauer 1990, 253). In response to these developments, the CR replied with a new discourse—the qualifier "natural" before the word "family" is an example of this. CR family theology is thus both a restatement of what conservative Christians believe God intends and a new common sense; that neither God nor Jesus contributed to this doctrine is neither here nor there.

New Family Theology

As we have discussed, the CR's familial ideology, in skeletal form, is that the family unit consists of one man, one woman, and their progeny, is

God given, and hence "natural," or, put differently, "natural" and therefore God given. In putting flesh on the bones of the "natural family," the CR's new doctrine both reiterates traditional characteristics, such as heterosexual marriage, and takes notice and to some extent incorporates contemporary social change, up to a point. In addition to being based on marriage, then, the CR's natural family also reflects changing views of the roles of women and men.

In terms of the moral and legal basis of the "natural family," marriage plays a crucial role in legitimating the union before God. Although traditional definitions of marriage have incorporated the notion of "for life," the CR has, in recent years, become careful always to preface the word "marriage" with the word "lifelong." Any topical CR text, as well as any CR organizational mission statement, emphasizes this point. The Geneva Declaration of the World Congress of Families II put it thus:

> [T]he natural human family is established by the Creator and essential to good society. . . . [T]he natural family is the fundamental social unit, inscribed in nature, and centered on the voluntary union of a man and a woman in the lifelong covenant of marriage.

This statement encapsulates the two key elements of the CR's new family theology: that the "natural family" is based on marriage and heterosexuality. The CR's antigay politics have now been well documented, while the "defense of marriage" has become one of the CR's primary, and most successful, domestic campaigns (Bull and Gallagher 1996; Diamond 1998, chapter 8; Durham 2000, chapter 3; Hardisty 1999, chapter 4; Herman 1997). That marriage and heterosexuality are at the core of the CR's "natural family" is well known; less discussed, however, are the ways the new family theology is integrating changing perceptions of gender. This assimilation is particularly significant for the CR's international activism, which, to have any impact, requires that the CR UN embrace a few "bottom-line" premises, particularly in relation to women's rights. How, then, has the CR's natural family doctrine responded to this challenge?

Until relatively recently, the Christian Right was very convinced about the "proper sphere" of women. Although gender has always been a site of contestation and reconstruction *within* conservative Christian communities (Ammerman 1987; Klatch 1987) the public face of the CR movement clearly embraced the view that God, nation, and nature intended and required women to stay close to hearth and home.[5] While the contemporary CR still subscribes to a theory of relatively distinct gender roles, in practice the very activism of CR organizations, many of them led by women, has partially undermined these older certainties. The CR does not now advocate that women *must* stay at home and raise children to be proper Christian women; they argue, however, that society must not discriminate against those who do, and, they contend, it is absolutely clear that young children thrive best when looked after at home by their mothers (providing a father is also on the scene).

In reevaluating the "proper sphere" of women, the CR, or at least many sections of it, has similarly taken on board the idea that women suffered historical discrimination that, to some extent, needed redressing. The struggle for women's right to vote, for example, is cited by several CR writers as a legitimate one (see Carlson 2000c; Ruse 1999e). While CR sources increasingly acknowledge discrimination against women, they tend to characterize it as corrected "past history" (though rhetoric during the U.S. attack on Afghanistan complicated this stance) (see Green 2001). The modern women's movement, the CR argues, has gone to extremes in *de*valuing the "speciality" of women—as nurturers, as moral guardians, as reproducers, in particular. Elizabeth Fox-Genovese, for example, an academic whose work at one time might have been described as feminist (and indeed was derisively labeled as such by one CR author in 1990 [Christensen 1990: 27–28]), in her speech for WCFII argued that both gender equality and essential gender difference should be valued.[6] Even the word "feminist" has come to have a more ambiguous meaning in some CR circles. In a 1999 interview, CR UN activist Austin Ruse explained that the CR prefers the term "radical feminist" to describe its enemies, because "some conservative women consider themselves to be feminist" (1999c), while Allan Carlson uses the phrase "extreme 'equity feminism'" to describe the UN's perceived "antifamily" stance (Carlson 2000a; see also discussion in chapter 6).

Thus, both CR women's activism and the external women's movement have helped shape the CR's new family theology. Other influences include the men's movement (see Kintz 1997, chapters 4, 5), rearticulated in CR terms as both a "fathers' rights" and a "fathers' duties" discourse (see also Collier 1999), and the late-twentieth-century self-help/therapy genre. Most conservative Christian bookstores in North America, for example, will feature several shelves brimming with self-help books for women, men, and married couples, as well as for those seeking to exit the "homosexual lifestyle." And, despite the CR's historical and contemporary antipathy to outside interference in childraising, such stores are replete with books offering such advice to Christian parents.[7]

These developments point to an interesting phenomenon within conservative Christianity, one that has affected the CR in much the same way as it has the social movements to which it is opposed: the increasing domination of professional expertise. CR professionals, including academics, have taken the religious foundation as given, and laid upon it a dome of scientific expertise that has served several functions for the movement, both pastoral and political. CR intellectuals adopt the basic premise of "the natural family," upon which much CR politics is based, and construct an elaborate analysis of the many "righteous purposes" of the family in the modern era. A notable example of this potent mix of devotion and data is the work embraced and produced by the Howard Center, a leading CR organization domestically and internationally.

The Howard Center produces a monthly publication entitled *The Family in America*. Each issue usually contains one lengthy paper, for example, on parental rights, family autonomy, or the social sciences, followed by a section entitled "New Research." This section summarizes various articles published in a range of social science journals.[8] Many of the pieces abstracted in *The Family in America* are written by conservative social scientists eager to "prove" a link between divorced and single-parent families, and a host of social ills. In practice, single parent means single *mother* (see also Mann and Roseneil 1999). Within this expert discourse, "fatherless families" are held responsible for, among other things, child psychosis, sexual abuse, and ill health generally, adult depression, increased rates of homicide, teenage sex, abnormally early puberty in female children, children taking guns to school, and an increased prevalence of "sudden infant death syndrome."[9] Allan Carlson's accompanying commentary in *The Family in America* also makes a typically conservative correlation between fatherlessness and race (see also Roberts 1998). In several instances, Carlson links African American "female-headed households" to a series of social catastrophes, including high rates of murder and the failure of black children to achieve well in school (Howard Center 2000g, 1999).

According to the Howard Center scholars and other CR intellectuals, such as fathers' rights advocate David Blankenhorn, the family is (or ought to be) the primary vehicle for childhood socialization, the key economic unit for its individuals, and, in tandem with the church, the foundation for spirituality and religious devotion (see Blankenhorn 1999; Carlson 1988; Christensen 1990, 1991). For many on the CR, the family is in opposition to the modern state, that most secular and anti-Christian of institutions, at least in the west: "[I]n the name of democracy the State steals customers from the living society, hoping for a dead society and a living State" (Carlson 1988). In terms of global activism, the family, for the CR UN, stands opposed to "international government," represented most graphically by the United Nations (see chapters 2 and 3). CR experts and academics have contributed enormously to a critique of the "welfare state," including its international incarnations.

Although the public rhetoric of Allan Carlson and the Howard Center, as well as other individuals and organizations on the CR, is not overtly religious in tone, their espousal or rejection of "expert discourses" (e.g., Popenoe 1988 and 1996) is intimately related to their conservative Christian ideologies. Thus, in considering CR "pro-family" activism, it is important to see how CR family politics, including CR secularized expertise, is rooted in its religiously based understanding of the "God-given natural family." The CR's understanding of the heterosexual, married, nuclear unit as God given, expressed in the new family theology, underlies much CR UN activism on the international stage. As we discuss in subsequent chapters, the CR UN has expended huge efforts fighting what it perceives to be the "international feminist agenda," as well as spearheading domestic struggles against the lesbian and gay rights movement. Although the CR's public discourse, particularly in the international realm, quite deliberately rarely makes reference to religion, it is not possible to fully appreciate its international political activism without attending to these religious foundations. This is not the place to undertake a full-scale analysis of CR "expert discourse" on the family; what we have tried to do is briefly encapsulate some key developments pertinent to our project, and to link this expertise with the CR's religious foundation, which critiques of "pro-family forces" often fail to do (e.g., Stacey 1996, 1999).

We are not suggesting that theology alone accounts for CR family activism. The relationship between religion and politics is a dynamic one, and, we would argue, there is little to be gained by trying to find *the* source for CR family activism in either religion or politics. If we have erred on the side of emphasizing the influence of old and new theology on CR UN activism, it is because the international activism of conservative *Christians* has been so overlooked in the literature.

The Second Coming

In the summer of 2000, the *New York Times* best-sellers fiction list was headed by a new entry: *Indwelling: The Beast Takes Possession.* Written by Tim LaHaye and Jerry Jenkins, *Indwelling* was the seventh installment in the authors' "Left Behind" series about the end of the world. Although the *Guardian* newspaper amusingly described the authors as "science fiction novelists," it is perhaps more accurate to understand them as CR social movement activists who have turned to fiction to sell religious vision (Kettle 2000). Tim LaHaye, the husband of Beverly LaHaye, founder of Concerned Women for America, is a longtime participant in CR politics and the author of numerous works of CR nonfiction (including a seminal antigay tract [LaHaye 1978]), in addition to the "Left Behind" series (see, for example, LaHaye 1998; LaHaye and LaHaye 1994). While there is clearly some element of drama and "play" to the "Left Behind" opus (as with Pat Robertson's similar efforts [e.g., 1995]), the series remains, at its core, a statement of how the authors and many other conservative Christians believe this world will end and a new one begin. In their detail, the "Left Behind" "novels" are indistinguishable from many works of ostensible "nonfiction" penned by other CR writers.

In this section, then, we consider the CR's "prophecy genre," in both its fiction and nonfiction manifestations, to shed light on how a significant portion of the American Christian Right understands global events. It is important, however, to appreciate that the global vision we analyze here is not shared by all the individuals or organizations we discuss in this book. The prophecy genre we explore most fully is that of the Protestant Right. As we discuss later in this chapter, Catholic beliefs about the Second Coming can take a different form, and, as we note, Vatican "wrongdoing" is at the heart of much of the Protestant genre. Nevertheless, it is our argument that the underlying motivation of many CR UN activists cannot be properly understood without considering the role played by their Second Coming belief system. Indeed, we argue that in terms of endtimes thinking and the new family theology, there may be an ever-increasing convergence in ideology among the different sectors of the CR.

Premillennial Belief about the Second Coming

The CR as a whole is united in terms of its religious orthodoxy about an inevitable future for the earth. All sections of the movement are convinced that the Second Coming will occur, all non-Christians will disappear one way or another, and Christ will rule the earth. Indeed, this belief is one of the defining features of conservative Christianity and therefore the CR. The questions of how and when Christ will return, however, are more controversial. For many decades, the predominant endtimes belief among American conservative Protestants, and therefore the CR as a whole, was premillennialism.

Premillennialists find the primary authority for their Second Coming beliefs in the final book of the New Testament—the Revelation of John.[10] Most historians view Revelation as an inspiration to believers during intense persecution by Roman tyrants at the time of writing, 81–96 C.E. (see, e.g., Gager 1983). However, orthodox Protestants have for centuries considered it a prophetic blueprint for the earth's end, Christ's return, and the ultimate establishment of Christendom throughout the world (Boyer 1992; O'Leary 1994). They have no doubt that these events will unfold; the sequence is inevitable, even if the exact timing is unknown.

In addition to Boyer's and O'Leary's exhaustive studies of the genre, the details of this scenario have been analyzed, critically and otherwise, by a range of theologians, historians, sociologists, journalists, and others.[11] Historically, there have been various versions of the premillennial Second Coming, all based on readings of biblical prophecy. Generally speaking, for Christ to reappear, a series of events must occur. The Gospel must be preached around the world and, as a result of this Great Commission, as it is known, many new adherents will be brought into the fold. At a certain point, this task will be as complete as it can be given widespread apostasy, and "true believers" will be "raptured"—they will literally ascend to heaven to sit with Christ and watch the horrors unfold. This period will also see the rise of the Antichrist—the charismatic leader who will unite huge regions of the world behind him in an anti-Christian drive for global power.

The earth will then (or at the same time) enter the stages of Tribulation—plagued by terrible disasters, floods, fires, earthquakes, wars, and so on. Many millions of people will die horrible, excruciating deaths. At this point, thousands of Jews will see the light and convert (however this is far too late for Rapture and most of them will perish in the disasters and final battles). As regional power blocs engage in war, the Second Temple is rebuilt in Jerusalem: this signals the return of Christ and the saints. They kill all nonbelievers, including the Antichrist, and usher in the peace and harmony of the millennium. During this period, according to Billy Graham, "Jesus Christ will be the King over all the earth in His theocratic world government" (1983, 227). At the end of one thousand years, Satan rises again, only to be defeated by Christ once and for all. The earth is then no more; only heaven exists.

The role of the Antichrist figure is particularly relevant to CR analyses of "the global" (see also Martin 1999). The Antichrist has a long history in Christian discourse (see McGinn 1994) and, more particularly, in the American apocalyptic genre (Fuller 1995). We cannot do justice here to the long history of Antichrist representation; instead, we will simply note several elements that have a bearing on our subsequent analysis of CR UN activism. First, the Antichrist must be distinguished from other key figures. The Antichrist is not Satan. He is a satanic force, furthering an anti-Christian satanic agenda, but he is rarely considered the literal embodiment of Satan.[12] There are also two other characters associated with the Antichrist who are important to premillennial belief—the False Prophet and the Beast. The False Prophet is, in many scenarios, a kind of envoy for the Antichrist, a precursor who is similarly evil, but who is not destined to achieve the Antichrist's glory. The Beast, on the other hand, is sometimes understood as a collectivity of regional power (usually Asian) that will engage in battle with the Antichrist during the Tribulation. In LaHaye and Jenkins's seventh and eighth novels in the "Left Behind" series, the Beast plays a central role (2000a, b). Frequently, however, the Beast and the Antichrist are viewed as one and the same (e.g., James 1991).

Second, the Antichrist is usually depicted, within Protestant premillennialism, as fully human. While he seems to possess strange and fantastic powers, he is not a demon. In premillennial novels, for example, we often learn a great deal about the Antichrist's family background, as well as other factors shaping his character and talents. The Antichrist, within conservative Protestantism, is perhaps best understood as a truly evil man, whom Satan has invested with supernatural powers.[13] Third, the Antichrist is intent on amassing political and economic power. He will accomplish great deeds in his drive for total domination, leading more and more people and nation-states to follow him. Historically, various Jews and Muslims were viewed as potential Antichrists, as well as many popes and monarchs (Boyer 1992, 61–62, 153). As Bernard McGinn has suggested, "The history of the Antichrist can be conceived as one way of writing the history of Christianity or at least the history of the hatreds and fears of Christians" (1994, 3).

In the first half of the twentieth century, signs of the Antichrist's rise were seen in the ascendancy of fascist dictators, the expansion of Soviet communism, the creation of the state of Israel, and the nuclear arms race. More recently, conservative premillennial Protestant belief about the Antichrist coalesced around the idea of "one world government."[14] Within this form of thinking, the Antichrist will successfully unite large swaths of the world under a superficially appealing philosophy of global unity. The emergence of the United Nations, with its subsequent growth and empowerment, has played a crucial role in confirming, for believers, the truth of this scenario, a theme we take up in the following chapters. Finally, it is worth noting that, during the Tribulation, true Christian believers (e.g., those who turn to Christ following the Rapture) are able to see through the Antichrist's lies and deception. It is their job to create a resistance force, and ultimately, for those who survive, to stand with Christ at Armageddon.

Popularly, speculation about the endtimes has generated a wealth of best-selling literature aimed at predicting and representing the end of earth. In a popular 1970s and 1980s scenario, the USSR, together with its allies, Iran, Libya, and others—Revelation's "Kings of the North"—would invade Israel. There they would do battle with the "Kings of the East" (China, Japan, and so on) in the final Tribulation (see, e.g., Robertson 1982, 213–22). Belief in a version of this scenario persisted into the 1990s (e.g., Price 1998). In that decade as well, many premillennialists believed the Gulf War signaled the Second Coming (see Jones 1992). In the latter part of the twentieth century in the United States, the imminent apocalypse was also associated, intimately, with cultural degeneration, secularization, sexual immorality, worship of the state, crime, drugs, and so on (see Herman 1997). By the late 1990s, prophecy writers were concerned with a number of "fin de siècle" issues, including, for example, world economic collapse, worship of the environment, "new age spirituality," the Internet, and the perceived resurgence of communism (see, for example, James 1997a, 1997b, 1998). No doubt the attacks of September 11, 2001, will provide similar fodder for such speculation.

Some readers of this book may find these ideas fanciful at best. However, many millions of Americans, including political policymakers, read Revelation for signs, buy prophetic literature, and believe fervently in the scenarios (see Barkun 1987, 168; Boyer 1992, 141–44; O'Leary 1994, chapter 7). This is perhaps not surprising, as recent survey data suggest that one in three Americans (a declining proportion over time) believes the Bible contains the actual words of God (Gallup and Lindsay 1999, 35–36). The Revelation scenarios are also powerful because they embody a fear of conspiracy that runs deep in American culture (Davis 1971; Fenster 1999; Johnson 1983). Premillennialism thus helps to shape, in important ways, approaches that believers take on social and political issues generally (see Lienesch 1993). Premillennialism informs many of the political positions adopted by the CR in the United States. For example, the CR's enthusiastic support for Israel (see McLaughlin and Chaddock 2002; Mouly 1985) cannot be fully explained without an understanding of the role Jewish people must play prior to the Second Coming, namely to return to Israel and convert or die (see Dyer 1993; Hagee 1996, 1998; Henry 1971; Hunt 1998; James 1998; Levitt 1997).[15] Similarly, the CR's pro-defense and patriotic stance is, for some, linked to the preordained role the United States is destined to play in the final days (see Boyer 1992, chapter 7; also Cassara 1982). Tim LaHaye (1998), in a "nonfiction" essay, links these two themes together, arguing that America will be spared end-times annihilation because it has been friendly to Jews and Israel. Similarly, the CR's vehement opposition to increased trading links with China is shaped, to some extent, by its belief that "Godless China" will play a satanic role prior to the Second Coming (Hutchings 1998; James 1998, 13–14; see also chapters 3 and 4 in this volume).

Protestant Postmillennialism

For many decades, postmillennialism languished in relative obscurity in terms of beliefs about the Second Coming. More recently postmillennialism has had a reawakening (see Barron and Shupe 1992). The basic foundation of postmillennialism can be expressed simply: conservative Protestants must establish God's kingdom on earth *before* Christ returns to rule for a thousand years. The Second Coming does not therefore occur in the context of apocalypse, and "Rapture" is a concept rather derided by most postmillennialists (Shupe 1997). Postmillennial theology has been articulated in detail most forcefully by the conservative Protestant movement known as Reconstruction.[16]

Rousas John Rushdoony, the "father" of Reconstructionism, has written over one hundred books articulating the theology (e.g., Rushdoony 1978, 1991). Other important figures in the movement include Gary North, Greg Bahnsen, David Chilton, and Joseph Morecraft. Reconstructionism, sometimes described as a stricter branch of postmillennialism and referred to as "dominion theology" (see Barron and Shupe 1992), posits strict biblical inerrancy (as do many conservative Protestants), that social life be governed according to Old and New Testament laws (including forms of slavery and the death penalty for recalcitrant homosexuals), and that "true" Christians should battle now to make Jesus's law reign supreme over all the earth. According to Rushdoony, "Christ is King of the nations. This is the Christian expectation and must be the Christian program for action; the sovereignty of Christ over all things and all nations" (1978, 185). "This means to ground the totality of our lives, thinking, institutions, and world, including church, state, and school on the Name of Christ the King, *under* His authority, power, law-word, and government . . . the state must serve the Lord" (1991, 8–9). Rushdoony's basic call is for what he unabashedly terms a "theocracy" (1991, 63–68): a Christian state run by Christian men—because "the Christian man is the only truly free man in all the world, and he is called to exercise dominion over all the earth" (1991, 1115).

It is clear that Reconstruction has had an important influence on the thinking of CR activists about American domestic politics. Rushdoony and Gary North have been frequent guests of the Christian Right, including past appearances on Pat Robertson's *700 Club* and D. James Kennedy's televangel show. Several prominent CR activists have written of their admiration for some Reconstructionist tenets, while disavowing formal allegiance to the movement as a whole. For example, John Whitehead, president of the Rutherford Institute, a leading CR legal firm that was very active in the CR battle to depose Bill Clinton, credits Rushdoony with being an important influence on his thought (Boston 1993, 191). Indeed, the Rutherford Institute originated as a project of Rushdoony's Chalcedon Foundation (Clarkson 1994, 6). Although the links between Reconstruction and CR UN organizations are far from clear, there is increasing reason to believe that a broader "dominion theology" may be taking root there as well.

Several scholars have noted the increasing prominence of postmillennial belief among the Protestant Right generally (Barron and Shupe 1992;

Ammerman 1991, 54). We would argue that postmillennialism provides a more coherent Second Coming belief for CR activists in both theological and pragmatic terms. Theologically, postmillennialism makes more sense of religious activism: if Christ's return is almost in some way conditional on the establishment of a Christian world, rather than its inauguration, contemporary Christian activism, particularly its global dimension, is fully vindicated and indeed a rational choice. Pragmatically, postmillennialism is also useful in that it appears more compatible with, and less hostile to, the Catholic activists in the CR UN alliance. Indeed, the growing international alliance between conservative Protestant and Catholic activists could be read as a "sign" of the resurgence of postmillennialism, or, perhaps more accurately, the decreasing significance of premillennial doctrine (which has often been virulently anti-Catholic [e.g., Hunt 1994, 1998]). The failure of premillennial fin de siècle prophecy no doubt plays a role here as well. As Balch et al. (1997) have argued in a different context, prophetic blueprints, once proved unreliable, may encourage religious believers to become more pragmatic and goal oriented.

Having outlined pre- and postmillennial Second Coming perspectives, it is worth saying a particular word about Mormon endtimes belief, given the significant role played by Mormons within the CR UN. Mormon prophetic belief, like Catholicism, has source material in addition to the Bible upon which to rely. Mormonism is arguably millennial in terms of beliefs about Christ's return; however, there has been some debate as to whether it is pre- or postmillennial (Introvigne 1997). The uncertainty this question raises is, in itself, interesting. What seems very clear, however, is that contemporary right-wing Mormonism has been heavily influenced by Protestant millennialism in the wider culture (Introvigne 1997), as it has been by Protestant fundamentalism generally (Mauss and Barlow 1991; Mauss 1994, chapter 11).

A Word about Catholic Second Coming Beliefs

Although the predominant individuals and organizations of the American CR are Protestant, Catholics play an important role, particularly in the global arena. Arguably, the Catholic Right has a less developed Second Coming theology than its Protestant coactivists. Its depiction of the Antichrist figure, for example, is vaguer and far less personified (McGinn 1994, 226–30; Thompson 1996, 185). While there is clearly a separate, indeed isolationist, movement of an apocalyptic Catholicism anchored in a conspiratorial framework that is often anti-Vatican (Dinges 1995), the mainstream Catholic Right, as both Cuneo (1997a, chapter 4; 1997b), and Dinges and Hitchcock (1991) have argued, is rather distanced from it (see also Weigel 1995). Even so, Vatican statements about the church's mission do have resonances with Protestant millennial discourse (Thompson 1996, chapter 8).

Mainstream conservative Catholics would tend to agree with Protestant millennialists that the world is in an anti-Christian spiral, and that, eventually, Christ will return to usher in Christendom. Catholic CR activists would not necessarily subscribe to an apocalyptic Second Coming scenario (Cuneo 1997b) and, in contrast to postmillennial Reconstructionists, would not advocate a biblically based rule of law. Like Mormons, the sources for Catholic perspectives on the Second Coming are also more varied than for most Protestants. In addition to biblical texts, conservative Catholics rely on Vatican pronouncements for authority, and many are also inspired by prophecies emanating from Marian apparitions (Cuneo 1997a, chapter 5, and 1997b; Thompson 1996; Vásquez and Marquardt 2000; Zimdars-Swartz 1995).

Cuneo (1997b) has argued that the separate movement of Catholic apocalypticists has also been heavily influenced by Protestant premillennial writing, and there is no reason to think that this is not true for the mainstream Catholic Right as well. Indeed, Thompson (1996, 178) suggests that the proliferation of Marian prophetic apparitions has quietly succeeded in undermining traditional, antimillennarial accounts of the Second Coming. Arguably, the Second Coming beliefs of Catholic CR activists may be more compatible with a broader *post*millennarianism that entails building a Christian world in the here and now. Thompson, for example, in his analysis of late-twentieth-century shifts in Catholic endtimes thinking, traces a "new optimism" (1996, 180) that, we would argue, is in keeping with theological movements within conservative Protestantism. Wendy Wright, of the Concerned Women for America, described this new approach:

> There's different opinions. . . . for those that ascribe to the pre-millennial viewpoint, they would believe that the world is going to get worse and worse, then Christ will come back. There are some who believe that viewpoint that then say, "Hands off. Let's just *let* it get worse and worse because then Christ will come back." But there are others who say, "No,

Christ said, 'to occupy until I come' and so we have a responsibility to be influencing our culture as . . . he commanded us to, to preserve our culture and to be a light within our culture." So, the premillennialist viewpoint for some has incapacitated them but I think we're almost coming out of that. The premillennialist viewpoint started growing in the 1970s, 1980s, but as people are beginning to see how because Christians have removed themselves from society it is starting to affect their families, starting to affect their kids. So, they are starting to realize, "Wait a minute. We need to be involved, we've got to be involved." . . . We have a mandate from Christ that we have got to be involved. (Wright 1999)

The Natural Family after the Second Coming

It is perhaps unsurprising that the brief biblical passages referring to the time after Jesus's (or the Messiah's) Second Coming say nothing about the family, given that the Bible provides little detail about families at any point. We know that "lions will lay down with lambs," all illness and disability will be eradicated, and so on, but there is no indication of the structure of human society once satanic force is vanquished. If the Bible is silent on the question of millennial families, one might think that contemporary CR writers would have stopped this gap. This does not appear to be the case, however.

On the contrary, in the very few pages that conservative Christian writers devote to the time after the Second Coming, it seems clear that there are in fact no families, or, rather, that there is only one large global family, with Christ as the father and the church as its mother (e.g., Van Impe 1996, 207–9). It is questionable whether children will continue to be born, as most people seem to be able to live forever. The relationship between women and men is also vague; this Christian utopia seems almost devoid of gender altogether (e.g., James 1991, 118–19; Graham 1992, 312–14). In one CR novel, people do seem to live in conventional families during Christ's rule; however, this all changes at the millennium's end, as everyone joins "one great family of God" (Meier and Wise 1996, 308). Ironically, then, in the next world imagined by many conservative Christians, there seems to be little room for "the family," or even for gender distinction, two things they fight so hard to retain in this world.

The purpose of this chapter has been to introduce and explore two key concepts animating CR UN activism: the natural family and the Second Coming. We have argued that the CR's "new family theology" reflects a complex mix of religious referencing, as well as conservative social science, and that while it has a clear historical trajectory, it is also a response to the discourse of opposing social movements. We also suggested that conservative Christian beliefs about the Second Coming and the "endtimes" generally are in flux, and that, perhaps, a revised form of postmillennialism is proving to be an important basis of unity among diverse CR actors. We now move on to consider how different sectors of the CR understand the United Nations and its international role.

2.

Constructing the Global: The United Nations in Protestant Thought and Prophecy

> The United Nations is trying to establish a long list of universal values to guide nations and individuals. These values . . . will not be Christian values. They will be the values of the politically correct humanists, witches, mystics, goddessworshippers, peaceniks, environmentalists, and a wide assortment of other ungodly activists who deem the blood of Jesus a repulsive thought and bow down before the altars of Satan.
>
> **Daymond Duck, "Harbingers of Humanism's Hurricane"**

To develop our analysis of the CR UN's global vision, we will explore how the most predominant sector of the CR, the domestic Protestant Right (PR), constructs its most important international, institutional enemy: the United Nations. We focus on the Protestant Right for several reasons. It has produced the most voluminous amount of material on the United Nations, and the predominance of PR thinking in CR domestic politics is very significant. Particularly relevant to our project are the ways that domestic PR understandings of the UN have evolved, are contested, and are reshaped by both Catholic and Protestant UN activists.

Our analysis draws on two primary source materials: the nonfiction and fiction of the Protestant Right. We consider how these texts envision the UN, then explore the role of the UN in the premillennial prophecy-writing genre. This material highlights what might be called the PR's "domestic discourse" on the UN. The genre we explore here is intended to be consumed by conservative Protestants within the United States. In chapter 3, we examine more closely the shifting conceptions of the UN deployed by CR UN actors, as well as the tensions resulting from these reconceptualizations.

Constructing the United Nations

Animating Philosophy: Globalism

The American Christian Right's international concerns are, first and foremost, focused on what they perceive to be the construction of a "new world order" (NWO). This new world order has several characteristics. According to the Protestant Right, the NWO is animated by a small number of overlapping philosophies that include socialism, feminism, and environmentalism. The PR uses the term "globalism" as a catch-phrase to encompass all of these elements. From the PR perspective, leading the drive to extend the NWO are several key organizations, including the United Nations, the European Union (Herman 2000b), and the World Trade Organization. According to the Protestant Right, this NWO has been established by globalists for a specific reason: to engage in battle with Christ's forces, now and as the Second Coming approaches, in an (ultimately unsuccessful) attempt to thwart the inevitable reign of Christ on earth. In this sense, the NWO is both an enemy to the Protestant Right and necessary, inasmuch as the NWO fulfills prophetic scripture. For this reason, the PR is both fascinated and repelled by the NWO and its component parts.

A wide range of recent PR opinion on globalism can be found in two collections edited by William T. James (1997b, 1998), a well-known name in the prophecy genre. The contributors to these anthologies include a mix of Christian political activists, theologians, evangelists, and prophecy writers. According to these writers, the United Nations is a kind of think tank for the dreams and aspirations of globalists. Globalism, for the PR, is above all a secular worldview, requiring, as Concerned Women for America argues, "an international system to govern and unite 'nation states'" (CWA 1998c).

It is clear that, for the PR, globalism occurs on two levels. On the surface exists a rhetoric of world peace, harmony, and prosperity. Concepts such as the "global village" or "one world" epitomize the utopian aspirations of globalists. Beneath this rhetoric, the PR argues, lies a sinister agenda that includes economic and military centralization, the emasculation of the nation-state, and the inculcation of socialist, feminist, and, most fundamentally, anti-Christian values. Berit Kjos, a PR education expert, finds a covert code buried in the words and phrases of UN agencies; concepts such as "sustainable development," "caring for the earth," and even "lifelong learning" all form part of the UN's hidden agenda for total ideological control (1997). It is what Christopher Corbett, an influential PR journalist, calls this globalist "ideological construction project" that the PR finds most disturbing (1997, 210).

The PR tends to focus on four major themes when analyzing the globalist agenda: economic and military centralization, environmentalism, new age spirituality, and feminism. The PR points to the UN's economic and military agenda as positive proof of the globalist mission. According to several PR authors, the UN's economic program is aimed at destroying American sovereignty and compelling the U.S. government to engage in economic relations with anti-Christian regimes. UN auspices and philosophy are seen to be behind the creation of the General Agreement on Tariffs and Trade (GATT), the North American Free Trade Agreement, the World Trade Organization, the International Monetary Fund, and the World Bank (see Jeffrey 1995, chapter 13; Van Impe 1996, chapter 5). Some PR perspectives on these treaties and institutions share, with the left, a critique of global capitalism. However, what the PR objects to are the secular values and morality they believe accompany, indeed underpin, economic globalization (see, e.g., James 1997a, 36).

In terms of military policy, UN peacekeeping missions are viewed by the PR as part of a covert plan to construct a world army ready to take power from nation-states following compulsory, universal state disarmament (see, for example, CWA 1998c). This development is inevitable, and, as we discussed in chapter 1, a fulfillment of PR prophecy. The PR's critique of global economic institutions, and moves toward multinational armed forces, has strong resonances with an American public fiercely proud of its independence and "way of life." The deepseated PR antipathy toward forms of international economic regulation, however, poses a dilemma for CR UN activists seeking to make alliances with conservative Christians in the developing world. On the other hand, the PR's total opposition to supranational military forces may play well with the Christian Right's conservative Islamic partners, such as the Organization of the Islamic Conference.

The PR also focuses on environmentalist norms as among the principal tenets of this NWO "ideological construction project" (see also Guth et al. 1995). Espousing a "pseudospirituality backed up by pseudo-science" (Corbett 1997, 210), UN-sponsored events, such as Habitat II or the Kyoto Meeting and Protocol on Climate Change in 1997, were, for the PR, just two examples of this "anti-family and anti-American ideology" in action (see also Corbett 1998; CWA 1997f, c). Arguably, the PR's vehement objection to international environmentalism is in large part due to the latter's association with New Age spirituality: "Preserving the planet becomes the act of worship, and Christians the enemy" (CWA 1998c, e). The UN is thus seen to be behind the construction of a one-world religion—namely, New Age spirituality (see Corbett 1998; Gairdner 1992, 235; Lindsey 1994, 43; Marrs 1987, 37–41). The link between international environmentalism and "the New Age" is very clear to the PR: environmentalists are creating "a religion out of the environment," according to Daymond Duck, a pastor and prophecy writer (1998, 82). Both environmentalism and New Age religion are, fundamentally, about the anti-Christian worship of the earth.

For the PR, environmentalism also goes hand in hand with feminism. The two come together in an "earth-centered" discourse—ideas of the earth as mother, *gaia,* goddess spirituality, and so on (see Palmer 1997b)—but feminism is perceived to have a further agenda on the family and sexuality that the PR opposes with all its might (see CWA 1999b; Corbett 1997, 214–18; Van Impe 1996, 79–80). The United Nations is seen to be a key promoter of feminism internationally, through conferences such as the 1994 Cairo Conference on Population and Development and the 1995 Beijing World Conference on Women. An analysis of the focus on "international feminism" reveals the PR's *feminization* and *sexualization* of globalist philosophy itself. For example, one writer refers to the "sirens of globalism" who, "like the twin sisters who lured away sailors to their deaths in Homer's *The Odyssey*—sing their lovely, mesmerising songs of New World Order" (James 1997a, 26). Berit Kjos identifies the feminist organizations, individuals, and movements providing inspiration and leadership to the new world order project; these include Bella Abzug, Hilary Clinton, and the Women's Education and Development Organization (1997; see also Marrs 1993). Feminism and feminists, thus, are a (and in these writers' view *the*) driving force behind secular globalist philosophy. At the same time, globalism is, according to some PR writers, a distinctly feminine project in terms of its seductive qualities.

Why might the PR gender globalism in this way? Identifying evil as "woman" is not unprecedented and is by no means a peculiarly PR attribute. However, seductresses and "harlots" play a particular role in conservative Christian theology. Eve, of course, was perhaps the first character to star in this role, seducing Adam to sin and causing the fall that only Christ's Second Coming can reverse. But in literalist Protestant prophecy, the "loose woman" returns again at Armageddon in the figure of the woman—the "mother of whores"—who rides the Beast (Revelation 17:1–8). In the epigraph to this chapter, for example, Daymond Duck (1998, 82–83) explicitly links witches, environmentalism, and Revelation's harlot to show the extent of the conspiracy foreseen by prophecy. In the more virulently anti-Catholic genre of PR literature, the Vatican itself is feminized in this way and likened to this final female degenerate, while Marian apparitions are viewed as both a confirmation of "feminist power" and a herald of the endtimes. Author Dave Hunt describes this power:

> Worldwide, today's women are asserting themselves as never before in history. Contrary to public opinion, "women instigate most domestic violence [and] hit men more frequently and more severely [than men hit them]" and violence is far more frequent in lesbian relationships than between husband and wife. Women are taking over what were once men's jobs, and there is a growing acceptance of women at the highest levels of leadership in business, government, and religion. Only God could have given John, 1900 years ago, a vision that so fits our day—a *woman* in control. From current trends, it seems inevitable that a *woman* must ride the beast. And of all the women in history, none rivals Roman Catholicism's omnipotent, omniscient, and omnipresent "Mary." (1994, 456)[1]

Often, indeed usually, international feminism is directly fused to lesbian sexuality. Corbett, for example, out of hundreds of workshops that took place at the Beijing Conference, mentions only the following:

"Lesbianism for the Curious; Spirit and Action: Lesbian Activism from an Interfaith Perspective; Lesbian Flirtation Techniques; Beyond the Trinity Creator" (1997, 218). If globalism in general is heterosexualized as a siren seductress, a kind of femme fatale reeling "men" in through the mesmerizing rhetoric of peace and prosperity, then global feminism, like its domestic sister, is homosexualized. Concerned Women for America, in analyzing the Beijing Conference, claims: "For the first time in U.N. history, a clear place was given to lesbianism" (CWA 1997d). When CWA places Hilary Clinton on a plane to China with "a load of lesbians," the organization makes clear that conservative Christians must internationalize the PR's antigay domestic battles (CWA 1997a). Finally, then, globalism is gendered and sexualized because of the resonances this has with the PR's domestic antifeminist and antigay analysis and rhetoric (see Herman 1997).

Implementing Globalism: United Nations Mechanisms

If globalist philosophy animates the UN, what are its principal socio-political goals, and how does the organization, at a practical level, implement this agenda? The PR provides fairly detailed answers to both of these questions. As discussed above, a large measure of PR time is spent on the UN's expanding military role. The growth of UN peacekeeping forces and hence the UN's direct involvement and intervention in the affairs of nation-states are seen by the PR to be ultimately about universal national disarmament and the establishment of a permanent global fighting force. For many PR propheticists, this global force will become the army of the Antichrist.

Second, the UN advances very specific economic goals. Although, for the PR, the major economic players are separate players to the UN as a whole (i.e., the World Bank, the IMF, the WTO), the UN nonetheless plays an important role in the globalist agenda to create a world economic order. It does so by advancing globalist economic philosophy through various UN agencies, such as the UN Development Programme (Robertson 1991, 57) and the International Labor Organisation (Van Impe 1996, 132), and through UN General Assembly resolutions and declarations (Robertson 1991, 207). The UN also serves as a governance model for the construction of other global economic alliances, all of which work together to achieve the complete centralization of economic power. Thus, the PR, in addition to being a leading proponent of domestic market economies, is one of the fiercest critics of international capital and its governance mechanisms. Hence the "strange bedfellow" alliance between PR and left-wing activists at the Seattle WTO protests in 1999 (see Antiwar.com 2000).

Finally, in terms of inculcating globalist social values, be they feminist, New Ageist, environmentalist, or gay rights, UNESCO, the UN's educational arm, and the UN-sponsored World Health Organization are two of the key players identified by the PR (Hagee 1996, 122; Marrs 1987; Van Impe 1996, 133). According to PR analysis, each organization, through its myriad arms and agencies, promotes and entrenches an anti-Christian mindset throughout the world. UN conventions, such as those focusing on the Rights of the Child or the Elimination of Discrimination Against Women (CEDAW), also come under furious fire. Grant Jeffrey, for example, a writer in the prophecy genre, argues that the Rights of the Child convention usurps parental control and constitutes one of the most "insidious and evil attacks on the family" (1995, 176). This view is echoed by John Whitehead, a leading CR legal advisor, who writes, "[T]he assertion of these child rights is virtually a libertarian charter of children's rights which, at best, dilutes and, at worst, could seriously impair the parental control of children" (1994, 93–94).

Concerned Women for America has made the campaign against CEDAW and the Rights of the Child convention one of its chief concerns (see CWA 1999b, 1997d, 1998b; Hurlburt 2001; MacLeod and Hurlburt 2000; Gairdner 1992, 578–84). CWA views CEDAW as nothing more nor less than a tool of the "radical feminist agenda . . . to destroy the traditional family structure in the United States" (MacLeod and Hurlburt 2000). CWA goes so far as to link CEDAW with same-sex marriage initiatives in Hawaii. The Rights of the Child convention is viewed by CWA as a means by which globalists, under the cloak of "rights," will sever children from their families and religious communities (see Buss 2000a). In addition to their critique of international conventions, UN-sponsored conferences are a constant target of PR attack. Daymond Duck, for example, presents a comprehensive list of UN conventions, conferences, and other activities, arguing that "the progressive deterioration of America is directly linked to our involvement with the United Nations" (1998, 87). All of the various methods at the UN's disposal inexorably lead, for the PR, to the construction of a vast international Leviathan.

The Significance of the United Nations in Second Coming Scenarios

Despite the PR's intense critique of globalist developments, many conservative Protestants in North America believe these events to be inevitable and could almost be said to look forward to them. Arguably, an understanding of PR prophetic belief is essential for comprehending why the PR's international agenda and vision take the shape they do. An interesting place to begin this exploration is with the books of Hal Lindsey, one of the most popular PR prophecy writers for over thirty years. Lindsey's first book, *The Late Great Planet Earth* (1970), was an attempt to foretell how the world would end, given the politics of the period. Though his prophecies did not prove correct, that is not what concerns us here. Of more interest is his approach to the new world order.

In this early work, Lindsey simply has nothing to say about the United Nations and its global role. It does not figure in his text at all, even though extensive material is devoted to world power bases and alliances. Perhaps this is unsurprising; with the cold war a major preoccupation at this time, it is "predictable" that the USSR emerged as a major actor in PR prophecy texts. However, Lindsey does not hesitate to target western configurations; the European Economic Community (as it was known at that time) is one of his chief protagonists:

> As the United States loses power, Western Europe will be forced to unite and become the standard-bearer of the western world. Look for the emergence of a "United States of Europe" composed of ten inner member nations. The Common Market is laying the ground for this political confederacy which will become the mightiest coalition on earth. It will stop the Communist take-over of the world and will for a short while control both Russia and Red China through the personal genius of the Antichrist who will become ruler of the European confederacy. (172)

Although the cold war and the rise of European integration are two explanations for Lindsey's lack of interest in the United Nations, another must be that the UN itself was a rather different entity during this period (Cassesse 1986). Within the UN, the United States led the battle against the "evils of communism." The UN organization itself was relatively weak, and rendered somewhat ineffective by this cold war contest. At the same time, the postcolonial states were only beginning to make their UN presence felt.

Unlike Europe, the UN may well have been seen by Lindsey and others of the PR as a relatively unimportant or even benign influence. For it must also be recalled that the 1960s and 1970s were not, generally, a time of PR preoccupation with the American state and its liberal, atheistic ethos. Although conservative Christianity has always been a fierce critic of domestic liberalism, the American state itself was not, historically, a primary target; it was "society" and, in particular, "the permissive society," upon which the PR critique focused (see Herman 1997, chapters 2, 7). As a result, the United States government and its membership in the United Nations would not have loomed large in PR endtimes scenarios.

For the Christian Right, the 1980s, despite the Republican stronghold on government within the United States, was a period in which the sovereignty of America was severely undermined by the rise of the globalist philosophy described above. By the early 1990s, this was combined with a new threat: the ascendancy of the Clinton liberals. For the PR, the increasing power and role of international organizations, combined with the entrenchment of "globalists" within the White House itself, resulted in the United Nations becoming one of the principal protagonists in the drive to establish the secular new world order. This understanding mirrored a slightly different one on the part of the international community as a whole—that the end of the cold war signaled a new, powerful (in a positive sense), interventionist role for the United Nations.

The "new face" of the UN, as seen by the PR, was signaled by Pat Robertson in 1991. In *The New World Order*, Robertson explained the ways the UN and other international organizations were pursuing strategies that could result in a "one-world dictatorship" (1991, 54). Hal Lindsey, in his 1994 follow-up to *The Late Great Planet Earth*, *Planet Earth—2000 A.D.*, took up the mantle. Despite the UN playing no role whatsoever in his earlier prophetic work, Lindsey in 1994 explains how it is now the key actor: "[T]he hallowed halls of the United Nations—the world's leading promoter of globalism and world government—have become a hotbed of idol-worship and the kind of militant paganism that the prophets warned us would arise and spread in these last days" (43). Although he still believes the Antichrist will be a European leader (217–18), Lindsey describes Boutros Boutros-Ghali, UN secretary-general at that time, as "the most influential individual on the face of the planet" (51), and depicts Clinton's UN-sponsored intervention in Somalia as a blatant example of liberal one-worldism at work (54). But Lindsey has not left his concern with Europe behind; *Planet Earth—2000 A.D.* maintains his belief that the European Union is the ten-nation confederacy referred to in Christian prophecy.[2] Nevertheless, the UN has now taken a place as the leading philosophical (if not political) force for globalism (see also Van Impe 1996, 89).

The year 1998 saw the publication of Lindsey's next installment— *Planet Earth: The Final Chapter.* In contrast to his previous book, Lindsey's preoccupation with the UN has notably diminished here. As far as he is concerned, the UN is a spent force, a "paper tiger" (147). It will, Lindsey argues, "join its predecessor, the League of Nations, on the scrap heap of history" (148). The reason for this, he says, is that the UN has spread itself too thinly: "The problem is, there are too many diplomats, not enough decision makers. It is too political, too fragile, too unwieldy to function as a dictatorship as profound and universal as the one predicted by Scripture" (148). For Lindsey, it is the European Union that will fulfill this scriptural role (150).

Although Lindsey may have retreated from portraying the United Nations as the key global power, others have not. Grant Jeffrey, for example, takes the reverse view; he argues that the institutions of the European Union are but a "preview" to the UN becoming "the nucleus of a powerful world government" (1995, 96–97). Christopher Corbett also argues, though with slightly less assuredness, that the United Nations will absorb state sovereignties to become a ruling government in itself (1997). There is, therefore, a difference of opinion among the PR as to how seriously the UN should be taken. Is the UN the source of the international satanic agenda? Is it a benign institution in itself, but one that has been captured by anti-Christian globalists? Or is the UN globalism's red herring, with the European Union and the Antichrist potential of European leaders of far more importance? As we explore in the next chapter, differing conceptions of the UN and its role are reflected in the discourse of CR global activists.

Another source for exploring the construction of the UN in PR endtimes belief is the novel, one of the most popular of the prophecy genres (see also Fenster 1999, 167–74). Pat Robertson's first foray into this form, entitled *The End of the Age* (1995), follows the usual pattern in that a series of terrible events, commandeered by evil men, bring on the end of the world. Although all true Christian believers are raptured away to watch from above, those left behind who come to see the light (i.e., are born again) become a kind of resistance force for Christ. In Robertson's novel, the United Nations is mentioned just once, as a kind of relic that failed to deliver the new world order. Instead, Robertson's Antichrist figure, U.S. president Mark Beaulieu, "a descendant of an aristocratic French family" (166), creates the Union for Peace, a United Nations–type organization under his complete control (260).

In *Left Behind* (1995), Tim LaHaye and Jerry B. Jenkins construct a similar story, but one with an explicit role for the UN. Their Antichrist, "Nicolae Carpathia of Romania," becomes secretary-general of the UN (412). A CNN reporter conveys the breaking news to the despairing Christian believers:

> In the most dramatic and far-reaching overhaul of an international organization anyone can remember. . . . Romanian president Nicolae Carpathia was catapulted into reluctant leadership of the United Nations by a nearly unanimous vote. Carpathia, who insisted on sweeping changes in direction and jurisdiction of the United Nations . . . [intends that] the United Nations headquarters will move to New Babylon . . . [and that] member nations will . . . destroy ninety percent of their military strength and turn over the remaining ten percent to the U.N. (412–13)

By the time of the third book in LaHaye and Jenkins's series, *The Rise of Antichrist Nicolae* (1997), Carpathia is firmly ensconced as the "Global Community Potentate" and, under the guise of attempting to spread international peace and prosperity, he has succeeded in destroying much of the world's surface and population. By 2001, the authors had released the ninth installment, *Desecration: The Antichrist Takes the Throne*. The series as a whole has sold over forty million copies.

Whether in the fiction or prophecy-writing genres, premillennial conservative Protestants predict, in graphic terms, that catastrophic consequences will result from movements for world peace and global unity, much of this represented by developments at the UN. Because these contemporary movements are not motivated by orthodox Christianity, they are, and must be, false. But it is not that the PR opposes world peace and global unity; on the contrary, their vision of a millennium ruled by Christ and the saints is just that: a world where only "true" Christians exist, everyone else is dead, peace reigns, and Christian orthodoxy rules the day across the globe.

Domestically, the PR, despite its antistatist rhetoric, is not against "the state"; rather, it opposes *this* state, or the *types* of states that currently exist (Herman 2000a). Christian orthodoxy generally is explicitly progovernment and government regulation—providing that the government is a "truly" Christian one and that regulations promote orthodox Christian values. On the international front, the PR is nothing if not consistent. It is not world government or a new world order per se that is problematic; it is a secular world order, and a perceived atheistic global government that is the force for evil. Ironically, nothing resembles world government more, not any plans of contemporary "globalists," than the global Christian monarchy to which the PR so much looks forward:

> Ultimately, globalism will triumph—but not the false globalism of the Antichrist and today's spirit of antichrist. . . . But the kingdom of Christ will truly triumph. All nations will bow before His throne as He rules from His capital in Jerusalem. That is a true globalism which every Christian will enjoy. (Corbett 1997, 229)

> [L]et us remember that the triumph of God's world order is certain. (Robertson 1991, 268)

> When the Tribulation ends by the return of Christ. . . . He will set up His Kingdom . . . and he will reign over the world for 1000 amazing and remarkable years. (Breese 1998, 335)

> Jesus Christ will be the King over all the earth in His theocratic world government. (Graham 1992, 310)

The Christian Right, Its Enemies, and Globalization

We have suggested above that the Protestant Right and the globalists it demonizes both advance a rather similar blueprint for world domination—one religious, one ostensibly secular, or at least interfaith. However, the subjects of the globalist vision are, presumably, the world population, while the entrance way to premillennialist peace and harmony is restricted to (conservative) Christians only. Because the PR views globalism as "false" and sees its underlying animation as satanic, one-worldism without Christ at the helm is an illusion and an impossibility. Of course, it is also more than this; globalism and its attendant politics are, as we have discussed, fundamentally anti-Christ.

One question we have not yet addressed directly is, to what extent does the PR see globalism as originating from within the United States, or is it something "out there," infecting the American polity? Certainly, the PR is clear that domestic proponents of feminism, environmentalism, and monetary centralism, for example, abound, and the PR spends much of its time fighting battles with these domestic adversaries. Yet at the same time, there are definite threats outside American borders. Although the CR UN takes a somewhat different approach (see chapter 3), the domestic PR rarely identifies Americans as key globalists on the international stage.[3] Although Al Gore, for example, was a favorite target of the PR, he was generally portrayed as a dupe of international environmentalists. When globalist archenemies are identified by the PR, these are often people occupying positions such as UN secretary-general, or president of the European Commission. In the 1990s, for example, both Boutros Boutros-Ghali and Jacques Santer were often represented in terms reminiscent of Antichrist descriptions (see Herman 2000b). Another figure loathed by the PR is Maurice Strong, a Canadian environmental advocate and a significant player in UN-sponsored environmental initiatives.[4] And, as we have noted above, within the PR the Vatican is often (though not always) demonized in this way. An exception to this tendency to see the main globalist protagonists as outside the United States is Hilary Rodham Clinton. This is perhaps partly due to her direct foray into global politics through participating in UN conferences, and to her publication of *It Takes a Village* in 1996. The PR expended much energy denouncing this text and Clinton's subsequent trips to view African villages. Her election to the Senate in 2000 propelled her even further into the Christian Right's spotlight, as did her advocacy on behalf of Afghan women's rights during the "war on terror" (see, for example, Shepard 2001).

The question of "enemy origins" is important for CR politics, both ideological and strategic, and for developing an analysis of the CR's international activism in the shadow of globalization. We would argue that the PR, and to some extent the Christian Right as a whole, can no longer be as sanguine about the origins of "enemies." It is the PR's very inability to "know" where the danger comes from, inside or outside, that marks an important transition in PR approaches to governmental and international institutions. In the earlier decades of the twentieth century, the PR could easily identify trends and individuals in civil society of which it disapproved. "Bad apples" within state institutions could be rooted out; leading state figures, such as J. Edgar Hoover, wrote regularly in mainstream Christian publications explaining how they were advancing God's Plan in government (Herman 1997, chapters 2, 7). Although there were domestic adversaries, the "evil of Communism," for example, was clearly something with distinctly foreign origins. But now, when Hilary Clinton and a "load of lesbians" embark on an international excursion, just what is it they are doing? Are they exporting American feminism abroad? Will they bring some new danger "home"? Is there a meaningful distinction to be made between "home" and "abroad"?

The processes, effects, and, just as important, perceptions of globalization, such as the emergence of fluid boundaries, international identity movements, and instantaneous communication are developments that help to create a kind of postmodern miscegenation between the United States and the rest of the world.[5] By this we mean that, for many conservative Christians, globalization is facilitating the dilution (and pollution) of what is perceived to be historically, romantically, and essentially "American." It then becomes impossible to tell where the United States ends and the "rest of the world" begins (and vice versa). For the PR, such a contamination is highly toxic, both for those who believe a Christian America could withstand the Tribulation and for those who seek to construct islands of bounded, authentic purity, be they "the family," "the church," or "the nation."

3.

Nation, Church, Family: The Christian Right Global Mission

In the previous two chapters, we traced Christian Right constructions of the international order and the role of prophecy belief in animating an anti–United Nations stance among CR activists. Our analysis demonstrated that for the CR, the UN figures prominently as an agent of the Antichrist, playing an important role in the consolidation of world power into a single, global government, leading to the apocalypse. We now turn to look at CR activism with this very same UN. Starting around 1994, the CR began to establish a more permanent presence at the UN. Organizations such as Concerned Women for America and Focus on the Family became involved in a series of UN conferences, of which the 1995 Beijing Conference on Women is the most notable. At the same time, CR newsletters and communiqués began to include more reporting on global politics. This "internationalization" of CR interests is significant in a movement that has a deeply formed theological and political opposition to the UN, and a more general hostility to things international.

The decision by CR activists to become involved at the UN denotes a shift in CR thinking on the nature of the UN, and the possibilities for a CR politics at the international level. Moving away from a view of the

UN as a key institution leading to the apocalypse, a new strand in CR thinking has emerged in which the UN is seen as a good and potentially Christian organization, corrupted by certain forces. The emergence of this new vision of the UN is partly attributable to the parallel establishment of a global interfaith alliance. The prospect of a community of conservative religious actors working together against a shared foe has provided the impetus for many on the CR to commit to an international politics.

While the advent of a conservative religious alliance at the UN has invigorated CR international politics, it has also disrupted CR understandings of "the international" as a fundamentally anti-Christian space. Working within the UN has softened some CR rhetoric on the UN, suggesting a new political strategy emphasizing UN reform rather than UN abolition. In this chapter, we explore these changing conceptions of the UN and their impact on shaping CR international campaigns and strategies. We argue that while the emergence of a CR alliance has altered CR envisionings of the UN and its project there, CR UN politics are haunted by a conviction that the UN is an agent of world dominance, and hence essentially anti-Christian. The difficulty for the CR UN then becomes accommodating these divergent views into a coherent politics.

Our objectives in this chapter are threefold. First, we analyze CR UN constructions of the UN as a political space for a conservative Christian project. Through this analysis we outline the terrain on which the CR UN is waging its struggle, both as a framework for understanding the particular direction of CR UN politics and as a means for elaborating the broader "worldview" in which CR UN politics are embedded.

Second, we consider how CR UN politics are shaped, and sometimes constrained, by a deep-seated ambivalence about the international realm generally and the UN specifically. This ambivalence, we argue, directly impacts CR UN strategizing at the international level. More than an area of disagreement among the various CR actors, conflicting conceptions of the UN present serious obstacles as this interfaith alliance attempts to define its objectives at the UN. In this chapter, we outline the nature of this dilemma, looking at conflicting CR UN understandings of its long-term objectives at the international level. In chapters 4 and 5, we build on this analysis to explore specific tensions within the interfaith alliance itself.

Finally, our analysis in this chapter explores the nature of the CR

UN's global project. Despite deep uncertainties about the international realm, the CR UN appears committed to international political engagement. Rather than retreating into a more localized politics or advocating the return of some bygone era, CR UN politics, we argue, are very much directed to a future vision of the global order, albeit a fraught one.

Foes and Friends at the United Nations

We start this analysis of the CR's politics at the UN with "the enemy." Understanding the CR UN's construction of its enemy—or enemies—is key to understanding the CR UN's constructions of its friends, its politics, itself (Lechner 1993, 34; Aho 1994). This is not to say that the CR's global politics are merely a politics of opposition, that they exist simply to counter the international politics of its perceived foes. Rather, we take as our starting position that the global politics of the CR are based on a culture of a "friend-foe way of thinking" (Meyer 2001, 8), in which a politics of change is constituted through a process of contesting "the enemy" (Aho 1994, 14–15).

In the following discussion, we consider three distinct enemy types identified by CR UN activists: socialists/globalists, secularists/humanists, and feminists. In doing so, we are not suggesting that each of these enemies is a discrete category with separate, identifiable traits. Rather, the CR UN often ascribes very similar motivations and characteristics to all three enemies, and sometimes uses the labels of "globalists," "socialists," and so on interchangeably. Nonetheless, within CR UN literature, each actor is portrayed as pursuing a distinct global agenda, with implications for the "natural" family and religious values.

Socialists/Globalists

One of the key and recurring enemies for the CR UN are socialists/globalists. We have grouped socialists and globalists together because the CR UN depicts the move toward a global government (and the demise of the nation-state) as the ultimate goal of an enemy bent on a socialist world order.[1] In this view, the disintegration of the state, together with the removal of territorial boundaries, will reinforce the global centralization of power in the hands of a few key people (Reid 1999; Wright 1999). The United Nations, in this scenario, is positioned as the "governing body" of a globalized (i.e., "nation-less") world order (Wright 1999; Benoit 2000), and large financial donations to the United Nations by wealthy

American businessmen, such as Ted Turner and Bill Gates, are evidence of the alliance between monetary interests and the UN (Reid 1999; Wright 1999).

While the actions of "globalists" and the move to a centralized global authority is a recurring concern in CR literature, little explicit attention is paid to "globalization" per se. To the extent that it is addressed, it is defined almost exclusively in terms of a universalization of social policy. Harold Brown of the Howard Center, a leading think tank for CR international politics, explained the relationship between globalization and social relations in his speech to the second World Congress of Families:

> Globalization is the concept or ideal that tells us not that small is beautiful, but that small is pitiful and out of date. The nation replaces the family, as in the U.S.A. public welfare replaces the father, and instead of individual nations . . . we shall create a "world community." (Brown 1999)

This conception of "globalization" thus includes a structural dimension—the centralization of a global governance—which is threatening primarily for its perceived impact on the intimate, familial level. With its challenge to domestic boundaries—of the nation and the family—globalization is seen as dangerous for the impact it has on the configuration of the nation-state, the nuclear family, and gender roles. Globalization, in this respect, is seen as imposing one form, "a cookie-cutter standard," of social relations on all people, without accounting for the "differences" of culture and religion (Wright 1999; see also Ruse 1999c).

Missing from this analysis of globalization is an explicit reference to, or engagement with, economic factors—capital mobility, foreign direct investment, and the liberalization of financial markets—that impact upon global change (Held et al. 1999, chapter 4). The CR UN maintains, sometimes imperfectly, a rigid separation between the globalization of social relations—the "cookie-cutter" phenomenon—and economic globalization.[2] In an interview, Austin Ruse, president of the Catholic Family and Human Rights Institute and a key spokesperson for the CR UN, dismissed economic globalization as not a concern of the CR UN. "[T]he left has a problem with [economic] globalization. . . . we believe that globalization is trying to do a one-size-fits-all question on reproductive rights" (1999c).

This lack of an explicit economic analysis is surprising given the domestic CR's procapitalist economic analysis (see Lienesch 1993, chapter 3). For the domestic CR, a neoliberal economic order in which the state plays, at best, a minimal role, is linked to the achievement of other aspects of a conservative Christian social policy (such as the promotion of the "natural family," home schooling, and so on). Some domestic CR actors have also developed this further into a detailed economic critique of globalization. The Eagle Forum, for one, opposes United States membership in the World Trade Organization on the basis that it, alongside the UN conference system, the Law of the Sea, and international environmental agreements, constitutes a policy of "global governance" in which international agencies such as the UN will "dictate" laws and policies to the United States (see, for example, Eagle Forum 1997).

For the most part, however, CR activists have avoided an explicit critique of the economic dimensions of globalization in the context of their global political project, focusing instead on the homogenization of social relations considered to accompany global change. The "cookie-cutter" phenomenon is seen as both a consequence of globalization and characteristically socialist. Thus, the goals of socialists and globalists are the same: a single global order, dominated by a strong centralized government (the UN), which pursues a welfarist, interventionist government policy. Who are these globalists/socialists? In some analyses, they are influential individuals holding key positions in the UN (see, for example, Carlson 1999a), while in other accounts they are the "radical" governments of "[t]he US, the European Union, Canada, New Zealand and to a certain extent Japan," whose pursuit of "radical" reproductive rights marks them out as socialists/radicals (Ruse 1999c).

Secularists/Humanists

Within CR thinking on world government and the role of the UN, there is a clear overlap between the means and effects ascribed to socialists, globalists, and secularists. For the CR UN, the movement to a one-world government signals a homogenization of social values that is both socialist in its universal reach and secularist in its presumed rejection of religious values and the traditional family. The relationship between globalism and secularism is central to CR theology and politics at the UN, but it is a relationship that is far from clear. We have separated the secularist enemies from the globalists in our analysis because the CR also separates them within its own discourses on the UN. This

separation, however, belies the complex and sometimes problematic relationship the CR envisions between secularism and the move to global
government.

In CR domestic politics, secularism figures as the large, amorphous
development that is both resisted by and justifies CR involvement in the
political process (see Lienesch 1993). CR battles over such things as abortion, prayer in schools, and taxation are all described in terms of resisting
creeping secularism. At the international level, the battle against secularism is more generally encompassed within a broad "natural family"
politics, which is largely focused on resisting human rights. For the CR
UN, the promotion of rights for women and children is a direct attack
on religious values (see Buss 2000a):

> [T]he new global civilization . . . is militantly secular, ferociously anti-
> traditional, fundamentally hostile to autonomous families, the enemy of
> robust marital fertility, and a threat to the newly conceived child every-
> where . . . *including* the new Christian child. (Carlson 1999a, 39)

In this view, the secularist threat at the UN is bent on destroying
the "natural family" as part of a larger effort to secularize the international domain (see, for example, Francis 1998; Ruse 1999c; Landolt
1999; O'Leary 1998). The means and effects of the secularist threat are
described in relatively narrow terms: secularists want a godless world
and they are attacking the family because it is central to a Christian
society. No explicit link is made here between the secularist threat and
globalism. In effect, these are treated as separate, though overlapping
phenomena with secularism helping the cause of globalism, and globalists definitionally secularist.

However, upon closer reflection, globalism and secularism are inextricably connected, with one necessarily leading to the other. The
link between the threat to the family, secularism, and the prospects of a
global government are explicitly drawn by Austin Ruse, president of the
Catholic Family and Human Rights Institute, who describes the CR's
project at the UN as the defense of three sovereignties, nation, church,
family:

> The way that I talk about work at the United Nations is that from
> certain quarters, not all . . . there are three sovereignties that are under
> attack, sovereignty of the nation, of the church, and of the family and

each in their own way are defenders and protectors of us as we make our way through life, and we believe that each was instituted by God in a certain way. (1999c)

Ruse's comments are instructive on a number of levels. First, he makes clear that the CR UN is not just resisting a narrow range of policies. From its perspective, secularism and other threats at the international level are directed at the family, institutionalized religion (Christianity), and, crucially, the structure of an international order predicated on the nation-state. The secularist threat is thus connected to a globalism that seeks to undermine the state as a God-given institution.

Second, Ruse identifies the UN as the principal locale for this threat to family, church, and nation. This relationship between the UN and secularism is not unproblematic. For some, such as Ruse and Allan Carlson, the UN itself is not necessarily secularist, nor essentially anti-family. It has been corrupted by antifamily forces but can be redeemed and returned to its original, family-friendly roots. In a series of essays on the history of the United Nations, Carlson traces the source of secularism at the UN to the influence of a few, key individuals who promoted "a socially radical form of Scandinavian democratic socialism" (1999a, 6; see also 1999b, 2000b). The proponents of this "democratic socialism" pushed for measures, such as population control and a devaluing of "traditional" marriage, that undermined the "natural" family (1999a, 6–10).

Carlson's essays attempt to distinguish between the UN as a relatively benign institution and the people (socialists/secularists) who have influenced its policies. He argues that in its formative stages, the UN expressed explicitly "pro-family" policies, evidence of which can be found in the 1948 Universal Declaration of Human Rights and its references to the family as the fundamental unit of society.[3] After that period, key individuals, primarily from Scandinavian countries, enjoyed an unprecedented degree of influence and were able to redirect UN energies in an antifamily direction (Carlson 1999a, 6–10; 2000b).

In Carlson's analysis, the UN, because of the influence of individual policymakers, is developing into the instrument by which secularists are establishing a "global civilization" that is antifamily by definition (1999a, 39). In a strategic sleight of hand, however, it is not the UN itself that is under attack here; it is UN agencies and the implementation of seemingly inauthentic international human rights guarantees that are the real antifamily instruments. Later in this chapter we explore the different conceptions of the UN that abound in CR UN publications and that have, we argue, consequences for the direction of CR global activism. For now, it is important to note that Carlson's image of the UN, as good but corrupted, contrasts with another view of the UN as fundamentally anti-Christian. This view sees the UN not just as an instrument of secularism, but as intimately connected to secularism and definitionally antithetical to Christianity. Denesha Reid of Concerned Women for America explains it thus: "The very essence of Christianity is the realization that God is the ultimate ruler and that God is our provider. The concept of the UN is that government is the ultimate ruler and that government will be the provider and decide what is best for you" (1999). No matter how "family friendly" the UN may be, it will always be a threat to Christians because it will always be a form of big government that seeks to replace God (Ingraham 1994). As we discuss later in this chapter, these divergent views prove difficult as the CR UN endeavors to develop its project at the UN.

Feminists

Conservative Christian opposition to feminism is well known and well documented. As we explored in chapter 2, Protestant premillennial discourse on the UN is emphatically antifeminist. This is equally true for the CR UN. It is not surprising, then, to find that the global politics of the CR are often explicitly directed at "radical" feminists and the perceived radical feminist agenda. The term "radical feminist," or, as is sometimes used, "gender feminist," are CR UN expressions used to distinguish between a feminism acceptable to the CR UN and a radical feminism defined as antifamily and antichild (see, for example, CWA 1996a; Hsu 1995a). This distinction parallels a shift in domestic U.S. CR strategy. Sara Diamond argues that the CR has had to adjust its antifeminist rhetoric in light of the increasing importance and competence of women in fighting *for* family values. "Even on the Right," she says, "it is no longer politically correct to make direct attacks on women's equality. . . . one does not read or hear arguments from the Right that women *should* be paid less than men for the same work" (Diamond 1998, 127). The distinction between types of feminism allows the CR UN to answer the criticism that it is antiwoman. By targeting "radical" feminists rather than just feminists, the CR takes the position that it is not against policies directed at helping women, but against "antifamily" policies. As a number of CR UN representatives interviewed for this book commented, it is difficult to be *against* human rights for women and children (Moloney 1999; Reid 1999; Wright 1999). This does not mean that "feminism" is embraced by the CR UN. Far from it. But this attention to terminology suggests a tactical shift in CR politics in which its antifeminism is defined in terms of combating a larger evil. This theme is developed further in chapter 6 where we look specifically at CR UN political activism around women's rights and UN conferences such as the Beijing Conference on Women.

In the context of this discussion of enemies, "feminists" occupy something of a paradoxical position in CR UN politics; they are center stage in CR UN discourses as the real "face" of the anti-Christian/antifamily forces, but at the same time they are sidelined by CR UN attempts to define a larger enemy behind global "antifamily" politics. The result is that while CR UN activists minimize the "feminist threat," feminists are most often the actors that the CR UN identifies as the forces behind the "antifamily" measures of women's rights, reproductive freedom, population policy, and so on.

According to the CR UN, feminists have managed to secure a strong grip on the UN and hence have an upper hand in influencing the international agenda. Conservative religious organizations, by contrast, are "outnumbered and outspent," and have to counter UN bureaucracy and unfair treatment used to keep them out of important UN meetings.[4] These claims are not entirely baseless. Feminist NGOs have demonstrated effective organization and consequently have been successful in influencing the international agenda on issues such as human rights, development, and population policy (Joachim 1999; Sen 1995; Stienstra 2000). Moreover, some states, such as Canada and the United States during the Clinton presidency,[5] have occasionally included feminists on state delegations sent to UN conferences and meetings, thus giving some feminists access to negotiation sessions at which NGOs are otherwise unrepresented.[6] Finally, many of the current CR organizations active at the UN came to international activism without much experience. Arriving on the doorstep of conferences such as Cairo and Beijing, CR UN activists sometimes found themselves not only encountering a strongly organized feminist NGO sector with some "inside" connections, but also a draft agreement, the bulk of which had been negotiated months earlier. In effect, they arrived too late to set the negotiation agenda and, in their view, were left countering only the most extreme effects of feminist policies.

The CR UN portrayal of the "feminist threat" goes further than simply recognizing their organizational advances. Feminists are seen as having successfully infiltrated key UN agencies and as working to secure the implementation of their agenda through UN bodies. Thus, feminists are reported to have "secret meetings" with UN "antifamily" officials to "mastermind" the reinterpretation of existing international rights to include "implied rights for abortion and homosexual rights" (Real Women of Canada 1998).

According to the CR UN, abortion and homosexual rights are central to the "radical feminist" agenda, which is ultimately an agenda to "free" women from childbearing.

> [I]t seems . . . the most important thing to them [radical feminists] is complete freedom from their reproductive systems, which some feminists have referred to pregnancy as a kind of sexual slavery. . . . So at the end of the day, perhaps they are looking for complete transformation in mankind, but along the way, I think they want to be freed from the constraints of nature. (Ruse 1999c)

Thus, while women's rights may seem like a laudable aim, they are rejected by the CR UN because they cloak a much more nefarious agenda variously described as the promotion of "abortion and sex education" (Wright 1999); the separation of women from their "religious and cultural ties" (Real Women of Canada 1999a); the exploitation of children; the destruction of the family; "the foe of every religion, the very Angel of Death" (Carlson 1999a, 23); and the promotion of a "boundless society" (Reid 1999), leading ultimately to the acceptance of homosexuality (Wright 1999).

Feminists are clearly seen by the CR UN as part of the "antifamily" camp at the UN, but their role in the secularist/humanist conspiracy is less clear. The extensive CR UN literature on "the feminist threat" at the UN, at first glance, seems to suggest that feminists are the principal enemy confronting the CR UN and "the natural family." However, in interviews, CR UN activists made it clear that while feminists have a strong influence at the UN, the UN is not a mere puppet of a feminist hegemony. Rather, feminists work "in partnership" with the various anti-Christian agents at the UN (Reid 1999). This argument depicts feminists as almost a "single issue" actor, promoting a "misguided" equality between women and men that denies the dictates of biology (Ruse 1999c). The CR UN may oppose feminists, but this is not the only enemy they seek to counter.

Sitting alongside feminists, in CR UN politics, is an emerging international threat: "the homosexual." While the CR UN depicts feminists as a separate actor, it sees a large degree of overlap between feminism and lesbian and gay activism. Many CR organizations active on the American domestic scene have historically made little distinction between feminists and lesbians (Herman 1997, chapter 4). Indeed, Concerned Women for America argues that the feminist movement at the UN is largely "peopled" by lesbians, and that women's rights inevitably lead to homosexuality (Reid 1999; McFeely 1999). The view of many in the CR UN is that some groups, primarily feminists, are trying to introduce language into international agreements that will amount to a de facto acceptance of homosexuality. However, as we discuss in chapters 5 and 6, the homosexual "threat," while looming large on the horizon, is often subsumed within the larger villains of globalism, secularism, and "radical feminism."

Each of these villains—globalists/socialists, secularists, and feminists—is identified by the CR UN as part of the danger motivating a CR UN politics. Each enemy represents a different type of danger facing the "natural" family, but no one enemy has emerged as *the* force of evil at the international realm. Sometimes these enemies are portrayed as acting in concert, but each remains a distinct actor, with different, usually overlapping agendas, requiring a particular CR UN response. The CR's portrayal of multiple and shadowy enemies can be read in several ways. The lack of a clear certainty about "the enemy" might suggest a movement uncertain of its direction. Or it might suggest a movement potentially divided along ideological and theological lines in its worldview. Or it might simply suggest a movement whose politics play to a number of different concerns and different agendas and for whom the lack of specificity about "the enemy" has certain strategic benefits. In our view, the CR UN's identification of its enemies reflects all of these. For our purposes, however, what is important about these multiple, and sometimes conflicting enemies is that they point to very different conceptions within the CR UN of its role at the UN, and indeed, to different conceptions about the UN as a political space within which to undertake a "natural" family, conservative Christian politics.

In the following section, we build on this discussion of the CR UN's enemies to look more closely at the CR project at the UN. What is it about these enemies—globalists/socialists, secularists, and feminists—that requires an international CR presence, and what does the CR UN hope to accomplish at the UN?

Taking It to the UN: Defining a CR International Politics

The entry point for the CR at the UN is the UN-hosted conference. Throughout the 1990s and into the twenty-first century, a series of intergovernmental negotiations, often referred to as "conferences," were held at which the international community agreed on "plans of action" for a number of topics, from the environment (1992), population policy (1994), and women (1995) to racism (2001) and HIV/AIDS (2001). These negotiations proved to be ripe terrain for social activists seeking to affect international policy and consensus building, and are generally lauded as facilitating the formation of social justice networks (Keck and Sikkink 1998a, 168–69; Riles 2000).

For our purposes, the proliferation of UN-hosted conferences in the 1990s and early twenty-first century has resulted in two key developments. First, it has facilitated the expansion and further institutionalization of NGO involvement in international law and policy making. Second, it has broadened the range of social policy issues on the international agenda. The conferences themselves have become international media events, attracting the participation of the world's press and a wide range of social activists, as well as top-level state delegates. For the CR UN, the involvement of NGOs, together with the perception that the UN conference is a hotbed of social activism, makes it both a dangerous "antifamily" arena and a promising political space within which an interfaith, "natural family" alliance can have an immediate impact.

CR UN activists often point to these conferences, particularly the 1994 Cairo Conference on Population and the 1995 Beijing Conference on Women, as the "birthplace" for a conservative Christian global politics (Ruse 1999c). In chapters 4 and 6, we discuss each of these conferences in more detail. In this section, we turn our attention more generally to the role of the UN conference in shaping CR UN activism. The

UN conference is both the entry point for the CR's global politics and a source of danger justifying that politics. For the CR UN, it is precisely because the UN conference has become a site for social activism that it is seen as a dangerous "antifamily" arena.

The 1995 Beijing Conference on Women was the first UN conference to attract a broad range of CR UN actors, who saw their participation as essential to countering the activist presence of feminists and safeguarding American law from the excesses of UN policy making (see, for example, Dobson 1995; Roylance 1995). While some scholars and activists have applauded the emergence of an active NGO sector as the laudable development of an international civil society, the CR UN is deeply suspicious of NGO involvement in international (including UN) matters (C-Fam 1999). For the CR, NGOs are the source of what Austin Ruse calls "all the wacky ideas in the world" (1999d), which then "percolate" through the UN system (C-Fam 2000d). As a forum at which NGOs have an active role, the UN conference is seen as similarly excessive. According to Katherine Balmforth of the World Family Policy Center, the Beijing Conference on Women, for example, promoted a "radical world view" and is being used as a tool for "social engineering" (quoted in C-Fam 2000b).

Thus, the UN conference, far from being a democratizing space, is seen by the CR UN as profoundly *un*democratic, allowing activists, such as feminists, to pursue a social policy agenda through the backdoor of international law and policy that was unsuccessful when introduced through the front door of domestic policy (see, for example, Ruse 1999c; CWA 1998b). Having failed at the domestic level, the argument goes, social activists—primarily feminists—are now turning to the international realm as an alternative arena within which to advance an "antifamily" agenda (Hirsen 1999, 31; see also Hafen 1999). This view of the "alternative" political space offered by international law and policy is, at some level, shared by many social activists who presumably have seized on the international realm precisely because it provides another way to affect social policy. The question this raises is, whose policy is being affected? Is it domestic U.S. policy or international policy? Or both?

For the CR UN, it is both. Within the CR's campaign literature there are two basic arguments about the effect of UN conferences. The first and most prevalent goes like this: "Antifamily" activists—"radical feminists, population control ideologues, and homosexual rights activists"

(Balmforth 1999)—push for international recognition of "new" rights that are framed very generally as, for example, "reproductive rights." This vague human rights language is a "trojan horse" that masks a more nefarious "antifamily" agenda (Hafen 1999). With each new UN meeting, language referring to "reproductive rights" is repeated and repeated until it becomes an accepted part of international law, in turn binding upon domestic states (see, for example, Bilmore 1998; Hirsen 1999; Wright 1999; C-Fam 2001b). Thus, the political activity that takes place at seemingly far-flung UN conferences is actually "a direct path to power" for these "antifamily" forces, allowing them to affect U.S. politics beyond the reach of democratic accountability (Balmforth 1999). The task for CR UN activists is to prevent international agreement on language such as "reproductive rights."

The second, increasingly prominent view is that social activists, such as feminists, are fundamentally changing the international order, making it a profoundly antifamily arena. In this view, the rationale for a CR politics is less specifically about protecting the United States than about stopping the global dominance of the "antifamily" forces. Proponents of the "natural" family need to act now because time is running out. Allan Carlson explains it thus:

> It is not hysterics, but objective observation, to suggest that the defenders of those "family moralities" that still *hallow* marriage and still *welcome* children have little time left, perhaps a decade, before the virulent secular individualism of the new so-called "Western" order completes its work. (1999a, 40)

Whereas both of these views—of a direct threat to U.S. domestic law and politics and an "antifamily" takeover of the international realm—are used to justify a CR UN political engagement, each entails different conceptions of the international realm and the nature of the United Nations. In the following sections, we outline the different views of the UN and the international realm, exploring how these, in turn, offer different visions of the CR UN's international mission.

Making Sense of "the International"

For many on the American political and Christian right,[7] the UN is the epitome of big government: a "big unorganized body" characterized by corruption, "inbreeding," and "nepotism" (Moloney 1999). As a large, lumbering institution, the UN is seen as somewhat ineffective: a "backwater" (Ruse 1999c), "isolated and in-bred" (Wright 1999). In this conception, the UN is considered largely incompetent: "[W]e laugh because what is actually productive about the UN is that it is unproductive" (Moloney 1999). But this image of an ineffective UN is seemingly in contradiction to the international threat to Christianity and family values that motivates CR international activism. If the UN is so incompetent, why bother with it? To a certain extent, this is the view taken by many in the CR who oppose American involvement in the UN but have gone no further. The turning point for the CR UN, however, appears to be the perception that this "backwater" is becoming a threat, precisely because it is a big inefficient organization operating on the margins of domestic politics. As a large, faceless bureaucracy, the UN is seen as more susceptible to infiltration by radical NGOs and democratically unaccountable, sympathetic UN bureaucrats (see, for example, Moloney 1999; O'Leary 1998; Ruse 1999c). As with the work of Allan Carlson, in which the UN is seen as good but corrupted, the UN, in this analysis, is depicted as a passive, arguably feminized institution that "has become all too vulnerable" to the "invasion" of "powerful" antifamily forces; "all too easy a conquest" (Gusdek 1998). In contrast to the feminization of globalist philosophy outlined in chapter 2, in which the "sirens of globalism" denote the "evil power" of woman, this construction of the UN elides the feminine with power*lessness*. It is also a UN in distress and in need of rescue by the forces of good.

This view of the UN is also facilitated by a conceptual split between the UN itself and its constituent agencies, which are seen by CR UN activists as being more specifically the instruments of the antifamily movement. This is particularly the case with UN agencies, such as the World Health Organization and the United Nations Population Fund, which are vilified in CR campaign literature as instruments of "population ideologues" (Balmforth 1999).

A contrasting image is of the UN as an essentially un-Christian, negative force. For some groups like Concerned Women for America or the Eagle Forum, the UN is, and always will be, a force for the international centralization of power. As the size and scope of international agreements grow, some CR activists see an expanding UN as leading to a world government, with the "Secretary General . . . positioned to become *the* premier global leader" (CWA 1998h). As a form of big government with global aspirations, the UN must be resisted:

> Coming from a Christian perspective, walking into the UN and listening to these conferences, it is a stark contrast to the principles by which Christians stand. The very essence of Christianity is the realization that God is the ultimate ruler and that God is our provider. The concept of the UN is that government is the ultimate ruler and that government will be the provider and decide what is best for you. (Reid 1999)

Linking these very different understandings of the UN is a shared conviction that international law, and the international arena more generally, is having an increasingly powerful effect on domestic governments. For example, the CR UN sees the UN-hosted conference as directly affecting international law, as well as domestic law and policy. For the CR UN, the existence of multiple documents with agreed-upon language on, for example, "reproductive rights," gives this language a normative quality. As such, these documents and related human rights standards are seen as becoming—potentially—agreed-upon standards against which U.S. law might be measured.[8] The "soft" quality of these conference agreements makes them even more dangerous. Because conference documents are "plans of action" and not formal treaties, the CR UN argues, they can be introduced into U.S. domestic policy through the "backdoor" of executive orders, rather than being subject to the more rigorous approval process required of formal treaties.[9]

The CR UN's depiction of the insidious but profound effect of UN conferences on domestic and international law and policy, while in some ways an overstatement of the operation of international agreements, is, in other respects, partly accurate.[10] Certainly, for some international lawyers, UN conferences are important but not central to the evolution of international law.[11] Under more traditional readings of international legal doctrine, UN conferences, with their consensus-based "plans of action," are more aspirational then legal; they are expressions of policy direction rather than formal, legal developments. For other theorists, however, social activism at the international level has changed both the direction of international policy and the way that international law develops. Like the CR UN, international legal scholars are beginning to look at the ways that legal norms are evolving internationally, and at the complex relationship between events such as UN conferences and human rights and international law (see, for example, Bianchi 1997; Mertus 2000; Spiro 2000).

In this respect, CR UN activism offers an interesting comment on the changing nature of international law. Within dominant thinking on international affairs, international law has occupied a marginal position as an aspirational, idealistic discipline out of step with the power politics said to govern affairs between nation-states.[12] Not only is state behavior governed by economic and military might, according to this view, but the idea of an international law regulating state conduct is seen as simply impossible in an international realm devoid of a centralized state with the power to punish noncompliance. How can this be law, the argument goes, if it cannot be enforced?

In a curious twist, we now find, with the CR UN, a discourse on international law that condemns it not for its aspirational quality, but for its power. For the CR UN, the international realm is a dangerous, "antifamily" arena precisely because the decisions made and the consensus reached there have the power to change domestic law and policy. This view of the reach of international law stands in sharp contrast to the realist critique of international law outlined above. But it is a view shared by many activists, such as feminists and environmentalists, who have turned to the international realm as an arena within which to achieve social change.

Having identified the power of the international realm, the more difficult question for the CR UN is how best to confront this power. What is the CR UN mission at the UN? With very differing conceptions of the United Nations and its role in a perceived "antifamily" international order, the CR UN appears divided about its task, and a much larger question remains for this movement: to what end is it working?

Defining a Purpose at the United Nations

While all of the CR UN organizations discussed in this text may agree broadly that they are needed at the UN to defend the three sovereignties— nation, family, and church—they differ in their long-term objectives. Very generally, the CR UN groups can be divided into two types: the "reformers," who see reforming the UN as essential to stopping the "antifamily" agenda; and the "illuminators," whose role is more narrowly defined in terms of raising public awareness.

Groups like the Catholic Family and Human Rights Institute (C-Fam) and the Howard Center argue for an active presence at the UN to both counter their enemies and reform the UN itself. Building on Allan Carlson's depiction of a benign UN corrupted by secularist forces, the CR UN's role is, for some, rescuing the UN from the brink of secularist domination. Initially, this requires resisting attempts by secularists and their supporters—such as feminists—to shore up the "antifamily" agenda. In concrete terms, this means attending UN conferences and other UN meetings to lobby against women's rights, children's rights, and population policy. Austin Ruse of C-Fam, for example, argues that the CR UN is doing "triage" at the UN: "Most of these documents [negotiated at UN-sponsored conferences] are just horrible and what we try and do is get out the worst of things" (1999c). But in the face of a secularist dominance of the UN, CR UN activists must do more than triage; they must also start to operate on the sick patient that is the UN:

> Our side has generally been content with scanning the document which the other side writes and trying to improve their language. This still remains the most important part of our work. But we will not win until we begin writing language and getting governments to introduce it for us. At Cairo +5 we did this for the first time. (Ruse 1999e)

More fundamentally, however, Ruse argues that the "antifamily" movement at the UN can only be stopped by ultimately changing not just the UN, but the whole world (1999c). In this view, western governments (in their globalist and secularist guise) are able to impose an antifamily politics on the third world because of global disparities in economic resources. So long as the west can "manipulate" third world governments, secularists will be able to promote their antifamily politics. The task then becomes changing the UN—ostensibly making it fairer to developing countries—and making the developing world less reliant on western aid:

> [A] lot of these things [antifamily policies] are allowed to come in the debate because the developing world needs money. So a developing world/country will say "O.K., we will allow this radical language and we may institute these changes in exchange for development money from the UN and the World Bank and IMF." So, I don't think until that monetary incentive is removed that this will change much. Sadly many on the American right don't understand that. (Ruse 1999c)

This ostensibly "liberal" position, taken by a self-defined "conservative Christian," is clearly not shared by others on the American right. Organizations like Concerned Women for America or the Eagle Forum are ideologically hostile to international aid, seeing in it an extension of the welfare state to the international level:

> Eagle Forum's position is that we should completely get out of the UN. We don't think our U.S. dollars should be funneled through this organization. . . . [W]e have a number of private organizations—religious and secular—that do international charity work. We don't think that it's necessarily [up to] American taxpayers . . . to [fund the UN] involuntarily. (Moloney 1999)

For others, international aid is part of a global plot to "channel Americans' wealth . . . into Third World countries" (James 1997a; see also P. Robertson 1991, 206–7). In addition, for these organizations, the UN itself is part of "the problem." Thus, no matter how effective the "natural family" lobby is at changing UN policy, the UN itself cannot be condoned.

The role that groups like CWA define for themselves at the UN is primarily to expose what goes on there for the purpose of then mobilizing Americans to demand changes in U.S. foreign policy and revoke U.S. membership in the UN (Wright 1999; Moloney 1999). CWA, for example, describes its role at the UN in largely passive terms: "CWA is committed to standing as a watchman on the wall in order to alert American families to an United Nations activity [sic] that will affect their future" (CWA 1997d). The Family Research Council, in contrast, sees a more activist role, but one that is still largely about monitoring rather than reforming the UN: "The Family Research Council's current United Nations Project is an attempt to call the U.N. to account for its failure to protect human rights around the world" (Wagner n.d.).

Despite these different roles, an increasing number of CR UN organizations, such as Concerned Women for America and Eagle Forum, are seeking formal recognition by the UN as nongovernmental organizations. This process of formal recognition entitles an NGO to more permanent standing at the UN, with greater and more immediate access to UN meetings. The decision by various CR UN organizations to seek this formal accreditation is part of a general expansion of CR UN activism beyond simple attendance at UN conferences. CR UN groups have become more permanent actors in the UN system, regularly monitoring UN agencies and departments, such as the World Health Organization and the Commission on the Status of Women, and attending sittings of the committees that oversee the implementation of human rights agreements.[13] Once again, the CR UN's concentration tends to be on women's rights and population policy, and an ongoing focus of CR UN activism is the committee that monitors the Convention on the Elimination of Discrimination Against Women (see MacLeod and Hurlburt 2000; Balmforth 1999) and the equivalent committee for the Convention on the Rights of the Child.[14]

This expansion of CR UN activism entails a number of difficulties for this movement, particularly in light of the different views taken by member organizations about the long-term objectives of a CR global politics. First, the CR UN's engagement with the UN, no matter how strategic, belies the hostility with which many CR activists view this organization. Despite the apparent willingness of many groups to work within the context of a global interfaith alliance, this overt hostility to the UN reasserts itself in often extreme anti-UN rhetoric. For example, Real Women of Canada, while ostensibly seeing merit in UN policies on disaster relief and peacekeeping, describes UN policies as:

> like a coiled serpent, ready to strike at the throat of a nation's cultural and religious values, and its very foundation—the traditional family, bringing them crashing down to a cruel death. The anti-life, anti-family serpent at the UN is determined to triumph as it holds the world prone to be swallowed up and digested. (Real Women of Canada 1999a)

While Real Women seems to separate the UN itself from its policies, suggesting that perhaps the UN can be redeemed (Landolt 1999), it is difficult to reconcile this with an image of the UN as a snake that "will return to attack again and again" (Real Women of Canada 1999a). For many, the prospect of an interfaith orthodox alliance is the vehicle by which a "natural" family politics is possible at this otherwise evil institution. Real Women, in the same newsletter quoted above, goes on to herald the interfaith alliance as a potential "tamer" of the UN "serpent":

> [S]omething positive is taking place at the UN. The NGOs from around the world, speaking many languages and representing many faiths, together with the Christian and Muslim delegations and observers, work

together in perfect harmony—understanding and trusting one another implicitly. It is truly a miracle which gives us the assurance that we are not alone and abandoned in our struggle against the UN serpent. (1999a)

Despite this apparent hope in the future of the UN, the CR UN's often virulent antiglobalist/anti-UN rhetoric may pose particular problems as this movement engages in mainstream political debate at the UN and other international institutions. Excessive rhetoric, for example, may prove counterproductive as the CR UN endeavors to promote a "natural family" politics as a reasoned alternative to the "excesses" identified in feminist politics. Similarly, the extreme language used to describe various UN agencies may make it difficult to sell a global activism to an otherwise resistant grassroots membership: if the UN is so evil and ready to "strike at the throat of religious values," what hope can there be for a CR UN politics?

As the CR UN becomes more "mainstreamed" within UN structures (as, for example, UN-accredited NGOs, a further difficulty arises for a movement that often defines itself as outside of, and hence somewhat immune to, the power politics of the global order. Through their participation at the UN, CR activists are becoming a part of the very activist NGO sector they disdain, and with the Bush administration, the CR UN may find itself with more ready access to the centers of power than it had expected. Under Bush, CR activists have been included as official representatives on the U.S. state delegation to UN conferences, such as the 2002 World Summit on Children, a position the CR UN heavily criticized when occupied by feminists (see above).[15] Thus, the CR UN's self-portrayal as the marginalized and maligned "innocent abroad," fighting against the privileged and powerful secularist, globalist, and feminist cliques at the UN may prove to have a limited shelf life as the CR becomes an established UN player.

Perhaps most problematically, the CR UN's uncertain mission at the UN exposes a larger difficulty for this movement: the role of the domestic state in a changing global order. Implicit in all variants of CR UN activism is a concern that the international realm—whether as a fundamentally anti-Christian space or an emerging power largely under the sway of antifamily forces—poses a threat to the domestic state both at "home" in the United States and in the "vulnerable" third world. This threat may be envisioned in different ways—as a move to world governance or as the secularization of all societies, domestic and international—but it shares a single feature: an attack on the power of individual nations to define their own religious and cultural practices.

Behind this concern with the growing power of "the global" is an implicit valorization of the nation-state as a bulwark against globalization and the universalization of social policy. This is a curious and not unproblematic position for a movement that in its domestic politics is highly critical of the domestic state. For the domestic CR, the state is a controversial player in delivering social policy. While many CR activists oppose any role for the state, others foresee a possible role for the state acting as a "moral leader" (Herman 1997, chapter 7). In the international realm, CR UN politics construct an implicit vision of an independent, muscular, domestic state. As the guardian of religious and cultural beliefs, it must be relatively strong, capable of resisting stronger (presumably "antifamily") states, as well as the involvement of international agencies such as the World Bank or the United Nations Population Fund. This state, then, must be financially independent (and hence above the ministrations of international agencies who come "bearing gifts") and secure from military and cultural incursion.

But is this a vision of the domestic state acceptable to all within the CR? And how is this strong state achieved in an era of globalization? Earlier in this chapter, we noted that the CR UN limits its critique of globalization to the social policy dimension, largely omitting any consideration or analysis of international economic factors. This is a curious omission given the domestic CR's comparatively well-developed economic analysis. The difficulty for the CR UN is that the neoliberal economic vision promoted by the domestic CR may not play well internationally, particularly in the context of a CR global vision of a "natural" family order, characterized by strong, independent nation-states. This leaves a number of questions unanswered: what is the vision of the "economic good life" underpinning a CR global politics? Is an empowered nation-state economically self-contained, or is it a player within an equal and accessible trading regime? Are all nation-states to be empowered, or only those evincing a religious orthodoxy? Can the "natural" family be protected within any society, or only those with particular political (liberal democratic) and economic (neoliberal) institutions? Is it enough to have an empowered, "family-friendly" state, or must international institutions themselves be reformed?

Conclusion

In this chapter, we have done three things. First, we have analyzed the scope and direction of CR UN activism, focusing on the particular forums and means by which the CR UN advances its political agenda. Second, we have considered how CR UN ambivalence about the UN and the international arena more generally have impacted CR UN politics. We have argued that the CR UN evinces different and sometimes contradictory conceptions of the UN. More than a curious anomaly, this uncertainty about the UN affects CR UN strategizing. Is this a movement advocating structural reform of the UN, or one that simply exposes the fundamentally flawed nature of this institution? The CR UN's failure to answer this question haunts its political project at the UN.

Third, we have shown that the CR UN is engaged in the processes of global change. Whether termed "globalization" or the "imposition of a cookie-cutter standard," what is at issue in CR UN politics is an attempt to participate in the negotiation of global social change. The CR UN may resist aspects of globalization—the perceived imposition of universal social policy, for example—but its political engagement demonstrates a commitment, on some level, to participating in the international realm. This is not a movement advocating a knee-jerk isolationism and a return to "simpler times." This is a "modernist" movement, responding to social and political change and deeply involved in contemporary processes (Caplan 1987a, 5; see also Lechner 1993, 30; Marty and Appleby 1993a). It is now fairly well recognized within social movements literature that religious fundamentalism is not the regressive, antimodernist movement as it was sometimes characterized (Lechner 1993; Marty and Appleby 1993a, 3). The above analysis takes this conclusion further to demonstrate that a CR international presence cannot be read simply as an "antiglobalization" stance. Rather than retreating into a regressive nationalism in the face of a globalized world order, the CR UN is developing a worldview that accommodates a changing understanding of self and community.

4.

The Death Culture Goes Global: International Population Policy and Christian Right Politics in Action

Our side did not wake up [to] the damage done by the UN until the 1994 International Conference on Population and Development, the Cairo Conference. At that time, Pope John Paul II called forth people of all faiths to go to Cairo and to fight the Culture of Death. He knew that rumors of great danger whispered from that ancient city. More than two hundred citizen lobbyists appeared out of nowhere . . . stopping the feminists from their desire to make abortion an internationally recognized human right.

Austin Ruse

For the war on population and the family is the most savage and brutal war ever waged by the greatest powers on earth against the weakest and most innocent of all God's creatures. From the sheer number of its victims alone, which now exceeds the number of those killed in all the great wars, what we are witnessing today is nothing less than the third world war. . . . A new paganism has taken over where once stood the mightiest Christian faith. Europe, therefore, must be rechristianized. Only then will we finally cast out the devil and see the return of the strong and vibrant families into our homes.

Senator Francisco Tatad

Population policy, more than any other issue, symbolizes for the CR UN the threat to family, nation, and church. Defined broadly as the amalgam of programs, institutions, and agreements governing efforts to limit population growth,[1] this area of international law and policy has raised the ire of religious conservatives opposed to abortion, contraception, women's rights, and environmental protection. International measures to address reproduction and reproductive health are seen by the CR UN as part of a global "death culture," which seeks to undermine the "natural family," the sovereign realm of the state, and the future of Christianity. In the area of population policy, the CR UN finds the most extreme manifestations of the evils besetting the international realm. Advocates of population "control," for the CR UN, are nothing more than the very foes of "the natural family."

Because international population policy brings together many of the issues motivating the CR UN—abortion, contraception, women's rights, the "internationalization" of social relations, and the global centralization of power—it provides a case study of CR UN politics "in action." Our first objective in this chapter is to provide an overview of CR UN politics in the population area as a way to explore the key areas of concern for the CR UN and the different levels at which their politics engage with international law and institutions. In doing so, we realize another key objective, which is to consider how some of the tensions outlined in the first three chapters of this book play out in the context of a specific area of CR UN politics. In chapters 2 and 3, we explored competing images of the UN within CR politics and theology. Various views of the UN were reflected in Protestant Right and CR UN discourses, including constructions of the UN as corrupt to its core and implicated in the global consolidation of power, and the converse view of the UN as an innocent victim of globalist forces, corrupt but salvageable. We suggested that this unresolved view of the UN haunts CR UN politics as it struggles to identify the multiple and shifting enemies with whom it must engage in battle. In this chapter, we pick up where that analysis left off, considering the various enemies depicted in CR UN opposition to population policy. We look behind CR UN rhetoric to discern who, in the view of the CR, is the force behind the population apparatus. Through this analysis, we consider and highlight some of the strategic difficulties stemming from CR UN ambivalence about the nature of the international realm and the possibilities of CR UN "natural family" politics.

CR UN uncertainty about the international realm, we argue, is in part a result of changes within CR UN organizations as they accommodate their worldview to an international politics. We trace a shift in CR UN rhetoric from an emphasis on abortion as the tool of an emerging Marxist world government to a "softer" focus on poverty, third-world development, and "the rights of poor women." This shift, we argue, may herald a change in tactics at the UN and may reflect the effect of coalition building among various conservative Christian groups. However, this change presents a dilemma for a movement that is fundamentally conservative in nature. The changing tactics around population policy suggest a new vision of the UN that is at times hopeful and surprisingly egalitarian. But is this a vision around which the CR UN can coalesce?

International Population Policy and the Cairo Conference

International population policy, while formally coordinated by the UN through the UN Population Fund (UNFPA), encompasses a vast range of projects administered and carried out not just by UN and related international bodies, but by state governments and nongovernmental organizations. Starting in the 1950s, western policymakers, particularly those in the United States, adopted the view that overpopulation not only prevented economic development in the south, but also represented a risk to world stability (Hartmann 1987, 57; see also Crane 1994, 351–93; Donaldson 1990). Programs designed to reduce overpopulation received a large infusion of funds from state governments, and large, primarily American, charitable organizations, such as the Ford and Rockefeller Foundations, began to invest substantial funds in such programs as well.

Initial efforts to control population growth were heavy-handed and focused on meeting demographic targets. The first World Population Conference, held in Bucharest in 1974, for example, saw third-world governments and some women's groups challenging the approach and the dominance of international population institutions. The result was a change in the language of "population control," reflecting an attempt to adopt more of an integrationist approach, where population was linked to socioeconomic transformations required in developing countries (Hartmann 1987, 107–8). Rigid demographic goals were deemphasized and the idea of women as decision makers in the population area was tentatively introduced. The "integrationist" language had little subsequent impact on the delivery of population programs (Hartmann 1987, 108–9), and the focus remained on limiting fertility in order to reduce the "negative externalities of childbearing" and promote economic growth (Crane 1994, 363). Following the Bucharest Conference, some developing states, contrary to their position at Bucharest, began to develop state-sponsored fertility control measures (Corrêa 1994, 12; Finkle and Crane 1985, 1). By the time of the second World Population Conference in Mexico in 1984, many developing states had accepted population control measures as essential for economic growth.

The Mexico City conference was dominated by political fallout resulting from a shift in U.S. policy on world population growth. Under the Reagan administration, U.S. foreign policy no longer addressed population growth as a problem, defining it instead as a "neutral" phenomena (Corrêa 1994, 2; Finkle and Crane 1985). Up to that point, the United States had been a principal source for funding international population programs. However, under the Reagan administration, a new approach was introduced, known as "the Mexico City policy," which prevented U.S. foreign aid from going to "any organization that performs abortions, advises women on abortion, or lobbies on behalf of abortion rights—even if these activities are supported by non-U.S. funds" (Stein 1996, 45; see also Hartmann 1987, 123–25; Crane 1994, 366). The result was a move toward a more decentered program delivery where funds were channeled through international population groups.

In addition to the privatization of population programs, the 1980s saw the rise of women's groups in both the economic south and north who challenged the family planning focus of population institutions. Feminist and other activists pointed out that substantial international funds were being poured into developing countries to establish extensive birth control and sterility services without considering or treating related health-care issues, such as sexually transmitted diseases, sexual health, and the sexual health needs of adolescents and infertile women (Germain, Nowrojee, and Pyne 1994). Feminist and other groups argued for a rethinking of international population initiatives based on reproductive health rather than fertility control. To a large extent, the language of reproductive health was adopted by population institutions and by the late 1980s was part of mainstream population rhetoric but without being fully integrated into program provision. In the view of feminist scholars and activists, the result was a language of reproductive health that maintained a focus on medical intervention over systemic changes, and reinforced the construction of women solely in terms of their reproductive and gender roles (Corrêa 1994, 62; Germain, Nowrojee, and Pyne 1994, 37–41).

In the lead-up to the 1994 Cairo conference, feminist groups mobilized to present a unified lobbying position at the negotiation sessions. Their principal objective was to replace the historic emphasis on demographics with a more "woman-centered" position that emphasized women's empowerment and rights to control their own fertility.[2] To advance this position, women's groups worked within the language of "population policy" and, where necessary, incorporated feminist concerns into those of the population industry (Higer 1999, 127–31).

The 1994 Cairo Conference on Population and Development

As the third of the world conferences on population, Cairo is particularly significant because the agreement reached there—the Programme of Action—provides a twenty-year blueprint for international population policy. Cairo is, at this time, the leading expression of international agreement on the scope, funding, and aims of population programs. A technical document detailing international development activities, the Programme of Action is also an expression of international consensus on a range of issues, from women's reproductive rights to the relationship between population growth and economic development. As such, it can be read as describing and delimiting the social meaning of contested terrain such as reproduction, environmental protection, gender relations, and economic development (Buss 2000b).

For many, the Cairo Programme of Action represents both a feminist success story and a "paradigm shift" in the understanding of international population policy (Sen 1995; Crane and Isaacs 1995; McIntosh and Finkle 1995). Principally, the Programme of Action moves away from a focus on demographics to a more complex approach that situates population issues in the context of other social, economic, and environmental issues. Rather than emphasizing reductions in fertility, the Programme of Action recognizes women's and men's rights to control their reproductive lives. Population policy, according to this agreement, must operate within a rights framework and address not just reproductive issues, but also related social justice concerns, such as women's empowerment and equality between women and men.[3]

But, as we stated earlier, the story of the Cairo conference does not end there. This conference was, in many respects, the "birthplace" of the CR UN (Ruse 1999e), and there are a number of aspects to the conference itself that were influential in shaping CR international mobilization. First, Cairo was characterized by the involvement of a large number of NGOs, including, as we stated above, a well-organized feminist presence. The preparatory process leading to Cairo reflected the input of feminist organizations, with the result that the language of reproductive rights was included in the draft Programme of Action. The Cairo conference, like other UN conferences, started with extensive preconference negotiating and drafting sessions, with the idea that by the time of the actual conference, the agreed-upon document would be largely in place, with any contested provisions put in brackets for final negotiation. Thus, in the lead-up to the actual Cairo conference, the draft programme reflected a certain degree of international support for what might be seen as a feminist "agenda" to introduce a reproductive rights framework. Cairo can thus be seen as something of a feminist success story, and was certainly a significant event in getting women's rights on the international agenda (Copelon and Petchesky 1995, 343).

The perception of the draft programme as a "feminist blueprint" was of particular concern for "right-to-life" groups, and more importantly the Vatican, whose subsequent campaign against the draft programme was, arguably, a second important development in mobilizing an international CR movement. Through its status as a Permanent Observer to the UN, the Vatican launched a vociferous opposition to the draft programme, which has been described as a "full court press against abortion involving the Vatican diplomatic service, the Roman Curia and bishops around the world" (Reese 1996, 263). The resulting publicity did much to inform and ultimately motivate a conservative Catholic and Protestant interest in international developments.

Third, the extent of the Vatican's opposition to provisions concerning birth control and abortion led it to pursue diplomatic alliances with fundamentalist Islamic countries, such as Iran and Libya, to provide a unified opposition to aspects of the Cairo programme (*Independent* 1994b; Stein 1996, 53). While the alliances forged by the Vatican were not as forceful as anticipated, the conference negotiations were stalled in the face of intractable disagreement over language perceived by the Vatican to condone abortion and birth control. The Vatican eventually backed down, but not before it achieved some compromise on key language on abortion (Cohen and Richards 1994, 153; Stein 1996, 54). Despite this, the idea of an international conservative religious alliance is one that has been picked up and pursued by CR UN activists, who see the Vatican's efforts in this regard as a positive step in the development of a conservative religious presence at the UN (Carlson 1999a, 39–40; Ruse 1999e).

Fourth, the Vatican's actions made international headlines at a conference that was already attracting enormous publicity. Following the precedent set by the Rio Conference on Environment and Development (1992), Cairo was typical of the new generation of United Nations conference: part negotiation session, part performance and public relations event. While previous population conferences had also been controversial, Cairo was unique in the scale of public interest and hostility it attracted. For example, in the lead-up to the conference, Islamic lawyers filed a lawsuit to prevent it from being held in Cairo and an extremist Islamic group threatened to attack conference participants (*Independent* 1994a; Fisk 1994). The Vatican's actions, however, stole the conference headlines. For media observers, the "battle" between the Vatican, feminists, and western governments became the defining event of the conference (see, for example, Connor 1994; Clough 1994, 10; *Independent* 1994b).

The enormous publicity the Vatican attracted, as well as the subject matter of the conference, galvanized CR organizations in the United States, many of which had previously ignored international events. CR groups made very public statements of support for the Vatican leadership in the international fight against abortion (Dobson 1995; Hsu 1997). In the following year, several CR organizations, such as Focus on the Family and Concerned Women for America, attended the Fourth World Conference on Women in Beijing to lend support to the Vatican and to continue the campaign against abortion, thus starting a new international phase for CR politics.

The Christian Right and International Population Policy

At the heart of the CR UN's opposition to international population policy is, not surprisingly, a rejection of abortion and, to a lesser extent, contraception. Population policy is, for the CR UN, the globalization of a "death culture," evidence of which can be found not only in the specific practice of abortion, but in other related areas that operate to denigrate the "natural family." Thus, while abortion is a defining issue for the CR UN, its politics on population policy go much further. In this section, we look at CR UN opposition to population policy, both to provide insight into the specific machinations of CR domestic and international politics in this area and as part of an unfolding CR UN worldview, revealing how that opposition animates various aspects of the CR UN's theology and politics.

For the CR, international population policy is a horror story of devastation and destruction visited upon women and the "natural family." CR UN documents invariably contain "horrible but true" stories of human rights abuses, usually coerced abortions carried out under a state policy to reduce fertility levels.[4] Those stories tend to focus on China and its one-child policy, though Peru, and more recently Kosovo, also figure prominently. One of the key CR UN actors in this area is the Population Research Institute (PRI), an organization devoted to monitoring international population policy. PRI describes its work as exposing "abuses of human rights in the name of population control . . . in China, Bangladesh, and dozens of other countries around the world," and debunking "the widely held, but fundamentally wrongheaded, development paradigm which places economic and population growth in opposition to each other."[5] Although describing itself as "nonpartisan," PRI is an affiliate of the conservative Catholic organization Human Life International. Austin Ruse, president of the Catholic Family and Human Rights Institute (C-Fam) is an occasional researcher and writer for PRI.

Allegations of Chinese human rights abuses figure prominently in PRI's work. PRI's president, Steve Mosher, lived in China for one year and gained some notoriety in 1983 when he was expelled from Stanford University "for alleged 'unethical conduct' during his research" in China (Crane and Finkle 1989, 30ff; Horowitz 1983). Mosher claims that his expulsion was due to pressure on Stanford by the Chinese government, embarrassed by Mosher's "eyewitness" accounts of Chinese human rights abuses (McManus 1999). Whatever the cause, Mosher has become a key China watcher and a source of information on other population policy-related human rights abuses.

Increasingly, the CR UN targets women's rights as a principal instrument through which population policy is enacted. Rather than protecting women from the abuses of the "population ideologues," the CR UN argues, the recognition of "women's sexual and reproductive rights," in the Cairo Programme of Action and other documents is a "Trojan horse" masking an explicit proabortion and antifamily agenda (Hafen

1999). Reproductive rights, in particular, are nothing more than a thinly veiled recognition of abortion, and, according to some, part of a larger project to make access to abortion a universal human right (Ruse 1998a; PRI 1999e). In this analysis, sexual and reproductive rights are homosexualized, appearing as one thing, but functioning as another. They are, according to the CR UN, "population control in drag."[6]

In addition to being a covert reference to abortion, reproductive rights are seen as advancing a population control agenda through an attack on motherhood and the "natural family." This happens in three ways. First, the motivating force behind reproductive rights, according to the CR UN, is feminism, which advances an agenda to "free" women from the biological constraints of their bodies (Ruse 1999c). Hence, the promotion of reproductive rights as the right of women to choose the timing, space, and number of their children is seen by the CR UN to be premised on a denigration of motherhood (Balmforth 1999; Hsu 1995b). Reproductive rights, the argument goes, are in fact the right of women *not* to have children (Tatad 1999; Carlson 2000b). It is, in this respect, fundamentally about undermining motherhood (Carlson 2000b; Ruse 1999e).

Second, women's rights, including reproductive rights, position women as autonomous, individual actors whose destiny lies outside the home (Carlson 2000b; Hamm 1995, 143). This, the CR UN argues, both denigrates the family further—by marginalizing motherhood—and undermines traditional cultures by setting women's rights above other rights, for example, to religion or self-determination (Balmforth 1999). Third, reproductive rights inevitably lead to the acceptance of homosexuality, itself an attack on the "natural family." For the CR UN, homosexuality creeps into reproductive rights in two ways. The first is through the language of "sexual rights" and references to famili*es,* rather than *the* family (Bartlett 1995). The second is through the use of the term "gender" and its presumed denial of women's biological particularity. The challenge to an essential "woman-ness" or "man-ness," for the CR, leads to the erasure of "the two" sexes, with homosexuality the inevitable outcome (Reid 1999; Wright 1999; Hamm 1995).

On the Home Front: The Christian Right and American Foreign Policy

Opposition to population policy has been a key political objective for the CR, both domestically and internationally. At the domestic level, that opposition has primarily taken the form of lobbying for the withdrawal of U.S. funding from international agencies involved in population policy, primarily the United Nations Population Fund (UNFPA), and preventing U.S. development assistance from going to groups in developing countries linked to abortion services. Legislation pertaining to the second of these areas—funding overseas organizations involved in any way with abortion services—has been a recurring feature of American politics since the early 1970s. At that time, the U.S. Congress stipulated that no U.S. funds could be used "to promote or carry out abortions overseas" (McIntosh and Finkle 1994, 273). As noted above, this policy was extended under the Reagan administration. Known as the Mexico City policy, it prohibited "overseas organizations from receiving U.S. funds, either directly through [the U.S. international aid agency] USAID or indirectly through U.S.-based NGOs that received USAID funds, if, with their own funds and in accordance with the laws of their own countries, they 'performed' or 'actively promoted' 'abortion as a method of family planning.'"[7]

Since the Reagan administration, Mexico City–type policies have been a central campaigning focus for both feminist organizations and the Christian Right. Concerned Women for America (CWA), for example, made the passage of a Mexico City–type policy one of its top three legislative priorities in 1997, arguing that the original Mexico City policy did not go far enough and that renewed efforts were needed to prevent "anti-life philosophies" from being "exported overseas" (CWA 1998f). CWA's work paid off. A Republican-dominated Congress voted in 1998 to strip twenty million dollars from the 1999 foreign appropriations budget earmarked for the UNFPA, and, in 1999, passed a provision similar to the Mexico City policy. Affecting U.S. funding for the 2000 fiscal year, this rule prevented U.S. funds from going to any organization providing abortions or involved in lobbying any government on abortion or abortion-related laws (Center for Reproductive Law and Policy 2000). Sometimes referred to as a "global gag rule," this restriction on U.S. aid spending has proved to be a hotly contested provision, constituting something of a tug-of-war between Congress and the presidency. Under the Clinton regime, the rule was revoked in 2000,[8] reinstated by George W. Bush in January 2001 on his first day in office, and is now the subject of a lawsuit brought by the Center for Reproductive Law and Policy.[9] Going hand in hand with Mexico City policies are other legislative enactments to limit funding for the UN Population Fund, strongly supported by the CR and a central campaigning focus for the CR UN.[10]

These efforts to target U.S. funding of population policy have taken place in the context of a larger campaign to limit U.S. funding of the United Nations more generally. As we discussed in chapters 2 and 3, the Christian Right has long distrusted the UN, viewing it as a big, corrupt institution strangled by its own bureaucracy. Together with organizations on the American right, such as the Heritage Foundation, the CR has supported cutting U.S. dues to the UN. In the 1980s and 1990s, the United States refused to pay all of its UN dues, arguing, among other things, that the dues were excessive and misused by a UN in need of reform (McDermott 2000, 99–116). In the 1990s, as the arrears in U.S. dues mounted, attempts to reach a compromise agreement between the Democrat presidency and Republican congress focused on reforms to the UN, reductions in the U.S. share of UN expenses (McDermott 2000, 103–5), and the inclusion of Mexico City–type policies (Martin 1999, 75). Together these campaigns—to reduce funding of population policy and to limit U.S. funding of the UN—constitute an important and successful component of CR domestic politics.

International Politics of Population: Genocide, Ethnic Cleansing, and the United Nations Population Fund

At the international level, the CR UN has concentrated its efforts on resisting international agreement on women's rights and discrediting UN population activities. CR critiques, while focused on the UN Population Fund (UNFPA), also include other UN organizations whose mandate the CR sees as straying into the population policy field, including UNICEF, the World Health Organization, and institutions like the World Bank (Ruse 2000b; Bilmore 1998; Morrison 1998).

Increasingly, the target for most of the CR's attention, however, is the UN Population Fund, the central, coordinating body of UN and related population programs. The UNFPA is singled out by Population Research Institute and other CR organizations for its role in facilitating an international population policy that is likened to the "the horrendous genocides by Hitler and Pol Pot," the Soviet "gulags," and "a peculiar case of ethnic cleansing, beside which Kosovo pales in comparison."[11] Not only does the UNFPA coordinate much of the UN's work in the area of population, but CR activists argue that it is "the biggest and fiercest member of the global anti-natalist collaboration" (Morrison 1997b). The UNFPA originally came under specific attack for its alleged involvement with China's population program. PRI and other organizations claim that the UNFPA is complicit in Chinese human rights abuses either by remaining silent and continuing to work with the Chinese government, or, according to CWA, by "shaping China's brutal one-child policy" (Morrison 1998; CWA 1998h).

A more current example of CR critique of UNFPA activity is the headline-grabbing accusation of UNFPA involvement in the ethnic cleansing of Kosovar Albanians. In 1999, the Population Research Institute sent Catholic Family and Human Rights Institute president Austin Ruse to investigate what it referred to as the "reproductive health campaign" waged by the UNFPA "against the Kosovar refugee population" in Albania (PRI 1999a).The Ruse-PRI report concluded that in these refugee camps the UNFPA carried out "ethnic cleansing . . . under the guise of 'reproductive health'" (Ruse 1999b). The report argued that the UNFPA was intent on providing abortion services to Kosovars and creating a demand for reproductive health services, such as birth control, where none existed. The PRI additionally claimed that the UNFPA had been invited into Serbia by President Milosevic to specially "target" the Kosovar population as part of a larger ethnic cleansing campaign. A *PRI Weekly News Briefing* alleged that the "UNFPA/Milosevic campaign" consisted "of the indiscriminate distribution of 'reproductive health' supplies to the largely Muslim Kosovar population." According to the PRI, Milosevic's goal, with UNFPA assistance, was to "engage in ethnic cleansing by reducing the Kosovars' high birthrate" (PRI 1999c).

This report was picked up and publicized by other CR groups and, more controversially, by the conservative media, such as the *New York Post* (see, for example, CWA 1999g). In an exchange of letters between Ruse, Scott Weinberg of the Population Research Institute, and Alex Marshall of the UN Population Fund, all published in the *New York Post,* Ruse and Weinberg argued that the UNFPA's alleged conduct in Kosovo and Albania was part of a larger pattern of UNFPA abuses (Ruse 1999a).[12] For example, under the headline "Don't Buy the Spin Control from the UN's Butchers," Austin Ruse claimed that the UNFPA's main (nongovernmental) "partners are the largest abortion providers in the world," while Weinberg reiterated the PRI position that the "UNFPA has a history of committing human-rights abuses" and "collaborating with government 'policies' such as China's one-child policy."

In much of the CR UN writing on international population, the UN Population Fund and other institutions are characterized as part of a large, monolithic population "superstructure" staffed by individuals— "ideologues"—committed to a world vision based on population control (see Morrison 1998). While population policy and the UNFPA are the subject of voluminous CR UN publications, there is very little comment on the identity of these population "ideologues." Who are they, what do they want, and why? Are they working toward a secular agenda, a feminist conspiracy, or a global takeover? In the next section, we consider CR UN constructions of population ideologues. Rather than finding one enemy behind population policy, we are left with an unnamed but ubiquitous force, seen as pursuing various agendas. This lack of clarity, we argue, reflects the CR UN's own uncertainty about the forces it faces at the international level but also, possibly, provides the CR UN with a certain strategic advantage. As we discuss below, a faceless enemy provides the CR UN with some flexibility as it attempts to reposition itself as an international actor.

"Exploding the Population Bomb": Looking Behind the Population "Myth"

The pervasive reach of the population "superstructure" is most evident, according to the CR UN, in the conspiracy to construct the myth of a population "bomb," due to go off at any moment with widespread social, ecological, and economic problems.[13] This version of the "population problem," according to the CR UN, is simply wrong. First, it is argued, the link between population numbers and economic, social, or environmental degradation cannot be scientifically proven (Eberstadt 1999). Not only is the correlation between population growth and economic decline denied, but, according to the CR UN, population growth is good and necessary for the global economy (see Reno 1998). Second, there is evidence that population growth centered on the "natural family" is an economic good (Aguirre 1999), and third, the crisis facing the world is not *over*population but *de*population (see C-Fam 2000h; CWA 1999a and 1998d; Morrison 1997a). Pointing to statistics demonstrating declining fertility in Western Europe and North America, the CR UN argues that the western world faces a number of social and economic problems stemming from an increasingly aging population. The main thrust of these arguments is a refutation of the very definition of the population

"problem." This refutation is based on a range of "social science" literature, and is a further example of the development we discussed in chapter 2, of a CR "natural family" science on which CR UN politics are increasingly based.

If the population "problem" is a myth, this begs the question: who
is behind the myth? The short answer is: no one and everyone. In CR
UN publications, population ideologues prove to be slippery characters,
either the embodiment of various named enemies—from secularists to
feminists—or an elusive, unidentified "structure" working on behalf
of a faceless antifamily agenda. For some, such as Allan Carlson of the
Howard Center, population policy is part of the secularist attack on the
"natural family" (Carlson 1999a; see also Francis 1998 and Real Women
of Canada 1999d). Through the promotion of a "contraceptive mentality," population "ideologues" are able to undermine the natural family
as a union between a man and a woman for the purposes of having
children (Carlson 1999a; Francis 1998). The family constitutes a major
bulwark against encroaching secularism and liberalism. By undermining the "natural family," the argument goes, secularists are confirmed
in their ascendancy at the UN. "UNFPA hopes to achieve its goals by
way of undermining, and ultimately destroying, the strong traditional
families in these developing nations. It believes that once the traditional
family structure breaks down, the cultural and religious values, which
have led to resistance to their policies, will then collapse" (Real Women
of Canada 1999c).

In other accounts, population policy intersects with a larger antifamily
politics and feminist agenda to promote sexual and reproductive rights.
Sometimes population policy is depicted as leading to the destruction of
the family, while at other times, it is the end goal of a secularist global
takeover (see Tatad 1999; Carlson 2000b). In either account, population
policy goes hand in hand with an agenda to promote women's rights. The
promotion of abortion, the denigration of motherhood, and the challenge to women's and men's "natural" roles within the family (through
the promotion of women's autonomy) are all the end result of women's
rights and serve, inevitably, the goals of population "ideologues" (C-Fam
2000g; Real Women of Canada 1999b).

Feminist activists are, invariably, at the forefront of population policy
discussions, but they are generally not depicted as masterminding population policy. Rather, it is the—still very shadowy—population "superstructure" that is co-opting the agendas of feminists and lesbian and gay

activists. In this analysis, feminists, lesbian and gay activists, and the population movement are separate entities whose agendas "converge" over a shared denigration of the family. But the principal force in this coalition remains population "ideologues," with feminism and homosexuality tools in the greater arsenal of the population "superstructure":

> [B]y eliminating the differences between the sexes, encouraging women to be breadwinners and not mothers, and by legitimizing homosexuality, one does in fact control population. By discouraging motherhood at all costs, and educating the girl child against so-called "gender-stereotypes," one will be able to reduce fertility. The links between the homosexual movement and the population control movement are not always easy to find, but they do exist. The most obvious convergence is in their incessant call for abortion rights and for women to have total sexual freedom—including access to contraception and sterilization. (Hamm 1995, 143; see also McFeely 1999)

The lack of clarity about who—or what—is behind the population superstructure is, perhaps, not surprising given the multiple actors and agendas encompassed within the CR UN. It may be the case that the different enemies that emerge in CR UN conceptions of population policy serve various agendas at different times. And, as we discussed above, there is an advantage to a newly emerging movement in keeping its "big picture" vague as it endeavors to fill in the details. Indeed, while CR UN explanations of the "population structure" may reflect a lack of coherence in aspects of CR global politics, it also suggests a social movement that is on the move. That is, we can see in CR UN population politics an example of how aspects of this movement's policies and perspectives are changing in the context of its political engagement at the international level.

Remaking Conservativism: The Emergence of a "Kinder" International Politics?

CR groups who actively speak out against international population policy draw an explicit link between environmental initiatives—such as sustainable development, the Framework Convention on Climate Change, and the Biodiversity Convention—and population policy. They argue, with some justification, that many environmentalists see population reduction or, at least population "management," as necessary to achieve some measure of environmental protection. Indeed, historically, population considerations have been tied to various environmental narratives. For example, Thomas Malthus argued in 1798 that population control was necessary because of limits in food production. Similarly, many contemporary environmentalists view population growth as anathema to environmental protection. Popular books and articles, such as Paul and Anne Ehrlich's *Population, Resources, Environment* (1970) and Robert Kaplan's lengthy article in *Atlantic Monthly,* "The Coming Anarchy" (1994; see also Harrison 1992), have contributed to a view that the world is in a state of environmental crisis brought about by overpopulation. The biggest threat to the environment, and hence an important aspect of the solution to world collapse, is population explosion (see Bandarage 1997, 34). While most population activists have not wholly embraced the Ehrlichs' doomsday approach to population control, "environmental threat" has been a recurring theme in discussions around, and rationales for, population policy.

Not surprisingly then, CR UN activists are deeply suspicious of environmental initiatives, especially international measures. In a series of articles published in 1996/1997, Concerned Women for America outlined a damning critique of international environmentalism, arguing that it was a threat to American sovereignty, an attempt to control the lives of Americans, and a means of justifying population control (see CWA 1996a, b; 1998g; 1997b; and MacLeod 1997). By signing international environmental agreements, CWA argued, the American government had surrendered sovereignty over key aspects of national life and, in particular, over American land. CWA viewed agreements such as the UN Convention on Biological Diversity[14] as amounting to a "U.N. land grab," in which the U.S. government "schemes" with the UN to regulate private property and "violate the rights of United States citizens" (MacLeod 1997). CWA articles published on this topic during the 1996/1997 period were principally concerned with the establishment of protected—environmentally sensitive or important—areas, known as biosphere reserves, which they considered a "subversive removal of private property ownership." Not only was this a "U.N. land grab," but it would also lead to further U.S. government regulation, evidence of which could be found—somewhat incongruously—in the regulation of "such outdoors equipment as recreational vehicles, canoes, or sleeping bags" (MacLeod 1997).

For CWA, at the heart of these seemingly innocent environmental initiatives was a concerted attack on American sovereignty. Environmental protection was dangerous because it ultimately required—or justified—the regulation of the private lives of Americans. Touching on various environmental initiatives, from sustainable development to protecting the biological diversity of plant and animal life, CWA argued that environmentalism, and sustainable development in particular, was ultimately about regulating the behavior of individual Americans. In a 1998 publication entitled *The United Nations,* CWA went further and argued that *international* environmentalism was fundamentally un-American, "predicated upon the belief that people are a 'plague' upon the earth and that a global economic disaster might be necessary to 'punish' the U.S. and other 'rich nation's' [sic] for harming the environment" (CWA 1998h). Interestingly, the language CWA used here echoes CR descriptions of the apocalypse preceding (in some accounts) Christ's return to earth (see chapter 2). In this scenario, however, it is the CR's opponents—environmentalists—who are depicted as, and condemned for, espousing apocalyptic scenarios as a justification for particular social, economic, and environmental reforms.

CWA's focus on sustainable development stems from the belief that sustainability will require a reduction in consumption in rich countries. In environmental law and policy, "sustainable development" is a loosely defined concept that posits a reciprocal relationship between development and environment, where economic development can—and must—be pursued in a way that is environmentally sustainable. Sustainable development entered into international environmental policy with the publication in 1987 of the Brundtland Commission report, which defined sustainability as "development that meets the needs of the present without compromising the ability of future generations to meet their own needs" (World Commission on Environment and Development 1987). While some environmentalists might argue that sustainable development logically leads to a reduction in consumption by rich nations, many others argue that in its very lack of definition, sustainable development is becoming an apology for expansive economic development (Elliott 1998, 170–91). For CWA and other CR UN organizations, sustainable development is a dangerous concept, masking other agendas such as population control.[15] "A hard core environmentalist view know [sic] as sustainable development would control individual choices regarding consumption. Some examples that would have a great effect are the size of your family, the size of your home, what you eat, and what type of transportation available to you *[sic]*. This embraces the idea that no one may consume more than is needed for physical survival" (CWA 1996b).

In the 1996/1997 period, CWA's concern with sustainable development also highlighted another problem area: the relationship between environmental protection and population control. Not only did concepts like sustainable development regulate American consumption patterns, they also justified population control in the name of environmental "sustainability." CWA identifies "radical environmentalism" as the motivating force behind population policy: "Radical environmentalism is the real agenda behind this discussion. The U.N. believes that the earth is being damaged by too many people on the planet" (CWA 1996a). In this analysis, population control is seen as the desired outcome, but environmentalism is the motivating philosophy. "Rabid green devotees," such as then U.S. vice president Al Gore, were described as subscribing to a misguided environmentalism that sacrificed "the babies of third world mothers on the altar of [sustainable development]" (CWA 1997b).

With each of these critiques of international environmental law and policy—as an attack on American sovereignty, as meddling in the lives of individual Americans, and as justifying population control—the unifying theme was a rejection of environmentalism as a fundamentally "Marxist" notion. Environmentalism was for CWA a "Marxist philosophical agenda" that included not just the regulation of American lives, but the undermining of American independence by an empowered UN: "This is America the land where our forefathers shed their blood to allow us the great privilege of independence. No. United Nations you can't have our independence. Let freedom ring . . . let freedom ring!" (CWA 1996b).

CWA's position in the period 1996/1997 reflected, in many respects, dominant Christian Right opposition to international developments seen as threatening to the United States and as emanating from a Marxist-tainted consolidation of world power (see, for example, James 1997b). For the CR, international aid was fundamentally misguided because poverty, and particularly third-world poverty, was best "understood in religious terms, as an artefact of the absence of a Judeo-Christian tradition" (Lienesch 1993, 135). In this view, not only environmentalism but other international measures—such as international aid—were seen as left-wing attempts to increase government involvement in the essentially private spheres of individual and market activity. In 1996, for example,

CWA attended the World Food Summit with the express purpose of opposing measures for the "redistribution of wealth . . . [and] entitlement to food" (CWA 1996b). In addition to its view that environmentalism goes hand in hand with an "anti-god paganism," CWA's opposition to international environmental initiatives was also consistent with a neoliberal rejection of governmental interference in social, political, and economic policy.

This concern with the political implications of environmentalism has, more recently, been deemphasized in CWA publications on population policy. CWA writings, from 1998 onward, appear to have shifted emphasis away from the Marxist, globalizing agenda of environmentalism and population and toward a focus on population policy as an instrument of western imperialism. CWA has begun to call for a more "humane" approach to international issues like poverty and famine. While still maintaining that the link between population and environment is dangerous, CWA now argues for a more complex understanding of that relationship (CWA 1999d). And rather than calling for U.S. withdrawal from international aid commitments, CWA now (appears to) argue for humanitarian aid and technology to remedy the effects of famine (CWA 1999d). While it is unlikely that CWA has changed its basic opposition to environmental initiatives, its publications suggest a new role for CWA as the voice of compassion urging the international community to recognize the "needs of the world's people" (CWA 1998a).

In the space of one to two years, CWA has seemingly changed its position from one that opposed "redistribution of wealth and the entitlement to food" to calling for the use of humanitarian aid and "the offer of technology to those who lack it" (CWA 1999d). How does this organization, which opposes big government, objects to the UN as a fundamentally anti-Christian organization, and, in the recent past, resisted measures to address access to food, now find itself calling for international aid and the transfer of technology to "those in need"?

In answering this question, we need to start by sounding a few notes of caution. It is probably premature—if not inaccurate—to describe CWA as adopting a liberal, pro-development politics. The change we describe may be more rightly categorized as a shift in emphases or tactics, rather than a wholesale rewriting of policy. Additionally, these changes may be due to the influence of individual policy entrepreneurs, rather than a dramatic shift in CWA policy.[16] For example, the author of many of the

CWA publications from the 1996/1997 period is Laurel MacLeod, whose name disappears, for a time, from publications after 1997.

Having said that, it is important not to underestimate the significance of the change in CWA rhetoric. This is an organization that resists any kind of governmental interference in the free operation of the market, but is now, at least at the level of rhetoric, calling for increased humanitarian assistance and emphasizing the need for third world "life-honoring development" (CWA 1998d). In addition, the influence of individual policy entrepreneurs does not fully account for the shifts in CWA policy orientation that parallel a change in its international activism. With a more concentrated involvement in the international realm and a working alliance with conservative actors from various faiths, the CWA is likely adapting its policies in the context of more direct, or mainstream, political involvement (Lechner 1993, 24; Marty and Appleby 1993a, 6).

For example, CWA's stance on international aid and technology transfer is now much closer to that of Austin Ruse, president of the Catholic Family and Human Rights Institute. Indeed, CWA's "softened" population policy rhetoric appears to reflect a possible Catholic influence, especially in light of CWA's obvious working relationship with the Catholic Family and Human Rights Institute.[17] In an interview with one of the authors of this book, Ruse commented that part of his job at the UN was educating the "American right" on the need to put money into development aid (1999c; see also discussion in chapter 3). It may be that Ruse is being successful in this regard. Notably, one of CWA's publications, arguing that the solution to issues like world poverty was not population control but "life-honoring development," was published in advance of a forthcoming joint CWA, Catholic Family and Human Rights Institute, and Population Research Institute press conference (CWA 1998d).

Perhaps most importantly, CWA's seemingly pro-development rhetoric is consistent with other aspects of CR UN population policy, which has begun to demonstrate a much more "third world friendly" approach.

Colonizing the Third World: Racism, Feminism, and Population Policy

In its opposition to population policy, the CR UN exploits a tension between the western community of activists and feminists who promote and implement population programs and the third world targets of those programs. Referring to the "colonizing" aspect of international population policy, the CR UN argues that feminism and the western aid industry are effectively exploiting poor women and developing countries reliant on western goodwill. The Population Research Institute, for example, argues that family planning for refugees amounts to a "foreign imposition of a radical Western agenda on the poorest and most vulnerable" (PRI 1999d). Developing countries, the CR UN argues, are "bribed and coerced" into population control by western countries who hold "development projects hostage" to third world compliance with population programs (Wilson 1999; Hsu 1997, 4).

The imposition of an "imperialist" western policy of population reduction in the third world is a new form of "colonization," with the west imposing "their own misguided worldview on developing nations by denigrating marriage and families, and encouraging promiscuous sexual behavior" (CWA 1998d). Through the imposition of this "colonial model," the west is portrayed as pursuing a destructive world politics that seeks to undermine the developing world. First, the west is privileging its own preoccupation with reproduction at the expense of more serious issues of particular concern to the developing world, such as malaria, clean water, or basic health care.[18] Second, according to the CR UN, the west's preoccupation with population reduction in the third world masks a more nefarious agenda: to maintain an unequal balance of power between the west and developing countries.

> This recent and hard-edged intolerance by the UN to traditional values is due to the alarm of the western nations and Japan regarding to the [sic] population growth of the developing world. The west regards this as a threat to its global domination. The west is also concerned that such population growth will precipitate both increased migration to the west and increased civil unrest, which could lead to a loss of access by the west to natural resources in the developing world. (Landolt 1999; see also PRI 1999b, Ruse 1999e)

In this language, the CR UN positions itself as the lone voice speaking out on behalf of third world interests and the rights of poor women. CR UN publications, as discussed above, highlight the human rights abuses committed against women in the name of population control (see CWA 1998i and 1999c; Kaufman 1998a). CR UN activists argue that, in contrast, neither feminists nor population activists are defending women from these human rights abuses (Ruse 1999c; Morrison 1998). The battle over population policy is thus described as one between "population control" advocates, including feminists, on one side, and "human rights" activists, such as the CR UN, on the other (see C-Fam 2000a, 4; CWA 1999e).

While the CR UN may be the voice of compassion, feminists are accused of using the concerns of poor women as a "smokescreen" behind which to advance a particular social agenda that is racist (CWA 1997d). In a 1999 publication, for example, the Population Research Institute argued that "today's feminist jargon" hides a "New Global Racism" focused on reducing population in developing regions, almost by any means (PRI 1999c). This approach is also reflected in PRI's campaign against UNFPA involvement in Kosovo, in which it accuses the UNFPA of being involved in "ethnic cleansing" in the region. In this analysis, CR activists allege that feminists do not act on behalf of women, but advocate on behalf of *some* women, namely themselves. The women left silent and obscured by this debate are third-world women, whose wants, needs, and rights are not just left unaddressed, but have been sacrificed to a western feminist social policy.

By arguing that population policy is irredeemably racist and imperialist, and by characterizing feminism as western and single-focused, the CR UN has introduced a new question into the population debate: who speaks most authentically for the third world? Using the language of racism, inequality, and the needs of the poor, the CR UN has laid claim to a progressive stance that it says is more authentic, more compassionate, and more sensitive than that of feminists. This argument may raise difficulties for feminists encountering the CR UN at international forums, and while it offers certain tactical benefits to the CR UN, it also poses difficulties for a movement that is, at its root, conservative and deeply suspicious of international development.

Conclusion: Where to from Here?

The CR UN's "development friendly" rhetoric on population policy suggests a number of tactical advantages. Most crucially, it offers an important point of continuity with orthodox religious constituencies from the economic south, many of whom might hold different views on the merits of development assistance than do some CR activists. The CR

UN's rhetoric on "western imperialism," global inequality, and the need for technological assistance to the third world thus may have greater purchase with some members of the interfaith alliance than do CR views that characterize third world poverty as resulting from religious affiliation.

This tactical advantage aside, the "third world friendly" rhetoric of the CR UN also raises a number of tensions and possible contradictions as this movement begins to articulate a population politics in the context of a broader "natural family" agenda. These difficulties stem largely from the effective promotion of international development as an alternative to population control. Arguably, this position is quite similar to that advanced by a number of progressive groups, including feminists (see, for example, Bandarage 1997; Corrêa 1994, 8–9). More problematically, the CR UN's new, seemingly positive stance on international aid is at odds with its long-standing and often vehement objection to international measures as amounting to governmental interference in the free operation of the market and undermining U.S. independence (see, for example, P. Robertson 1991, 206–7).

This shift in rhetorical emphasis by groups like CWA may be attributed, at least in part, to the effects of a CR UN alliance, and particularly to the infusion of conservative Catholic perspectives. Thus, on one level, the emerging "third world friendly" CR UN discourse could be taken as a sign that the interfaith coalition, at least among Christian groups, is taking shape. At another level, the rhetorical shift in some CR UN writings on global issues may suggest future difficulties as the different members of this coalition try to reconcile an activist UN politics with their own, deeply held religious and political beliefs based on an apocalyptic world scenario.

The issue facing the CR UN is: can it coalesce around a development-friendly politics? The answer is probably no, and the reason is that the CR UN remains unreconciled to its own image of a UN that is corrupt but salvageable. Issues like population policy lead the CR UN to positions that are incompatible with its basic opposition to the UN as a form of big, global government. The difficulty for the CR UN is, once again, deciding on its purpose at the UN. In the area of population policy, the CR UN is pursuing a politics demanding institutional change; in effect, a new global balance of power that will "liberate" the developing world from the oppressive politics of the west. But the difficulty is that this politics, at another level, reinforces the very institution the CR UN sees as facilitating a secularist/Marxist global order and threatening the "natural family." The CR UN may be able to pull the UN back from the brink of "antifamily" chaos, but does it want to?

5.

In Defense of the Natural Family: Doctrine, Disputes, and Devotion at the World Congress of Families II Conference

"Did you see the Muslim ladies?"
"Yes, we've really got something here!"

Conversation between two American CR women at the WCFII

The previous chapters have responded to the question, how does the CR understand the world, international policy and events, and global institutions? We now open the discussion to consider wider questions of policy, strategy, and alliance building in relation to CR UN international activity. In this chapter, we take the World Congress of Families II (WCFII), a conference held in Geneva in 1999, as a case study to examine CR UN coalition- and alliance-building initiatives in the global arena and the tensions and possibilities these might provoke.

The WCF forum is an unprecedented development; it constitutes the first sustained attempt by the CR UN to construct a permanent, global, interfaith institution.[1] The invitation to participate in the WCFII, however, was extended solely to conservative Christian, Islamic, and Jewish organizations, and it seems a deliberate decision had been made by the conveners to exclude nonmonotheistic faiths; polytheistic traditions were, at that time, beyond the pale. The conference played educative, political, and mobilizing roles, acting as a forum for sharing information, providing an interface for CR UN intellectuals and grassroots activists, and beginning the process of developing and strengthening the monotheistic coalition.

In chapter 1, we considered the "new family theology" unifying the CR both in terms of religious doctrine and as a new conservative common sense. We argued that the CR developed its concept of "the natural family" in response to social and political pressures. The "new family theology" emerged as a product of both CR religious and expert discourse and its defense began to take pride of place on the CR UN's global agenda. Given that the CR UN took this doctrine with them to the WCFII in Geneva, how did its exportation fare? Can the CR UN's understanding of the family form a basis of unity for an international, interfaith orthodox alliance, or might it provoke challenges and rearticulations? In chapters 2, 3, and 4, we considered in detail the CR's understanding of the United Nations, as well as battles in UN forums around population policy. Given that the WCF forum was largely established to combat the secular/feminist/liberal "takeover" of the UN, what are some of the other tensions and difficulties that might emerge for the CR UN in the international arena? Finally, is the WCF forum likely to have great longevity, or do its own internal contradictions doom it from the start? These are some of the questions to which we now turn.

Background

To set the scene, the WCFII conference was held in Geneva, Switzerland, November 14–17, 1999. It was convened by two American organizations: the Howard Center for Family, Religion, and Society (whose offices in Rockford, Illinois, also serve as the WCF's permanent headquarters), and NGO Family Voice (now the World Family Policy Center), a Mormon organization based in Utah. The WCFII was planned in 1998, according to the conveners, by "twenty-six women and men from the six inhabited continents . . . including Roman Catholics, Evangelical and Mainline Protestants, Latter-day Saints, Eastern Orthodox, Jews, and Sunni and Shiite Muslims" (WCFII 1999). This claim of membership diversity was not borne out at the WCFII itself. Twenty-eight co-convening or sponsoring organizations were listed in the conference program; twenty-one of these were American, and just two were non-Christian.

In addition to the Howard Center and NGO Family Voice, American organizations represented a mix of leading players from the Protestant, Catholic, and Mormon Right. Participating in the WCFII were, among others, Banner of Liberty, the Catholic Family and Human Rights Institute, Concerned Women for America, the Family Research Council, the National Center for Fathering, and United Families International. Several non-American organizations also sponsored the WCFII, including the Australian Family Association, AIDS Information (Switzerland), the Catholic Bishops Conference of the Philippines, the Endeavour Forum (Australia), the Family Centre of Croatia, the Latin American Alliance for the Family, and the Organization of the Islamic Conference. The Islamic Conference, together with Toward Tradition, an American Jewish conservative forum, formed the sole non-Christian sponsorship.

The vast majority of speakers and delegates were Christian Americans, with an eclectic group of right-wing Europeans (largely Catholic and Russian Orthodox) composing the next largest group. Several prominent members of the Canadian and Australian CR also took part, such as Gwen Landolt of Real Women (Canada) and Rita Joseph of the Australian Family Association. In terms of participation from outside the north and west, a small group of Iranian Muslims attended the conference; speakers representing this delegation included Fatemah Hashemi, active with the Women's Solidarity Association of Iran, as well as the International Union of Muslim Women. Several Africans attended the WCFII, all of whom appeared to be Catholic, including Margaret Ogola, a Kenyan health practitioner and activist, and Maria Morfaw, a lecturer from the Cameroons. The WCFII also attracted a few representatives from Central and South American Catholic Right organizations, most of these with links to the Vatican through various pontifical councils. Missing from the WCFII were any representatives from the "Pentecostal revival" that continues to sweep parts of South and Central America and Africa (Brouwer, Gifford, and Rose 1996; Maxwell 1998); all delegates from those continents appeared to have been drawn in through the international connections of the American Catholic Right (for example, Human Life International). Two prominent members of the American Jewish Right, Don Feder and Daniel Lapin (president of Toward Tradition), gave speeches at the WCFII; they appeared, however, to be the only Jewish presence there.

The conference opened with a plenary at an official UN venue, the Palais des Nations. The paradox of a CR conference being held in the heart of UN territory was further heightened by the opening address given by Raymonde Martineau, head of NGO Relations at the UN, who spoke of the many successes of NGOs in the field of women's and children's rights (Martineau 1999). Martineau's presentation, unlike other speeches (including those of speakers who did not actually appear at the event to give them, such as Jean Bethke Elshtain and Elizabeth Fox-Genovese), is not available on the WCFII Web site. Several hundred delegates attended the conference; women formed a large proportion of the audience, though this was not reflected in the slate of speakers, the vast majority of whom were men. Interestingly, almost all the women speakers were from outside the United States. At the conference's conclusion, the WCF issued the "Geneva Declaration," an agreed-upon statement of purpose, and began the planning process for the third WCF, scheduled for 2003. One of us (DH) attended the WCFII, and several of the issues and questions we raise in this chapter emerge from this experience.

Tensions (and Compromise?)

"Family"

The CR's "new family theology" raises several possible points of tension between the CR and its potential international allies. One of these is the doctrine's explicit embrace of the nuclear unit model as the proper family form. At the WCFII, American CR speakers reiterated and emphasized the overwhelming "naturalness" of this nuclear model. According to Richard Wilkins, an architect of WCFII in his capacity as director of the Mormon World Family Policy Forum, "[T]he well-functioning natural family is founded upon a strong, stable union between a husband and wife" (1999). Wade Horn, subsequently appointed by George W. Bush as Assistant Secretary for Children and Families at the Department of Health and Human Services, offered a critique of children's rights firmly anchored in the validity and unquestioned "rightness" of the nuclear model:

> The family is and should remain society's primary institution for bringing children into the world and for supporting their growth and development throughout childhood. . . . Parents are the world's greatest experts on their own children. They are their children's first and most important caregivers, teachers, and providers. Parents are irreplaceable. (1999)

Many other North American speakers (for example, in their advocation of tax breaks for married couples) took the two-parent-and-children unit as a (God) given, self-evident norm (see, for example, Hafen 1999;

Farris 1999; Schmierer 1999; Morton 1999; Gairdner 1999). Only one CR delegate, Harold Brown, an academic associated with the Howard Center, made any attempt to suggest there might be more to "family" than the smallest denominator: "[W]hether we think primarily of the so-called nuclear family of husband, wife, and children, or of the extended family, including grandparents, uncles, aunts, cousins, and in-laws, we think of a group of people bound together, more or less for life, by covenants both formal and natural" (1999). However, Brown's was a lone voice among the CR contingent in terms of valuing the notion of "extended family."

In contrast, speakers from nonwestern countries, several of whom were women, expressed a far more fluid and open-ended understanding of the family form, encompassing, without hesitation, the "extended family" model. Jehan Sadat, for example, clearly articulated the distinction between western and nonwestern definitions of "family":

> When a westerner describes the family, he is speaking of the father, mother, and children. But when an Egyptian speaks of family, he means the father, mother, children, aunts, uncles, nieces, nephews, and scores of cousins. And there are no strangers in Egypt. Everyone is generously welcomed whether by a rich uncle in Cairo or a distant and poor cousin in Aswan. We think of ourselves as belonging to one big family. (1999)

Similarly, Maria Morfaw, a Catholic academic and activist from the Cameroons, continually linked "family" to larger communal groupings in her WCFII conference speech (1999; see also Ugochukwu 1999).

An expansive, nonnuclear definition of family was also embraced by George Haley, the only nonwhite American speaker at the WCFII. Haley, who made much of the fact that he was brother to *Roots* author Alex Haley (a clip from the 1970s miniseries was even shown prior to his speech), was appointed U.S. ambassador to Gambia in 1998. He spoke with great passion of the support he had received from "a wonderful grandmother, my stepmother and a bevy of aunts, uncles and other relations . . . my family was expansive not only in numbers but also in terms of the roles played by the older generations" (1999).

Although such sentiments were greeted with polite applause by the largely white, American-dominated WCFII audience, nonwestern and perhaps African American conceptions of the family are arguably much closer to what white westerners usually mean by the term "community." Nonwhite, nonwestern delegates also seemed to employ a more metaphorical use of the term "family" as opposed to the literalist interpretation by the CR.[2] George Haley, for example, approvingly quoted his brother Alex, who apparently said: "When you start talking about family, lineage and ancestry, you are talking about every person on earth." Haley continued, "when you talk of family, you really are speaking about the love of humanity." This metaphorical deployment of "family" was expressly denounced by CR speakers. Harold Brown, for example, who had been prepared to accept "the extended family," was most emphatically opposed to any broader use of family terminology:

> [T]he idea of universal brotherhood achieves the opposite of what is intended. When all are forced to behave as brothers, then no one will actually have his or her own brother or sister. Indeed, the very concept of brother will lose all that it traditionally meant. . . . If all are brothers, then the word brother comes to mean nothing.

The family discourse at the WCFII was simply contradictory, rather than contentious, as there were no obvious definitional arguments or debates. Given that the defense of "the natural family" is the main (perhaps the only) basis of unity for the interfaith coalition, this lack of discussion was both surprising and yet not, given the potential of such a discussion to disrupt proceedings and consensus building.

Lesbian and Gay Rights

Despite the CR's "homosexualization" of the UN, globalization, and feminist NGOs (see chapters 2 and 3), not one session at the WCFII was devoted to antigay campaigning, and not a single individual paper presented at the conference focused on homosexuality exclusively, or even predominantly. Unlike domestic CR arenas, where antigay discourse and strategy abound (Bull and Gallagher 1996; Durham 2000, chapter 3; Hardisty 1999, chapter 4; Herman 1997), CR contributions at the WCFII tended to mention gay rights only in passing, and to do so in rather hushed tones. The few references to homosexuality were largely contained in speeches by Canadian and Australian participants. For example, Rita Joseph of the Australian Family Association spoke of people's "natural repugnance" toward homosexuality, while two Canadian speakers, William Gairdner and Ted Morton, mentioned the need to combat gay marriage initiatives. However, these references to homosexuality were few and far between.

One explanation for the relative muting of antigay discourse in Geneva might be that there were some representatives of CR "ex-gay" ministries at the WCFII (see, for example, Schmierer 1999). The Christian ex-gay movement, while in many ways an important sector of the American CR, is, at the same time, a separate trajectory with a different and often less virulent approach to homosexuality. As has been discussed elsewhere (Herman 1997), ex-gay discourse revolves around depicting lesbians and gay men as psychologically flawed and in need of "reparative therapy." This view is at odds with the predominant CR approach, which tends to represent lesbians and gay men as combining sin, stealth, and wealth. The presence of delegates from both of these arguably divergent if not conflicting traditions at the WCFII may well have played some role in the relative sidelining of gay rights as an issue.

Another possible explanation has to do with the relationship between the CR UN and its nonwestern allies in Geneva. Almost all the Muslim delegates to the WCFII were Iranian, and while a lesbian and gay movement does exist in Iran, the main battle there, and in similar states, is for the right of lesbians and gay men to be free from persecution or, in some cases, the very "right to life." Lesbian and gay rights, particularly current western issues such as gay spousal rights, are very far from being on the mainstream political agenda in Islamic religious states. In terms of the CR UN's other nonwestern WCFII partners, African Christians, there were no representatives from African countries with vigorous gay and antigay movements, such as Zimbabwe and South Africa (see de Vos 2000; Phillips 2000; Spruill 2000; Stychin 1998, chapter 3). African Christian delegates to the WCFII were predominantly (if not entirely) Catholics from Kenya, Nigeria, and the Cameroons. While gay rights could be said to be an emerging issue in these and other similar states, the gay rights movement is not a major force with which religious conservatives in these nations have had to contend.

Finally, and perhaps most significantly, the failure of international human rights law to advance lesbian and gay rights in any real way has, up to this point, made the issue less of a priority for CR UN politics. In the United States, lesbian and gay movements have been, in many instances, very successful at winning legal reform, but this has not been the case in international law. International lesbian and gay organizations have had a bumpy ride just in terms of their validity as NGOs, much less their ability to influence international law and policy agendas. While some attempt has been made by feminist NGOs to add "sexual orientation" discrimination as a protected ground in international agreements, these efforts have been fraught, compromised, and largely ephemeral. Even CR activists would agree that little progress has been made on this front: "Canada frequently introduces language like this. I mean, we're convinced that they do it simply to get our side all riled up and waste our time. Because it will not last, because the Muslim world will not allow it" (Ruse 1999c). Thus, the lack of an "encoding" of lesbian and gay rights in international law, as opposed to, for example, rights for children (Child Convention) or women (CEDAW), is no doubt partially responsible for the CR UN's deprioritization of the issue at the WCFII. As Austin Ruse has noted, "[T]he question of homosexuality does not come up here, it just does not come up in the United Nations" (1999c).

Nevertheless, it is also arguable that the relative silence on homosexuality at the WCFII was, in some sense, not very indicative of the CR's international activism on gay rights issues. As we argue in chapters 3 and 6, there is evidence that gay rights, particularly lesbian and gay claims to "family" status, are a growing concern to some CR UN global actors. For many activists in the CR, it is clearly only a matter of time before the UN "embraces" homosexuality as it has done with women's and children's rights (Reid 1999; Wright 1999). One of the organizations sponsoring the WCF, the Family Research Council, is increasingly involved in producing material linking gay rights to the secular/globalist UN agenda (see, for example, McFeely 1999). However, it is clear that where there is a foundational international human rights document in existence, the CR UN's activism is far more intense. This goes some way toward explaining why the discussion of children's rights at the WCFII had a high profile.

In Geneva as elsewhere, CR UN activists uniformly condemned the UN Convention on the Rights of the Child and the entire concept of "children's rights."[3] However, speakers from nonwestern countries were largely silent on this topic. The children's rights concerns of the CR speakers, predominantly centered on an American preoccupation with home schooling, sex education, and school prayer, were clearly highly parochial and out of place in the supposedly international context of the WCFII. When speakers from the developing world discussed children, they spoke of economic issues—child poverty and deprivation.

Another example of potential discord between the CR UN and its global partners (again, if not so much at the WCFII, then perhaps in the future), was the discussion of HIV/AIDS. Within their own domestic forums, American and European CR activists usually portray HIV/AIDS as a scourge visited upon sinners and they campaign vociferously against HIV/AIDS education in schools (see Bull and Gallagher 1996; Diamond 1989, 101–4). At the WCFII in Geneva, however, CR UN HIV/AIDS discourse was far more muted and, indeed, often invisible. Arguably, this was a calculated silence given nonwestern patterns (i.e., largely heterosexual) of HIV transmission and the recognition of HIV/AIDS as a tremendously important issue in some developing countries, one requiring international aid and intervention. As we discuss later in this chapter, while some conservative religious activists in Africa might have a measure of sympathy with CR theological perspectives on HIV/AIDS, there remain fundamental differences in how HIV/AIDS is perceived and responded to.

WCFII participants thus hardly sang from the same hymn sheet, and this was further illustrated by the range of organizations in the conference exhibition area. Most of the display tables were occupied by American and European Christian organizations. No Jewish organization appeared to be present, though several Islamic ones were. However, the materials distributed by the Islamic organizations, while clearly religious, were, on the whole, very pro–United Nations in tone.[4] Muslim women's organizations, for example, displayed pamphlets and newsletters largely concerned with furthering women's rights, albeit within an Islamic context.[5]

The Geneva Declaration

The Geneva Declaration was the final, agreed statement issued by the WCF at the conference's end. The WCF's organizers intended the declaration to function as both an encapsulation of the unity of purpose achieved by the Geneva conference and a future-oriented basis for further international, interfaith networking. We have argued that several potential tensions presented themselves at the WCFII in terms of the CR UN's alliance with other religious conservatives. Although the atmosphere in Geneva was cordial, possible lines of fracture in the future include conflicts over the meaning of "family," the approach to HIV/AIDS and children's rights, the relative importance attached to antigay politics, and the perception of the UN itself. How, then, were these differing and potentially conflicting agendas dealt with in forging the terms of WCFII's final mission statement?

For the most part, the declaration reflects the CR's worldview. The definition of family contained in the final document, while perhaps not striking as unequivocal a note as the CR might have liked, nevertheless gives no recognition whatsoever to extended or metaphorical families:

> The natural family is the fundamental social unit, inscribed in human nature, and centered on the voluntary union of a man and a woman in the lifelong covenant of marriage.[6]

The words "centered on" detract somewhat from the CR's preferred "is" and could be read as a small sop to the "extended" advocates. However, the addition of the word "voluntary" is clearly aimed at cultures, some of which are represented by the CR UN's ostensible international partners, where arranged or coerced marriages are the norm and is an interesting example of how the CR has been influenced by some aspects of "women's rights" (for example, the focus on "consent").

In terms of sexual expression, the declaration could not more clearly reflect the CR position: "[M]arriage between a man and a woman forms the sole moral context for natural sexual union." A section on "The Family and Life" is mostly concerned with a western medical agenda concerning embryo experimentation and genetic engineering, and a short paragraph on "Education" is entirely absorbed with an (American) agenda of home schooling, religious education, and an antistatist discourse of parental authority. Where issues of a more international nature are addressed, however, the declaration takes a vague and relatively unprescriptive approach. For example, a paragraph on population policy carefully avoids saying anything more directive than "no country should be coerced to accept policies of 'population control.'" The bulk of this section is focused on the lack of "replacement fertility" in the developed world.

Perhaps the most interesting evidence of conflict avoidance resulting in anodyne language at Geneva is in the declaration's paragraph on religious freedom:

> *Parents have the right to teach their religious and moral beliefs to their children and to raise them according to their religious precepts. . . .* Religious institutions should not accommodate cultural trends that undermine

the created nature of the family. One need not hold religious views to recognize that the family is part of human nature and the fundamental social unit. Religious institutions have the crucial cultural-leadership role of affirming that: the natural human family is established in creation and is essential to a good society; life and sexuality are gifts from the Creator, to be enjoyed respectfully and wholesomely; the family is sacred and has the unique authority, responsibility and capacity to provide for its members' education, health care and welfare; and all social institutions should respect and uphold the institution of the family.

This paragraph is as notable for what it omits as for what it contains. The CR has become, in recent years, increasingly concerned with the persecution of Christians in non-Christian states. Volumes of evidence and advocacy materials have been produced by the CR on the issue of Christian oppression in Muslim states, much of it often quite anti-Islamic in tone (for example, Marshall 1997). Clearly, however, at Geneva, where the CR UN mingled in apparent harmony with devout Muslims, this was an issue not to be raised.

The "Religion" paragraph in the Geneva Declaration also reveals the WCFII's reluctance to, or perhaps uncertainty of *how to*, engage with international allies on the subject of gender and sexuality. The phrase "religious institutions should not accommodate cultural trends that undermine the created nature of the family," is, presumably, a thinly veiled reference to a number of issues, including perhaps gay rights, women priests, gay and lesbian clergy, and so on. However, the failure to spell out the exact problem is important if, as we would suggest, it is the result of an inability to "ideologically converge" among the WCFII participants. Other similar instances in the declaration include just one (negative but not condemnatory) mention of homosexuality, and while abortion is condemned as "wrong," the declaration does not insist that it "not be allowed," as it does with genetic engineering. The failure to unequivocally state that abortion should be unlawful, arguably one of the most important political campaigns for CR activists within the United States and internationally, is perhaps the most telling instance of compromise on the part of the WCF's CR UN leadership.

Nevertheless, despite these concessions, the Geneva Declaration retains a predominantly CR character throughout, most conspicuously highlighted in the declaration's repeated denunciations of governmental interference and state usurpations. Antistate discourse, while almost a defining feature of the American (and, to some extent, the European) CR, is of little relevance to the CR UN's WCFII nonwestern allies. The Muslims in attendance generally came from religious states; for them, the state plays a key and wholly justifiable role in social life (as it would for the CR if the American state was perceived as Christian). For the Christian delegates from African countries, a politics of "antistate" seems equally irrelevant, given the pressing need for government intervention in a range of areas. However, it is not surprising that the Geneva Declaration is a "western" document—the drafting committee of ten contained just three members not based in the United States, one of whom was an Australian.[7]

Perhaps the most conspicuous evidence of underlying discordance, however, is in the declaration's reference to "the Creator," the only mention of a higher power that exists in the document. The word "Creator" is clearly a term of compromise, indeed of art, as its vagueness and ambiguity can encompass the varying conceptions of all three monotheisms. However, the use of this word, accompanied by the declaration's failure to provide any theological guidance whatsoever, despite religious belief being the basis for the WCFII alliance, underscores the vast chasms separating the alliance partners in terms of their normative vision. As we discussed in chapter 1, the CR UN knows that its Muslim and Jewish allies will either die or convert prior to Jesus's Second Coming; from within their own respective paradigms, orthodox Muslims and Jews also look forward to an inevitable future that includes only themselves.

Politics and Strategy

Thus far we have explored how potential tensions within the CR UN global alliance were expressed or not, and resolved or not, at the WCFII and in its Geneva Declaration. We now wish to ask: how do the underlying conceptual and theological conflicts at the WCFII resonate in any wider sense? Do the tensions we have identified reflect important disagreements over an analysis of "the global"? If so, they may be significant indeed. For example, does the third world appeal to "community" and the "family of nations" have more in common with the left than with the antigovernmental (until the Christian theocracy) approach of the CR? While the CR rails against the expanding remit of the UN and against the philosophy it perceives as animating this expansion, the non-CR participants in WCFII may have a very different international agenda, one that is reliant on a large measure of international aid and an activist role for the UN and its institutions. The African battle against HIV/AIDS is a case in point, as are the UN-friendly activities of the Organization of the Islamic Conference, one of the WCF sponsors.[8]

Returning to the Geneva Declaration, the drafters did address some economic and political concerns from developing countries, but these issues were placed firmly within the CR worldview. The section on "The Family and Population," for example, advised that "efforts to assist developing countries should focus on promoting family self-sufficiency, not dependency," and insisted that "creative human enterprise and charity offer the best hope for addressing the problems of poverty, hunger and disease." An obvious "third world family friendly" statement missing from the Geneva Declaration might have been one on liberalizing western asylum and immigration laws to allow for family reunification; unsurprisingly, the CR would never support such a move.

The failure to understand global events and institutions in the same way may also have strategic implications for the CR UN alliance. For example, might some WCFII third world delegates have more in common with lesbian and gay attempts to define the family away from the nuclear model than with their CR UN allies, who are promoting it? Are tensions within the alliance over children's rights and refugee and immigration laws key areas for anti-CR forces to exploit? For how long will the CR UN's third world allies, many of whom espouse unequivocal agendas about global wealth redistribution, tolerate the imposition of an overwhelmingly American agenda on the international "natural family" network (see, for example, Morfaw 1999; Taskhiri 1999)? How fragile and tenuous is this international alliance when so many fundamental issues seem unresolvable? Is it even accurate to cite the WCFII as evidence of an "alliance," when the participation, agenda, and organizational control are so overwhelmingly in the hands of the American Christian Right?

In reflecting on these questions, it may be worth considering another: what motivated participation in the WCFII? For the CR UN, the benefits of an interfaith, global, orthodox alliance are fairly obvious: there is strength in numbers; an international network looks less American on the surface; an interfaith coalition appears less doctrinaire; and a WCF-type of network is better placed to combat the international social movements to which the CR is opposed. It is difficult to escape the proposition that the WCF is simply an instrument to further the CR UN's global agenda. It is equally difficult to escape the conclusion that the WCF is a particularly cynical initiative for the CR to take, given its historical condemnation of organizations like the World Council of Churches for engaging in similar, interfaith coalition-building exercises.[9]

And what of the other participants at the WCFII? Although the event was heralded as the coming together of representatives from the three monotheistic faiths, the first point worth noting is that orthodox Jews can hardly be said to have been present at the WCFII at all. As we noted earlier, there were two Jewish speakers—Don Feder and Daniel Lapin. These two men are the "usual suspects" in terms of Jewish participation in CR activities. They are both regular speakers at CR events in the United States (such as the Christian Coalition's Road to Victory conferences), and their appearance at the WCFII cannot be said to be any real indication of Jewish involvement in the CR UN's international network. The relationship of American religious Jews to the CR movement is best characterized as ambivalent, to say the least. In one analysis, Wald and Sigelman (1997) have suggested that many of the most observant members of the American Jewish community retain a deep skepticism of the CR agenda, as well as an identification with liberal, not conservative, political issues. There is little reason to expect that conservative Jews elsewhere in the world would be any more welcoming of the CR UN and its agenda. The CR UN may have little to gain from pursuing Jewish links internationally, and continued anti-Semitism in the CR would also militate against such a development.[10] However, as Wald and Sigelman have noted in the U.S. domestic context:

> The mission to the Jews, if we may call it that, may be less important for its stated objective of political coalition than for its contribution to fostering an image of tolerance. That is, it may well be more for the Christian Right to be seen appealing to Jews than it is to attract them. Even if the effort bears little fruit in the way of political converts, it can still be deployed to answer critics who condemn the movement for religious insularity. (1997, 161)

Thus, although the WCF does not at present contain more than a token Jewish presence, the fact that the congress is nominally open to Jews may achieve, for the CR UN, a similar purpose.

Conservative Muslim participation at the WCFII was more substantial. The largest contingent of Islamic believers, still only a handful of participants, came from Iran. Why were they there? Presumably, like the CR, orthodox Muslims are keen to appear less like "religious fundamentalists" and more like "pro-family advocates" on the world stage. However, this can only be a partial explanation. As we discussed earlier in this chapter, several of the Muslim organizations present at WCFII were clearly ones with an approach to global issues that was very different from that of the CR. In other words, some members of the Islamic contingent at the WCFII were there because they see a positive role for the United Nations and international law and policy making. For example, material produced by the Islamic women's organizations at WCFII were broadly supportive of women's rights, and in terms not unlike those of many feminist NGOs.[11] The participation of orthodox Muslims in the WCFII is less paradoxical than pragmatic: for some, the UN can be reformed to respond more appropriately to the values of orthodox religious states, and the WCF provides a useful forum for advancing this campaign; for others, there is merit in making common cause against a shared enemy—western liberalism.

This last motivation also played a role for a third grouping at the WCFII, again very small proportionately, that could be described, for lack of a better phrase, as "third world Christians." Almost all of these were Catholic, and several had a long history of affiliation with American Catholic Right organizations. One interesting example is provided by the participation in the WCFII of Margaret Ogola, a director of a charity for HIV-infected children in Kenya. Although Ogola's presentation at the Beijing Women's Conference in 1995 largely focused on the need for governmental intervention in health care and education, in Geneva, her speech was a vague plea for the sanctity of marital love (see Ogola 1995, 1999). Ogola is involved with Human Life International, and although she did not make much of this in her WCFII presentation, she is a fierce critic of abortion, contraception, and HIV-prevention policies, such as condom distribution. Ogola's affiliation with the CR UN (she has also volunteered to help plan the WCFIII) has resulted in CR Web sites, publications, and organizational materials abounding with her quotations on population policy and HIV/AIDS. Indeed, John Howard, of the Howard Center, has even written a letter to *The Nation* magazine accusing William F. Buckley of "condescension" in his attitude to AIDS in Africa (Buckley wrote supporting condom distribution policies) and quoting Ogola's WCFII speech for authority (Howard 1999).

The apparent agreement of Ogola and other delegates from the developing world with the CR UN on many issues, the extent to which nonwestern religious conservatives, even Christian ones, share a "worldview" with the American CR remains to be seen. Alison Calhoun-Brown, in writing about the CR's attempts to court African Americans, has suggested that one reason for the lack of great success in this endeavor is that "black evangelicals do not really perceive the same societal threat that white evangelicals do, or (even with the perception of threat) black evangelicals do not symbolically interpret the threat in the same way" (1997, 119). We would suggest that a similar analysis may be applicable to the CR UN's intended international partners, who clearly do not demonize the United Nations and its agencies as does the CR, and some of whom even have important links to the international women's movement.

In addition to tensions within the CR UN's international network, the very existence of the alliance may prove problematic for the CR domestically. For example, the CR UN leadership's failure to use international platforms to publicize the issue of Christian persecution in Islamic nations would not sit well with the CR's core constituents in the United States. Austin Ruse's comment, that "we do not work on religious freedom, we work on life and family" (1999c), could be taken by others on the CR as an abdication of duty. The coalition thus poses a dilemma for CR UN activists vis-à-vis their international allies, particularly those from Islamic states. Although brushed aside at the WCFII, an alliance between the CR UN and Islamic conservatives might be perceived at home as a "pact with the devil," one that would have domestic reverberations for the CR organizations involved in global politics and that has already resulted in CR UN activists receiving hate mail from other Christian conservatives (Ruse 1999c). Needless to say, the CR's domestic conservative Jewish allies might be rather perturbed by the WCF receiving sponsorship from the Organization of the Islamic Conference, a virulently anti-Israeli NGO that refers, on its Web site, to "criminal Zionists."[12] Interestingly, CR UN organizations have been relatively silent in the aftermath of the September 11, 2001, attacks and the subsequent American attacks on Afghanistan. While CR UN Web sites were replete with patriotic statements (and this is notable in itself as it signals a revitalization of a pro-state discourse), little comment has been made about CR UN international alliances with conservative Islamic states, some of which have been accused of "harboring terrorists."

In interviews, CR UN activists appeared to hover between describing their international coalition members as friends or allies. Arguably, for the CR UN leadership, the lack of clarity over the "true nature" of alliance partners is a result of a combination of pragmatic politics and a suspension of disbelief, rather than contradiction or hypocrisy. Austin Ruse, in referring to the CR UN's alliance with Sudanese and Libyan UN delegations, for example, remarked that "we work very well with them, at the same time having revulsion for the things that they are doing to Christians in their own countries" (1999c). In interviews, these sentiments were echoed by activists with Concerned Women for America (Reid 1999; Wright 1999). Islamic fundamentalists can be friends and/or allies in the short term, and yet remain satanic agents for longer-term purposes. Indeed, the Protestant Right would take a similar view of its Catholic partners, and perhaps vice versa. The alliance on display at the WCFII, then, while clearly precarious and potentially quite volatile, is nonetheless fascinating both for its problems and its potential.

Concluding Remarks

Using the WCFII as a case study, we began this chapter by asking: how did the exportation of CR ideology fare on the world stage? In retrospect, it becomes clear, we hope, that this question needs to be broken down into smaller parts. We must ask, at the very least, exportation "of what," "by whom," and "to whom"? For example, at the WCFII the CR UN was not attempting to export its politics on gay marriage or HIV/AIDS. Yet at the same time that they adopted a quiet or pragmatic approach to these matters, one of the most visible issues at the WCFII was the very parochial one of home schooling. Similarly, a passionate discourse at the conference was an antistate rhetoric of little interest to the CR UN's international partners. While the CR's "new family theology" plays relatively well among non-American religious conservatives (despite, as we noted earlier, awkward moments about how "family" is defined), the CR's virulent antigovernmental rhetoric, which, to a large extent, lies at the heart of its anti–United Nations politics, undermines the doctrine's potential strength.

We may also wish to question whether "exportation" is a useful concept to adopt at all. Brouwer, Gifford, and Rose (1996) use it to refer to the global proselytizing agenda of Protestant fundamentalism; however, "exportation" perhaps misleadingly implies a process that is unidirectional. We would argue for a more diffuse approach to understanding the dynamics of power we have discussed thus far. The concept of "exportation" implies a "power over" process that tends to obscure the agency and vitality of those whom the CR UN encounters on the global stage (see also Maxwell 1998). Despite the agenda-setting success of the CR UN at WCFII and other similar venues, there is evidence that the social and political concerns of developing countries may be having an impact on the CR UN leadership. Austin Ruse, for example, told us how he had learned that pro-family policies in the developing world must be linked to economic progress and the alleviation of poverty. He noted, however, that he had an uphill battle convincing domestic CR allies that sensitivity to developing-world issues, such as economic exploitation and the legacy of colonialism, was in order (1999c).

While some might argue that the "third world friendly" discourse of the CR UN is cynical, self-serving, and insincere, we would suggest this may be less true for some members of the CR UN than for others. Austin Ruse and other Catholics on the CR UN have no doubt been influenced by the Vatican's more progressive analysis of poverty and deprivation in the developing world in such a way as to begin to take these issues seriously. To the extent that the American Protestant Right works ever more closely with Catholics and the Vatican on global issues, a more complex analysis of the "new world order" may come to underlie, or at least coexist with, what might have once been a purely opportunistic discourse for them. The relationship between the CR UN and its international allies is thus less imperialistic than that captured by the concept of "exportation."

Ironically, although we are arguing here for a more dynamic or reciprocal understanding of the relationship between the CR UN and its international allies, the CR UN itself takes a more "messianic" approach. In other words, the discourse deployed by CR UN activists suggests that the third world is passive, intimidated, and powerless in the face of a relentless attack by globalists and their secularist, socialist, and feminist compatriots. Only the CR UN alliance can come to the rescue, as a Concerned Women for American publication confirms: "[At Beijing +5] Western delegations offered many terms—'sexual orientation,' 'sexual rights,' 'reproductive rights'—with which developing nations were not too familiar and did not understand completely, if at all. To their relief, pro-family lobbyists . . . stepped in to educate and equip those delegates" (CWA 2000b; see also CWA 2000c; Ruse 1998b).

Our argument thus far raises a further question: in this chapter, have we focused unduly on the problems the WCFII alliance generates? To what concerns or values is the CR UN speaking that it has managed to be even this successful at building an international coalition? Over the past decade, an antiglobalization movement has emerged from the left, epitomized in the Seattle, Prague, and Genoa protests at the turn of the century. This movement, however, is unlikely to speak to religious conservatives who see left-wing ideology as antithetical to a religious one. At the same time, religious conservatives around the world are very concerned with what they perceive to be the negative consequences of globalization; for example, several nonwestern speakers at the WCFII spoke of the negative and destructive effects of globalization processes (see Morfaw 1999; Hashemi 1999; Tashkiri 1999). Enter the American Christian Right. The CR is a leading conservative critic of the forces of globalization, forces that are seen to have wreaked economic and social havoc on many developing world communities. The CR UN thus arrives on the international scene with a developed critique of (although not necessarily an opposition to) globalization, and one from a religious perspective. It is thus not surprising that the CR UN will find some willing religious allies in the developing world who also blame globalization for the disintegration of local communities.

The alliance may also take strength from a shared analysis of the "degenerate west." While opinion on the proper role and purposes of the UN may differ, the Islamic and Christian organizations represented at the WCFII would largely agree that a "common enemy" is currently in control of international governance. As we discussed in previous chapters, this enemy force is perceived as a potent mix of secularists, globalists, socialists, and feminists, all of whom are seen as united in their anti-God ethos. Although Peter Beyer has argued that the power of the CR will "wane" in response to globalization processes inhibiting the construction of "outsiders" to function as "enemies," we would suggest that the reverse may be the case (1994, 132–33). The CR's global enemies are very clear indeed. Paradoxically, a quintessentially western movement, such as the CR UN, may have found an antiwestern discourse that resonates with the concerns and fears of conservatives elsewhere in the world.

The coming together of this conservative Christian/Islamic network, evidenced at the WCFII as well as in ad hoc groupings at particular international venues, may have a powerful basis of unity belied by our earlier focus on the alliance's potential fissures. The adoption of a "pro-family," rather than a religious, banner may further expand the network's appeal in the same way that "mainstreaming" and "rights talk" have facilitated a broader reach of CR politics domestically in the United States (Herman 1997, chapter 5; Rozell and Wilcox 1996). However, we would not wish to overemphasize the potential success of the WCF in the long term. As a structured, long-term power bloc, the World Congress of Families seems an unlikely candidate. Despite our argument that the CR UN may be both learning from and speaking to developing-world issues, its domestic politics, with its anti-immigration, anti–civil rights, and "English-only" elements, suggest either significant discordance between the global and domestic CR leaderships, or must lead us to question the CR UN's real commitment to these issues.

6.

The Gender Agenda: Women's Rights, Radical Feminism, and Homosexuality

> The stakes are incredibly high. . . . Radical feminists will be every-
> where. EVERYWHERE.
>
> **Austin Ruse, newsletter, December 1999**

In the spring of 2000, under the auspices of the General Assembly Special Session "Women 2000," government delegates and nongovernmental organizations met to negotiate an agreement on progress made since
the 1995 Beijing Conference on Women. This conference, known as
"Beijing +5," was the site of a pitched confrontation between the Christian Right and feminist and women's groups. The final UN General Assembly Special Session, and the preparatory meetings leading to it, have
been described as "one of the most difficult UN negotiating sessions in
recent years," with a "climate of hostility" characterized by "rancorous debate" (Barnes et al. 2000).

Not only did the Beijing +5 process involve, once again, international
discussion on women's rights, controversial in itself, but it came at an
important moment in CR UN mobilization. Although some CR UN
organizations were active at the original Beijing conference in 1995, it
was not until after that event that the CR UN began to organize more

effectively and concertedly. The Beijing +5 process provided an arena within which the CR UN could flex its newly acquired muscle and (more important, from its perspective) strike a potentially fatal blow to feminists and other "radicals." According to Austin Ruse, if the CR UN could prevent international agreement at Beijing +5, the "defeat" of "radical" forces, such as feminists, would "be a rout" (2000a).

The CR UN thus "stormed" the Beijing +5 process, sending nearly four hundred delegates with the apparent intent of ensuring a disruptive CR UN attendance at every meeting (Butler 2000, 3).[1] More important, the CR UN appeared to have successfully followed through on plans to mobilize sympathetic state governments into a single, conservative religious voice. Negotiations during the Beijing +5 process were dominated by a small group of countries that included not only the "usual suspects"—European Union countries, Japan, the United States, Canada, Australia, and New Zealand—but more significantly, Pakistan, Algeria, Egypt, Sudan, Iran, Syria, and Libya (Barnes et al. 2000). This second bloc of countries was generally lauded by the CR UN for standing up for pro-family values during the Beijing +5 negotiations. Austin Ruse of C-Fam referred to them as "strong and brave" despite their "records on human rights" (Ruse 2000a; see also Human Life International 2000). In the face of this concerted opposition, rumors abounded of a plot to sabotage Beijing +5.

The debates and sticking points at Beijing +5, with some exceptions, mirrored the negotiations at the original Beijing conference, with suggested language on women's health, sexual and reproductive rights, and sexual orientation resulting in protracted debate and controversy (see Barnes et al. 2000). Once the dust settled, agreement was reached at Beijing +5. The consensus view, outside of CR UN circles, seems to be that the CR UN did not entirely undermine the Beijing +5 process and that important gains were reached in a number of areas including "health, violence, globalization, the economy, human rights and empowerment"(Barnes et al. 2000). For the CR UN, Beijing +5 may not have been the blow to feminists they had wished, but it was still seen as a victory for the "little guys" because the CR UN was able to prevent further substantial gains by feminists (Kaufman 1998b; Butler 2000, 9–11).

More than just another conflict between the CR UN and its feminist foes, the events at Beijing +5 underline the centrality of women's rights to the CR UN and a broader conservative religious interest at the UN.

As we have shown in previous chapters, the CR UN views itself as countering a much more significant and malevolent enemy than "just" feminists. But as we have also noted, feminism and women's rights occupy a central position in CR UN politics. In this chapter, we look at women's rights and feminism as the target of CR UN activism at the international level. Beijing +5 was chosen by the CR UN as a "defining moment" precisely because it was a chance to revisit the 1995 Beijing agreement. The original Beijing conference encapsulates, for the CR UN, the immediacy of the threats it perceives to family and Christianity. Together with the 1994 Cairo agreement, Beijing represents feminist ascendancy at the international realm, the establishment of a women's rights framework within international policy, and the inexorable move to the destruction of "the natural family" and the celebration of a "culture of death."

In this chapter, we shift our focus somewhat from individual CR UN organizations to look at another, but equally important, actor in the emerging international conservative religious presence: the Vatican. With an established history at the UN, the Vatican has become the principal voice speaking out against women's rights.[2] In this respect, it has provided both motivation for, and leadership of, the emerging interfaith orthodox alliance at the UN. Our discussion of the Vatican and women's rights is primarily focused around the 1995 Beijing Conference on Women. That conference, and the events leading to it, provide an important context for understanding the nature and significance of the Vatican's assumed role in the international debate around women's rights. Our analysis, however, does not stop with this agreement in 1995. Looking at Vatican statements in the following years, we trace the emergence of a broader discourse on "the family": the "natural" roles of women and men within the family and the threat of "homosexuality" to the family and the global order. Aspects of this discourse on the family echo some of the CR UN positions explored in chapter 5. In other respects, however, the Vatican's international vision, and the role of the family within it, suggest a very different view of the international order from some of the Protestant and Catholic groups discussed earlier.

Although this chapter starts with a specific focus on women's rights and "the feminist threat," our analysis inevitably takes us back to "the natural family" and its importance to CR UN activism. The Vatican's linkage of women's rights with a broader critique of "the family" in international law brings together many of the themes we've explored throughout this book: the interrelationship, within CR thought, between women's rights, the "culture of death," and the disintegration of the family; the growing, but not unproblematic, significance of "the family" as a conceptual touchstone in CR UN politics; and the increasing significance of "the homosexual threat" to the CR UN.

The Vatican: A Primer

The term "Vatican" is generally used to refer to both the city-state of the "Vatican" located within Rome and the "Roman curia," the offices located in the Vatican that assist the Pope "in governing the universal church" (Reese 1996, 5). The "Holy See," which is the official face of the Vatican at the UN, technically refers to the diocese—the "seat"—of Rome. In practical terms, "Holy See" refers to the Vatican's representatives at international forums and organizations. The actual "foreign affairs" department of the Holy See (though not officially called this) is run out of the Secretariat of State located in Rome (Hanson 1987, 68–69). In this book, we use the term "Vatican" because it has a broader meaning and includes both the Holy See and the offices through which the Pope functions and the church is governed (Reese 1996, 5).

The Vatican is, in many respects, a complex bureaucracy, the workings of which are beyond the scope of this book. However, an increasing amount of attention has been paid to the functioning of the Vatican in the context of a highly visible and active pope: John Paul II. Under John Paul II, the Vatican has undergone significant and sometimes controversial change. Described as a "conservative," John Paul has instituted a number of measures to centralize church structures and increase the authority of the pope (Keely 1994, 237; Reese 1996, 241–63). According to Vatican watchers, John Paul has surrounded himself with like-minded conservatives (Reese 1996, 34) and has supported a number of theologically and politically conservative organizations such as Opus Dei and the Neocatechumenate movement (Reese 1996, 188; Urquhart 1995).[3] The result is a tension in the church between "theologians and the papacy" and the increasing perception of a problematic "Papal fundamentalism" (Stephens 2000, 19).

This papal regime has also become a high-profile international actor (Hanson 1987), positioning itself as a "moral superpower in international affairs" (Reese 1996, 272). With a highly trained diplomatic service and a committed staff at the Secretariat of State, John Paul II has undertaken an active involvement in international affairs, with a focus on "human rights, economic justice, and peace" (Reese 1996, 231). Supporting the Pope's international work are a number of papal councils, the most important of which, for our purposes, is the Pontifical Council for the Family, which has provided crucial legwork for some Vatican interventions in the area of international population policy and women's rights (Reese 1996, 266; Urquhart 1997, 2–3).

While gender issues and "the family" figured prominently in the Vatican's international activism in the 1990s, international development and peace are also high on its international agenda. Even on topics like population and reproductive health, on which it takes a strong, oppositional stance, the Vatican is committed to addressing global inequality and ending poverty (see, for example, Holy See 1994a, paragraph 1). In addition, John Paul II has maintained the church's strong support for the UN, and has called for a strengthening of the UN's role in the international realm (see John Paul II 1996, paragraphs 14–15).

Despite the arguably multifaceted nature of Vatican involvement in world politics, its international work remains, justifiably or not, linked to its vocal opposition to sexual and reproductive rights, gender issues, and abortion. Starting with the Cairo Conference in 1994, the Vatican has taken a strong and active role in international conferences where issues relating—in any way—to population, abortion, contraception, reproductive health, and women's rights are discussed.[4] In this capacity, the Vatican does not see itself as either an "oppositional" or a "Catholic" actor. Rather it characterizes itself as a statelike entity with universal citizenship, whose role is to provide a moral voice in the international realm. John Paul II describes the Vatican's role at the UN as a "specifically spiritual mission, which makes it concerned for the integral good of every human being" (John Paul II 1996). In the context of women's human rights, the Vatican has defined its spiritual mission as defending women, children, and the family from the threat posed by radical feminists. In the following discussion, we examine the Vatican's opposition to women's rights, first at the Cairo Conference on Population and Development, and then at the Beijing Conference on Women. Our purpose is to explore the Vatican's position at these events to elucidate the larger world and spiritual view informing its politics at the UN. Once again, we resist categorizing the Vatican as simply "antiwoman." Rather, we consider its opposition to women's rights in the context of a particular ideology of "the family," in which women's rights, the sanctity of the family, and global solidarity are inextricably connected.

Frequent Flyers: The Vatican from Cairo to Beijing

As we discussed in chapter 4, the Vatican strongly opposed the draft Cairo Programme of Action. While the Vatican has played an active international role in the United Nations since its inception, the Cairo conference was something of a catalyst for this current phase of Vatican international activism. For a conservative papal regime committed to a particular morality in which abortion and contraception are seen as unrelentingly "evil," population policy in itself is problematic. The Cairo conference was especially worrying for the Vatican because it was seen as leading to international recognition of a right to abortion (see Holy See 1994b). As a result, the Vatican launched a high-level campaign prior to the final Cairo negotiations, lobbying state governments to resist aspects of the draft agreement. That campaign is described by Thomas Reese (1996, 263) as follows:

> [A]ll of the ambassadors to the Holy See in Rome were called in to have the Vatican's position explained to them by the Secretariat of State. The pope also wrote each head of state. Each office of the Roman Curia was told to emphasize family issues since 1994 was also the international year of the family. . . . Bishops' conferences around the world were asked to pressure their governments to oppose pro-abortion language in the Cairo document. Nuncios [Vatican representatives abroad] also worked at developing alliances with Muslim and Catholic countries that opposed abortion.[5]

In addition to abortion, the Vatican's objection to the Cairo programme focused on a number of key issues: the relationship between development and population, the meaning of "sexual and reproductive rights," and the perceived absence of a moral framework in reproductive decision making. Reflecting a long-term commitment to development issues, the Vatican expressed concern that a broad definition of development should be incorporated rather than an approach emphasizing "simple accumulation of wealth" (John Paul II 1994). In the area of "sexual and reproductive rights," the Vatican expressed reservations about the meaning of "reproductive rights," seeing in it the possibility of a backdoor legitimization of abortion (Holy See 1994b). References to sexual rights were strongly opposed on the basis that they promoted a view of the world in which all were sexually active, and the call for responsible sexual behavior was objectionable if not balanced with a moral framework within which decisions (e.g., "abstinence") could be made on sexual activity.

The biggest concern for the Vatican, however, remained abortion, which was described by John Paul II as "a heinous evil" (John Paul II 1994). Increasingly, however, at Cairo and later, the Vatican's opposition to abortion extended to include a more general opposition to sexual and reproductive rights. As we discussed in chapter 4, the Cairo Programme of Action was a notable departure from its predecessors in its emphasis on a rights framework as central to any policy on population. Essential to that rights framework was a commitment to the empowerment of women in all aspects of their lives. For the Vatican, linking women's rights with population policy was a dangerous move. "[T]o formulate population issues in terms of individual 'sexual and reproductive rights,' or even in terms of 'women's rights' is to change the focus which should be the proper concern of governments and international agencies" (John Paul II 1994). Although governments were "properly" concerned with development and the environment, the status of women and sexual and reproductive decision making came within the jurisdiction of the family. "[Q]uestions involving the transmission of life and its subsequent nurturing cannot be adequately dealt with except in relation to the good of the family: that communion of persons established by the marriage of husband and wife" (John Paul II 1994).

Responding to the Vatican's call for international opposition to the draft Cairo Programme of Action, organizations on the American Catholic Right also became active in the Cairo process. For example, the Catholic Campaign for America (CCA)—an organization with strong ties to the Republican Party and a commitment to increasing Catholic representation in American public policy making (Askin 1994, 13–17)—worked within the NGO process at Cairo to oppose aspects of the programme. During the Cairo conference itself, CCA put out a daily "Catholic Alert" fax bulletin detailing the work of the Vatican and criticizing its opponents in the U.S. administration (Gould 1994, 2–3).

The Vatican's opposition to abortion and abortion-related language delayed consensus at the Cairo conference. Eventually, however, agreement was reached on compromise language, and for the most part, Cairo was seen as something of a feminist success story. A year after the Cairo conference came the Fourth World Conference on Women, held in Beijing, China. Coming on the heels of Cairo, Beijing was, in many respects, a continuation of the debates at Cairo around reproduction, women's health, sexual autonomy, and women's rights.[6]

The Beijing Conference on Women was a large event, attracting over fifty thousand people to the official intergovernmental conference and the parallel NGO forum in nearby Huairou (Otto 1996b, 7). The final document agreed upon at Beijing—the Platform for Action—is a lengthy, dense document of over 350 paragraphs covering twelve "critical areas of concern": women and poverty, education and training of women, women and health, violence against women, women and armed conflict, women and the economy, women in power and decision making, institutional mechanisms for the advancement of women, human rights of women, women and the media, women and the environment, and the girl-child.[7] Much has been written on the Beijing Platform for Action (see, for example, Bunch and Fried 1996; Charlesworth 1996; Chow 1996; Larson 1996; Morgan 1996; and Otto 1996b), and a detailed assessment of the document itself is beyond the scope of this book. However, Beijing, on balance, was seen as a watershed event in placing women's issues on the international agenda. Aside from the details of the actual agreement (many of which are seen by feminists as positive gains for women), the actual event of the Beijing Conference and the parallel NGO forum facilitated international networking among various women's groups (Morgan 1996; Riles 2000). For many feminist participants, even if Beijing resulted in no other positive gains, its role in facilitating international networking on women's issues was victory enough.

While Beijing may have been an important event in encouraging feminist activism, it was also key in attracting the attention of the CR to international arenas. The high-profile position of the Vatican at Cairo acted as a clarion call for others on the Catholic and Protestant Right, who then mobilized to attend the Beijing Conference. For many of the individuals active in the CR UN, Beijing was their first exposure to international activism, and was a key motivator in their decision to engage, on a more permanent basis, with the international realm (see, for example, Roylance 1995). For our purposes, however, Beijing is most important for providing a forum within which the Vatican, and to a lesser extent the CR UN, outlined, and to a degree consolidated, their views on women, the family, and the role of the international order.

In the lead-up to Beijing, the Vatican took a number of steps to clarify its position on women's issues and to distance itself from its image at Cairo as the principal opponent of women's rights. In addition to the Vatican's active participation in the preparatory process, John Paul II issued a number of statements on the topic of women, such as his "Letter to Women," and his "Address to Mrs. Gertrude Mongella, Secretary General of the Fourth World Conference on Women." These statements appeared to be part of an effort by the Vatican to redefine itself as a progressive international voice, responsive to the needs of women. In this vein, the Vatican appointed, as head of its Beijing delegation, Mary Ann Glendon, a Harvard law professor. As a law academic, Glendon presented a professional face for the delegation, and as an established scholar, she arguably brought a degree of sophistication and insight to the Vatican's negotiating positions at Beijing.

Through the interventions of John Paul II and Vatican representatives at Beijing, a coherent policy on women, family, and human rights unfolded. In this policy, the Vatican portrayed itself as representing an inclusive world vision in which the needs of women were promoted in the context of larger struggles against poverty and global inequality. In this way, the Vatican's position was not simply "antiabortion" or "antiwoman." The Vatican had, instead, a commitment to recognizing women's "dignity" as essential to an international society in which human rights, "the family," and "womanhood" are inextricably connected. For our purposes, the Vatican's position at Beijing focused on the following key areas: women's "natural" roles, "women's rights" and the importance of "the family," gender and equality, and the distinction between "real" and "radical" feminists.

John Paul II and the "Vocation and Mission of Women"

On 10 July 1995, the Vatican released a letter from John Paul II addressed to the world's women, in which he both thanked women and apologized "if" the Catholic Church had contributed to their historical oppression (John Paul II 1995b). In particular, John Paul thanked all women who as "mothers," "wives," "daughters and sisters," including those "who work," are "consecrated," or are simply "women," for contributing to humanity. Recognizing women's historical disadvantage, John Paul called for "real equality in every area: equal pay for equal work, protection of working mothers, fairness in career advancements, equality of spouses with regard to family rights and the recognition of everything that is part of the rights and duties of citizens in a democratic state." His letter clearly identified and to a degree supported the many roles women play, not just as mothers, but also, for example, as "workers." However, this recognition of women's diversity is balanced against a very specific description of what "true" womanhood means, one steeped in a conservative definition of "the family" and women's roles within the family as mother and helpmate.

For John Paul II, women achieve their "deepest vocation" by "placing themselves at the service of others." "The creation of woman is thus marked from the outset by the principle of help," and this special "genius of women" is "part of the essential heritage of mankind." The Vatican thus supports the strengthening of international commitment to improving the status of women, provided that commitment is consistent with a vision of women's unique roles as mothers and wives. For the Vatican, this means recognizing women and men as equal but different. Women and men are "human beings to the same degree," but they perform different and complementary roles in life. This complementarity results from the fact that women and men "are marked neither by a static and undifferentiated equality nor by an irreconcilable and inexorably conflictual difference" (Holy See 1995; John Paul II 1995b). While the complementary roles performed by women and men are dictated by their different biologies—women, for example, are "wives and mothers"—the Vatican says it rejects the view that biology determines fixed and static roles for women and men.[8] Rather, the nature of men and women's roles can change over time, allowing women to be, for example, "employees" and "mothers." While rejecting the phrase "biological determinism," the Vatican nonetheless uses "complementarity" to signify a sexual division of labor in which women's reproductive capacity means they will be "mothers" and "wives." The Vatican seems to suggest that this construction of gender roles is not biologically determined because it accepts that some women will perform roles other than just being mothers and wives. However, women's roles as mothers and wives are essential both to achieving their true vocation and as part of the "heritage of mankind," the very nature of (global) society.

If women's roles as mothers and wives are part of the "heritage of mankind," then their (married) union with men is the fundamental building block of society. According to John Paul, "It is only through the duality of the 'masculine' and the 'feminine' that the 'human' finds full realization" (John Paul II 1995b). "Women's rights" can only be realized within this context. The Vatican thus supports a strengthened international response to the victimization of women, provided such a response is consistent with this vision of women and men's separate roles.

When Women's Rights Are Not Human Rights

While the Vatican may support rights for women, it does not support women's rights. The difference, for the Vatican, could not be more fundamental. In the 1990s, a number of feminist and women's groups became active in the campaign to make "women's rights human rights" (Friedman 1995). Their argument was that international human rights law has, for a variety of reasons, failed to address the human rights needs of women (see, generally, Peters and Wolper 1995). The solution was not simply to "add" women to existing human rights guarantees. To a certain extent, that had already been done and was a resounding failure (Larson 1996, 697–702). Rather, what was needed was a rethinking of the way international human rights assumes and incorporates western masculine norms about the nature of human rights, state involvement, and the hierarchical nature of human rights violations (Charlesworth 1995). Thus, the phrase "women's rights are human rights" is as much a campaigning banner as a shorthand reference to a rethinking of existing human rights principles to better account for the ways that women suffer human rights abuses that are particular to them as women.

Through very careful language, the Vatican makes clear that it distinguishes between rights for women and "women's human rights." For example, Vatican statements (see John Paul II 1995; Navarro-Valls 1995b) often refer to the "human rights of women" in the context of statements on the universality of human rights, with the implication that women's rights are encompassed within existing human rights agreements (Riles 2000, 81). In its reservations and interpretative statements to the Beijing Platform for Action, the Vatican stated that it interpreted the phrase "women's rights are human rights" to mean only that "women should have the full enjoyment of all human rights and fundamental freedoms." That is, the Vatican refused to accept that existing human rights were unrepresentative of women, or that recognizing women's particular positions of disadvantage entailed rethinking rights in a way that recognized that disadvantage.

Christian Right activists make a similar distinction. For the CR UN, "women's rights" as used by feminists is a dangerous concept because it represents "new" rights that have not been agreed to through democratic means, and that act as a vehicle for the infiltration of other "radical" feminist ideas. In this analysis, "women's human rights" are not "true" human rights, but are a new invention by feminists that have the effect of undermining, first, "true" universal rights, and, second, the "natural family" (Bilmore 1998; O'Leary 1998). According to Katherine Balmforth, former director of the conservative Mormon organization, World Family Policy Center, by broadening the meaning of human rights, feminists and other "antifamily" forces succeed in moving international policy "into private areas traditionally reserved first to families and religious institutions" (Balmforth 1999). Their purpose in doing so, according to the CR UN, is to denigrate the "importance of motherhood" and promote "homosexuality, abortion-on-demand, and the removal of parental rights" (CWA 2000a).

While not as polemical as some CR UN activists, the Vatican's opposition to women's rights mirrors that of the CR. For example, the Vatican, like the CR UN, argues that women's human rights undermine existing universal guarantees through the inclusion of "sexual and reproductive rights," and more problematically, a "right" to abortion (Holy See 1994b). Similarly, the Vatican argues that seemingly benign language, such as reproductive rights and women's right to health, are a feminist ruse to introduce more subversive rights.[9] For example, the Vatican opposes the phrases "sexual rights" or "women's rights to control their sexuality,"[10] claiming they legitimate promiscuity and homosexuality:

> The Holy See does not associate itself with the consensus on the entire chapter IV, section C, concerning health; . . . the Holy See cannot accept ambiguous terminology concerning unqualified control over sexuality and fertility, particularly as it could be interpreted as a societal endorsement of abortion or homosexuality.[11]

Finally, the Vatican, like the CR UN, views women's rights and the agreements reached at both Beijing and Beijing +5 as amounting to an attack on the family. First, the language around women's empowerment is seen as "antifamily" because it is not balanced with language recognizing women's unique roles within the family (Holy See 2000a). Second, the focus on women's sexual and reproductive rights is seen as advancing an "individualist concept of sexuality," when the "exercise of sexual expression by men and women" should take place only in the context of "the family" (Holy See 1999a). Finally, the Vatican, like the CR UN, argues that the Beijing agreements view the family in almost entirely negative terms (see, for example, Navarro-Valls 1995b). Evidence of this is found in calculations of the number of times "family" is mentioned in international agreements. For example, Austin Ruse offers the following analysis of the agreement reached in the Cairo +5 process:

> A cursory count shows the word "father" appears twice in the document, "men" once, "boy" four times. The word "family" appears 29 times but almost always in the phrase family-planning. The word "parents" appears once and then only to tell governments that parents should be taught about the need for childhood sex-ed. On the other hand, "sex" appears 62 times, "gender" 59 times and the term "reproductive health," always a code word for abortion, appears 103 times. (Ruse 1998c)

Dignity, Equality, and the Perils of Gender

Ultimately, the Vatican opposes "women's human rights" because it suggests a view of social relations inimical to its own. At the root of the Vatican's opposition is a view different from that held by feminists about the meaning of women's empowerment. For the Vatican, women's empowerment must be pursued within the confines of the strengthened traditional family form, in which women and men perform specific roles (John Paul II 1995a). The theory of complementarity, which lies at the heart of the Vatican's worldview, thus entails a rejection of "equality" or "equal rights" as undermining the important differences between women and men. What is needed, according to the Vatican, is not equality as "sameness" but an equal "dignity." The Vatican avoids, where possible, references to "equal rights" and instead refers to the "dignity" of women. Dignity as opposed to "rights" is achievable not on the basis of equality, but by the recognition of difference: "The Holy See considers women and men as being of equal dignity in all areas of life, but without this always implying an equality of roles and functions" (Holy See 1995, paragraph 2(a); see also Navarro-Valls 1995b).

The Vatican and other conservative groups also oppose the use of the term "gender." In the preparation process leading to the Beijing conference, the Vatican, supported by other groups such as Focus on the Family, succeeded in having all references to gender in the draft platform placed in brackets, meaning that it was subject to further debate (Baden and Goetz 1997, 11). The term "gender" was objected to because the idea that "male" and "female" are socially constructed categories is inimical to the Vatican's view of women and men as essentially complementary. For both the CR UN and the Vatican, "gender," used to mean the social construction of identities, is dangerous for two reasons. First, it is a profoundly elastic term, encapsulating a broad feminist rights strategy that includes abortion (Ruse 1998a). As discussed above and in chapter 4, any language seen as promoting abortion is also seen as an attack on the family (Hamm 1995; O'Leary 1998). Furthermore, by challenging the "naturalness" of an essential "femaleness," the Vatican and the CR UN see feminists—through the term "gender"—undermining the complementarity of women and men, and hence the "natural family" (O'Leary 1998).

Second, and more problematically, the CR UN and the Vatican see "gender" as a "code word for gay rights" (Ruse 1998a). At Beijing, opposition to "gender" by the Vatican and the CR became a major debate in the negotiations. CR UN groups repeatedly made the argument that the term "gender" referred not to male and female, but to five genders in total. James Dobson writes:

> Relating again to "the deconstruction of gender" . . . the goal is to give members of the human family five genders from which to choose instead of two. When freed from traditional biases, a person can decide whether to be male, female, homosexual, lesbian, or transgendered. Some may want to try all five in time. (1995)

In this analysis, "gender" was seen as the means by which "the lesbian caucus was hoping to achieve their agenda" (Hamm 1995, 137). Not only was the term "gender" objectionable, but women's rights themselves were seen as tainted by a "gender agenda," violating the "vision for women, family, and human dignity" reflected in the Universal Declaration of Human Rights (O'Leary 1998).

Contesting Radicals: The Vatican's Alternative to Radical Feminism

At the 1995 Beijing conference, the Vatican's opposition to women's rights was framed not as an outright rejection of women's rights, but as a condemnation of a liberal, western rights strategy. In arguing this position, the Vatican depicted itself not as antifeminist, but as opposed to "radical" feminism. Whereas the Vatican portrayed itself as the only truly inclusive voice at the international level, occupying a feminist "middle ground," "radical" feminism represented an impoverished, western-centric view of women that failed to account for women's differences. This characterization is important because it came at a particular historical point when feminist groups had achieved a degree of success in lobbying for changes to international human rights.[12] The threat of looming feminist dominance was a significant mobilizing force for the CR UN. The Vatican's construction of feminism as outdated and unrepresentative was, however, a more insidious critique that posed important questions for feminist international activism. The tactic of marginalizing feminists as raging radicals is predictable. Damning them as "mainstream" is, arguably, a more sophisticated critique of feminists. In this section, we examine how the Vatican has endeavored to marginalize feminism by constructing it as, first, a western-dominated movement that is unrepresentative of women from the economic south; second, as an outdated version of feminism that is unrepresentative of even western women; and finally and most critically, as relying on a mainstream and limited rights discourse that is of little value to women.

In the lead-up to Beijing, Dr. Joaquin Navarro-Valls, director of the Holy See's press office, wrote that the conference was under threat by an attempt to impose on the world "a Western product, a socially reductive philosophy, which does not even represent the hopes and needs of the majority of Western women" (1995b). This threat of (an albeit unrepresentative) western imperialism was seen in the "disproportionate attention [paid] to sexual and reproductive health."[13] According to the Vatican, the entire chapter in the Platform for Action devoted to women and health was seen only in a reproductive context that was unrepresentative of the interests of women in developing countries. In particular, it argued that the platform gives "preference to sexually transmitted disease or those which refer to reproduction," while diseases of more concern to women from the south, such as "tropical ones—which each year become more contagious and cause more deaths than sexually transmitted diseases—are not given serious consideration" (Navarro-Valls 1995b, 4). The Vatican thus denounced what it saw as an attempt to "reduce the human person—woman in this case—to social functions that must be overcome" (Navarro-Valls 1995b, 2). The promoter of this troubled view, according to the Vatican, was "feminism," whose characteristics are "a negative attitude towards the family, acritical support for abortion and an angry anthropology in which feminine problems are linked solely to sexuality and contraception" (Navarro-Valls 1995b).

The Vatican's opposition to the "angry anthropology" of feminism appears restricted to a particular type of feminism, which it characterizes as outdated, speaking only for a minority of women. In its report in preparation for the Beijing conference, the Vatican argued that

[t]he collapse of myths and utopias associated with the dominance of ideologies in the Sixties and Seventies, has brought with it a tendency to move beyond a radical "feminism"; complete uniformity or an undifferentiated levelling . . . of the two sexes is no longer seen as a goal; instead there is a growing sensitivity to the right to be different . . . in other words, the right to be a woman. (Holy See 1995, paragraph 4 [3])

This view of two feminisms—a new and an old—is clearly linked to the Vatican's own views about the biological construction of gender roles. The new feminism described here sits comfortably with Catholic doctrine concerning women and their different but complementary roles, while the old feminism is described as an "angry anthropology" concerned solely with "sexuality and contraception" (Navarro-Valls 1995b, 2).

As evidence of feminism's dated views, the Vatican offers a stinging indictment of the reliance on a limited rights strategy with its emphasis on an "exaggerated individualism" (John Paul II 1995b, paragraph 8). In its reservations to the final Platform for Action, the Vatican condemns the final document as a product of

an exaggerated individualism, in which key, relevant, provisions of the Universal Declaration of Human Rights are slighted—for example, the obligation to provide "special care and assistance" to motherhood. This selectivity thus marks another step in the colonization of the broad and rich discourse of universal rights by an impoverished, libertarian rights dialect. Surely this international gathering could have done more for women and girls than to leave them alone with their rights! (paragraph 11)

The implication is clearly that the responsibility for this "impoverished" outcome lies largely with the feminist movement and its perceived exclusive focus on reproductive health and sexuality issues. The compelling nature of the Vatican's arguments is reflected in the very powerful last sentence in the above quotation. By this remark, the Vatican evokes a number of images: of abandoned children, an uncaring community, and a feminist movement preoccupied by formalities at the expense of the lived experience of women and girls. Importantly, through this comment, the Vatican also seeks to distance itself from the Beijing process. While others may have abandoned women and girls, the suggestion is that the Vatican is still fighting for them. In this way, the Vatican positions itself as the only true radical voice advocating women's human rights. Unlike western feminists, the Vatican argues, its emphasis is on development issues, poverty, and the interests of women from the south. According to Robert Moynihan, writing for *Inside the Vatican,* a Catholic magazine supportive of the church hierarchy, at Beijing the Vatican had

> a double strategy: to ally with all those forces which are "progressive" to increase women's role in society (including some Western secular feminists, but not including strict Muslims, who oppose this development) but at the same time to build an "anti-radical" alliance against the proponents of radical feminism. (1995)

That alliance, as we have shown throughout this book, has begun to emerge in the post-Beijing period, and the Vatican maintains its role as an informal leader of the "natural family" movement at the UN. In the following section, we look more closely at this leadership role in conservative religious politics at the UN and at the Vatican's increasingly hostile position to feminism and lesbian and gay rights. With the Vatican, we see a crystallization of a "natural family" politics that has come to provide the grounding for opposition to issues like abortion, contraception, feminism, and lesbian and gay rights.

Of Hedonism, Homosexuality, and "Human Race Feminism": Leading the Pack in Defense of the "Natural" Family

Earlier we discussed the Vatican's view of itself as a global moral voice, speaking on behalf of a universal constituency. In many respects, this role is confirmed by organizations on the Christian Right who applaud the Vatican's leadership in opposing women's rights. Groups like Concerned Women for American or Focus on the Family look to the Vatican as the voice of "conscience" at the UN (see, for example, Wright 1999; Reid 1999; Moloney 1999). In the Vatican, they see an autonomous international actor, not tied to the geopolitics of international aid and hence immune from the pressures imposed by western aid benefactors. Because of its independence, the CR UN argues, the Vatican is able to ensure that moral standards are articulated at the international realm (Wright 1999), and the CR UN is supportive of the moral positions taken by the Vatican. In this respect, the CR UN accepts the Vatican as more than just an independent voice. It is seen as a moral standard bearer, representing "faith" at the international realm.

In some respects, this seemingly unqualified support for the Vatican's leadership is surprising. As we discussed in chapter 2, many on the CR have historically viewed Catholicism, and the Vatican in particular, with outright hostility. Indeed, the pope has often figured in CR endtimes scenarios as an Antichrist figure. In addition, the Vatican supports a strengthened United Nations that will provide leadership in an international realm characterized by solidarity and a commitment to global equality (see, for example, Holy See 2000b and 2000c). As we discussed in chapters 2 and 3, the prospect of a strengthened international realm is anathema to a CR deeply suspicious of both the UN and the prospects of global interdependence.

How is it, then, that this same CR now looks to the Vatican to provide international moral leadership? There are probably a number of factors that have contributed to this. The first is the actions of John Paul II, who has brought in not only a new era of Catholic conservatism but also a commitment to interfaith dialogue. Second, and parallel to this, are moves within both the Catholic and Protestant Right to join political forces in pursuit of common aims (Hitchcock 1991). In the 1990s, this was most clearly evident in attempts to include a Catholic subsidiary of the Christian Coalition (Xanthopoulou 1995, 1). While the idea of a Catholic Alliance linked to the Christian Coalition never really took hold, this move reflected the growing recognition among religious conservatives that they often had more in common with other orthodox believers than with the more liberal members of their own faith (Butler 2000, 5–6). The attempt to build an orthodox alliance at the UN is an outcome of this thinking.

The pivot around which the orthodox alliance functions is the shared commitment to a "natural family" politics. It is in this way that the various CR UN political positions and objectives are distilled into a concentrated political agenda that is able to bring together the various factions within the CR UN as well as the Vatican. In this "natural family" position, there is much to ally the CR UN with the Vatican. Both the CR UN and the Vatican have placed their opposition to various international issues, from women's rights to population policy, in the context of a larger aim to protect "the natural family." In the following discussion, we look at the Vatican's "family" politics in the context of its interventions at the international realm. Protecting "the family," as defined by the Vatican, has become an important rhetorical device, providing the framework within which the Vatican articulates a particular view of social relations. This "family" politics, while potentially limited as a worldview, provides an important point of continuity with CR UN politics. This "natural family" platform, for both the Vatican and the CR UN, has become a basis from which to challenge the perceived growth of "gender ideology" and "pro-homosexual" politics at the UN.

Family, Women, and the "Heritage of Mankind"

"The family" figures prominently in Vatican statements on international policy. Depicted as the central building block in society, the Vatican resists any measures, such as women's rights, which it sees as undermining the family (Holy See 1999a). For the Vatican, the family provides a "community" through which "cultural, ethical, social and spiritual values" are taught, and "the young, the aged, and the disabled are sustained" (Holy See 2000c). In its educative, nurturing, and economic functions, the family is essential to a society in which public and private spheres are maintained. Without the family, "the State must increase its interventions in order to solve problems directly which ought to remain and be solved in the private sphere, with great traumatic effects and high economic costs" (Pontifical Council for the Family 2000b).

The Vatican defines "the family" as the "union of love and life between a man and woman from which life naturally springs," and which is sanctified by marriage (Pontifical Council for the Family 2000a). As we discussed above, this "union" is based on a "natural" division of roles, in which women are crucially "helpmates," providing "service" to their families (John Paul II 1995b, paragraph 12). Womanhood, according to John Paul II, is "part of the essential heritage of mankind," and the family unit, as described above, is part of "a common patrimony" (John Paul II 1995b, paragraph 12; 2000). In this way, "the family," defined by marriage between a man and a woman, is both essential to and the "property" of the global order.

As we discussed in chapter 5, there is a tension in an orthodox "natural family" alliance between those organizations (primarily the Christian Right) whose definition of the family is narrowly focused on the nuclear family, and those organizations that refer to an extended family. The Vatican's definition is much more closely aligned to the latter view, and building on this, sees the family as the building block of (global) society: the "Family of Nations" (John Paul 1996; Holy See 2000c). Within this family of nations, however, the Vatican recognizes a problematic inequality with pronounced gaps "between rich and poor countries," resulting, to an extent, from omissions "on the part of developing nations" (Holy See 2000c). "In too many cases, some countries ignore their duty to cooperate in the task of alleviating human misery. Instead of producing shared prosperity, this age of globalization, characterized by greater interdependence among nations, has led to an even greater disparity in wealth and increased exploitation" (Holy See 2000c).

This conception of "the family of nations" offers interesting parallels to the family as a union between a man and a woman. In the family of nations, like the family defined by marriage, the language of duty is used to convey a universal responsibility to a communal good. However, unlike in the context of marriage, the family of nations is described, albeit aspirationally, in terms of an "equality" among the various members. While all may have duties to this family, each member of the family is nominally equal, and all have a responsibility to ensure that equality. In contrast, the family defined by marriage between a man and a woman is characterized by an explicit difference and an arguable *in*equality. While both women and men may have duties in that marriage, the best they can hope for is an equal "dignity," realized through their different roles. There is no suggestion that the family of nations is similarly characterized by an "equal dignity" achieved through difference. For example, while women's unique role as "helpmate" is part of the common heritage of mankind, the developing world is not seen as playing an analogous role as the "servant" to the western world. Indeed, the idea of complementarity, so essential to the Vatican's definition of marriage, is not translatable to the international realm. To suggest, for example, that the family of nations, like the family defined by marriage, is characterized by a role differentiation, where one party provides "service" to the other, would result in a very inhumane, unequal world order.

Although promoting a global order predicated on equality is an important objective for the Vatican, that objective is increasingly sidelined by a preoccupation with protecting the family defined by marriage. In the post-Beijing period, the Vatican has made increasingly pronounced condemnations of the forces it sees as threatening the family. As discussed above, its position at Beijing was arguably characterized as an attempt to occupy a feminist middle ground. However, in the post-Beijing period, the Vatican has seemingly abandoned this position in favor of a more concerted opposition to the foes of "the family," which it defines as hedonism, homosexuality, and "human race" feminism.

Confronting the "Culture of Death": Hedonism and the "Ideology of Gender"

John Paul II has long condemned the western "culture of death," which he sees as encouraging "divorce, birth control, homosexuality, abortion and euthanasia" (Urquhart 1995, 172). In recent years, the Vatican has more specifically identified the proponents of this amorphous "culture of death" as "minority" groups advocating a dangerous, antifamily politics. These "minority" interests remain largely unidentified by the Vatican, but are characterized as representing a "narrow" or "small" segment of the population, who are pushing a dangerous "ideology" on the international community (see, for example, John Paul II 2000; Holy See 1999b; Holy See 2000b).

Given the Vatican's opposition to women's rights, we can assume that this reference to "minority interests" includes feminists who support women's rights to sexual and reproductive health. But it is not only feminists the Vatican sees behind the western "culture of death." Rather, it is a more general western hedonism (John Paul II 1998), manifest in the promotion of an "ideology of gender" (John Paul II 1996; Pontifical Council for the Family 2000a). The proponents of this "ideology" are, of course, "radical feminists," but also advocates of lesbian and gay rights. In this way, "gender ideology" becomes the link between feminists and lesbian and gay advocates, who are portrayed as joined in a shared project to undermine marriage and the family. According to longtime Vatican watcher Gordon Urquhart, Bishop Tarcisio Bertone, secretary of the Congregation of the Doctrine of the Faith,[14] identifies "human race feminism" as the source of the attack on "the family," by which he refers to the attempts by "gays and lesbians to abolish the two sexes of male and female, replacing them with a single neuter gender" (Urquhart 2000).

Eliding gays and lesbians with feminists is, of course, nothing new (see, for example, Herman 1997). As we discussed in chapters 2 and 3, many in the CR UN view "radical" feminists as lesbians, and hence, it is not surprising that they see the political and social objectives of these two groups as the same. Such a view is additionally supportable in the context of a view of feminism that distinguishes between "true" feminism and a radical feminism pursuing "minority" aims. In the context of the Vatican, this slippage between feminists and "homosexuals" is important for signaling a growing preoccupation with the human rights claims by lesbians and gays. As the comment by Bishop Bertone suggests, the Vatican sees "radical" feminism and "homosexuality" as two sides of the same "gender" coin.

Confronting "Homosexuality": A Point of Convergence?

As discussed earlier, "homosexuality" has until recently occupied a curious nonposition in CR UN politics. For the most part, the CR has focused on feminism and women's rights as the immediate target of its activism. However, for some CR UN groups with an established domestic profile in antigay politics, such as Focus on the Family, the international realm was initially viewed as hosting a progay faction. For example, James Dobson's decision to send Focus on the Family delegates to the Beijing Conference on Women was motivated, primarily, by a concern about "gender feminism" and the promotion of homosexuality (Dobson 1995). To a certain extent, Dobson's views seem to be shaped by a conception of the international order more consistent with the views discussed in chapter 2, in which the international realm was seen as the playing fields of the Antichrist. With the growing commitment by the CR UN to an international politics, the concerns with lesbian and gay rights seemed to recede into the background, with abortion, population policy, and women's rights taking center stage. Austin Ruse, president of the Catholic Family and Human Rights Institute, for one, dismissed homosexuality as a "non-issue" at the UN: "The question of homosexuality does not come up here, it just does not come up in the United Nations. . . . I am surprised, honestly, I am surprised that they [homosexuals] are not here" (1999c).

Despite this comment, there now appears to be a growing and increasingly vocal concern among the CR UN about homosexuality, with groups like Concerned Women for America, the Family Research Council, and the World Family Policy Center including regular comments on homosexuality in their online newsletters and commentaries.[15] In part, this growing concern with international recognition of the legitimacy of lesbian and gay identities reflects the fact that advocates of lesbian and gay rights are beginning to have an effect at the international level. At both Beijing and Beijing +5, references to "sexual orientation" were included in draft sections prohibiting discrimination against women on a number of protected grounds (Otto 1996a, 25–26; Barnes et al. 2000). In both cases, the phrase "sexual orientation" was controversial, and in both cases it was eventually struck out because of a lack of international consensus. However, the impact of these debates is significant. In the context of the 1995 Beijing Conference, for example, a number of state governments agreed to interpret the phrase "other status" to include "sexual orientation" (Otto 1996a, 26).

For the Christian Right and the Vatican, these debates confirm their suspicions that first, feminists are in league with homosexuals, and second, that women's human rights guarantees can be used to promote "antifamily" politics, such as the acceptance of homosexuality. At the same time, the CR UN is also correct that lesbians and gays are not as active politically at the UN as are feminist and women's groups. There are many reasons for this, some of which we have already canvassed in chapter 5. In addition, the international realm is in itself inhospitable to lesbian and gay activism. Many countries strongly resist any recognition of the rights of sexual minorities, and human rights violations against lesbians and gay men continue with little apparent international condemnation (Amnesty International United Kingdom 1997). Perhaps reflecting this, lesbian and gay activists have met with resistance in their attempts to establish an activist presence at the international realm.

For example, the International Lesbian and Gay Association (ILGA), an umbrella organization representing various lesbian and gay organizations, tried unsuccessfully to become a consultative NGO at the UN, representing lesbian and gay issues. ILGA was accredited in July 1993, and by September 1993, their status was challenged by the United States, which argued that ILGA included an organization promoting pedophilia (Sanders 1996, 67–68). In September 1994, at the initiation of the United States, ILGA's consultative status was revoked "pending a review of its member organizations" (Sanders 1996, 68) and has not been reinstated, despite new applications by ILGA.[16] ILGA's experience at the UN certainly did not stop lesbian and gay groups from using UN mechanisms, but it did mean that there was no permanent organization representing lesbian and gay issues at the UN.[17]

The result has been that lesbian and gay issues have made it onto the international agenda only in a sporadic and partial way. Despite this, and paradoxically because of it, the CR UN is increasingly concerned about the threat of homosexuality, seen as lurking in the corners of various international agreements and UN agencies. For example, Tom McFeely, writing for the Family Research Council publication *Insight,* describes the UN as advancing "homosexual rights" by "stealth," "subterfuge," and "camouflage."[18] Evidence of the "covert" nature of lesbian and gay rights can be found in terminology like "various forms of the family" and "gender," both of which, he argues, legitimize "homosexuality." In an argument similar to that advanced in the context of women's rights, "homosexual" rights are seen as undermining "the family" as well as international law. The promotion of "homosexual rights" denigrates the "authentic body of human rights" found in, for example, the Universal Declaration of Human Rights. More problematically, homosexuality results in "calamities such as the AIDS epidemic now raging among male homosexuals" (McFeely 1999).

The Vatican has also taken an increasingly vocal stance against lesbian and gay rights, and, like the CR UN, is distrustful of human rights language that may suggest an acceptance of homosexuality. For example, the Vatican has long resisted the term "sexuality" used in provisions recognizing women's rights to control their own health, on the basis that sexuality "could be interpreted as a societal endorsement of . . . homosexuality."[19] Recently, the Vatican has turned its attention to the subject of "homosexual unions" (Pontifical Council for the Family 2000b). The prospect of international or domestic recognition of partnerships between individuals of the same sex is vehemently resisted by the Vatican. In same-sex partnerships, the Vatican sees the implementation of a gender ideology that "rejects the fact, inscribed in corporeity, that sexual difference is an identifying characteristic of the person" (John Paul II 1999).

Attempts to gain legal recognition of "homosexual unions" are seen by the Vatican as a profound attack on the family. The Pontifical Council for the Family report on "de facto unions," for example, condemns any union between a man and a woman not sanctified by legal marriage. The main thrust of that report, however, is arguably on "homosexual unions" and their destructive impact on society.[20] The legitimation of lesbian and gay partnerships is threatening enough, but holds an additional dangerous possibility of lesbian and gay families adopting children. The Pontifical Council, quoting John Paul II, concluded the following:

> In the case of homosexual relations, which demand to be considered de facto unions, the moral and juridical consequences take on special relevance. "Lastly, 'de facto unions' between homosexuals are a deplorable distortion of what should be a communion of love and life between a man and a woman in a reciprocal gift open to life." However, the presumption to make these unions equivalent to "legal marriage," as some recent initiatives attempt to do, is even more serious. Furthermore, the attempts to legalize the adoption of children by homosexual couples adds an element of great danger to all the previous ones. "The bond between two men or two women cannot constitute a real family and much less can the right be attributed to that union to adopt children without a family." (Pontifical Council for the Family 2000b, paragraph 23)

This report by the Pontifical Council is clearly motivated by, and reflects a concern with, the increasing profile of gay and lesbian activists, both domestically and at international forums like the UN or the European Union. The council's conclusions, together with the very strong statements by John Paul II, firmly proclaim the Vatican's unequivocal opposition to the recognition of gay and lesbian rights. The Vatican's position in this regard is important not just as a clear expression of its commitment to opposing homosexuality, but also as suggesting a potential shift in conservative religious thinking on human rights, women's rights, and a politics based on "the family." In the following concluding comments, we consider this "antihomosexuality" stance in the context of women's rights. Drawing together the various themes of this chapter, we look at international human rights as the central arena within which conservative religious politics have taken shape. Women's rights, as the focus of much CR UN activism, has, in many respects, become the dramatis persona in a larger politics based on protecting "the traditional family" but increasingly oriented to opposing lesbian and gay rights.

In Conclusion: From Women's Rights to "Homosexual" Rights

Our objective, at the outset of this chapter, was to consider the international politics of the Vatican in the area of women's rights, as reflecting a complex worldview based on a particular conception of social relations. Wanting to resist the too simple characterization of the Vatican as "antiwoman" or "antifeminist," we have examined its opposition to women's rights in the context of a social and political project defined in terms of protecting "the family" as defined by marriage between a man and a woman. At the 1995 Beijing Conference, the Vatican framed its objection to women's rights as, first, protecting the family from a "radical" feminism that sought to deny the complementarity of men and women, and, second, as rejecting an "impoverished" rights strategy that failed to offer a progressive vision of society and women's roles within it. In this way, the Vatican offered a nuanced argument against "women's rights" and "radical" feminism without explicitly rejecting either the rights of women or "feminism." It argued, instead, for a vision of society based on the family defined by marriage and against the use of human rights discourse as a vehicle for (a particular form of) social change.

In this respect, we can see the Vatican's opposition to women's rights as not only promoting its own vision of gender relations based on a sexual division of labor, but also reacting to what it sees as a feminist or western "hedonist" co-optation of international human rights. By challenging what it perceives as the overreliance on rights rhetoric, the Vatican sees itself as standing outside the dominant international framework within which questions of social relations are discussed. Not only does the Vatican challenge the definition and scope of those social relations, it opposes the way in which the international community "talks" about them (i.e., through the language of rights). In this way, the Vatican perceives itself as being at the margins of international human rights discourse, challenging the views of those in the mainstream: feminists and western governments.

Many would argue that the Vatican does not occupy a position at the margins of international human rights decision making, but neither does it lie entirely at the center. The Vatican's view of social relations, which reinforces certain dominant power relations (i.e., between women and men), combined with its years of power and influence, is not consistent with a "marginalized" social actor. But the rise of feminist international organizations and their impact on human rights, as well as the increasingly dominant discourse of rights, have altered the nature of international dialogue on social relations in a way that might appear to isolate certain actors, such as the CR UN. In this respect, the shifting terrain of international human rights discourse and its impact on the religious right can be compared to the CR's domestic politics in response to strengthened legal protection for women (De Hart 1991) and gays and lesbians (see, for example, Herman 1997). In the American domestic context, the CR mobilized to stop what it saw as the authentication of a particular view of social relations inimical to its own. While focused on the concrete policies of rights for women, gays, and lesbians, the CR's rationale is drawn more broadly as a protection of family and religion from the dangers of secularism (Herman 1997, 4).

In the international context, similar motivations apply. Moves to recognize the rights of women to sexual and reproductive freedom are seen as a nefarious attempt to undermine "nation, family, and church." In the domestic context, the CR UN distinguishes between legitimate rights (such as religious freedom) and the claims by illegitimate "minorities," such as lesbians and gays (Herman 1997, chapter 5). In the international context, the distinction is drawn between the "core" international human rights found in the Universal Declaration (such as the "rights of families") and the "new," and hence illegitimate, rights of women (O'Leary 1998; Ruse 1998a). In both the domestic and international realms, the unifying theme is the rejection of a rights strategy promoting a view of social relations that both the CR and the Vatican see as destructive to faith and family. At the international level, the stakes are seen in more "macro" terms as a battle not just against secularization but also against a globalization of social relations. For the Vatican, the threat to faith and family is also a threat to a global social order predicated on "the family" defined by marriage.

In the post-Beijing period, women's rights remain a central concern for the Vatican and the CR UN but are increasingly characterized as problematic to the extent that they legitimate "homosexuality." In this new focus on homosexuality, the CR UN and the Vatican have fewer concrete measures to confront. For example, there are no conferences or agreements on the meaning or scope of lesbian and gay rights. Perhaps because of this, the CR UN and the Vatican turn their attention to women's rights as the vehicle by which homosexuality is promoted. In this way, feminism and women's rights become subsumed within a larger antihomosexual agenda. While feminists are not often named in Vatican statements, they are obliquely referred to as promoting a "gender ideology" that promotes homosexuality. Women's rights are similarly seen as introducing fluid sexualities or promoting a sexual liberty that includes homosexuality. Thus, homosexuality, which has been a creeping subtext in CR UN opposition to women's rights, is increasingly articulated as a central concern for a "natural family" politics.

This is not to suggest that the CR UN and the Vatican do not continue to see women's rights and feminism as dangerous political developments in and of themselves. Groups adopting the "natural family" political banner, with its emphasis on marriage and the "traditional" division of labor between women and men, are necessarily suspicious of a feminist politics that seeks to empower women within and outside of the home. However, it is equally important to recognize the extent to which the CR UN and the Vatican have come to view women's rights as coextensive with lesbian and gay politics. As we have discussed in this and other chapters, the CR UN often frames its objections to women's equality measures, whether express human rights or other social commitments, as leading to homosexuality (as well as the destruction of the family). In the words of Wendy Wright of Concerned Women for America, "[W]hen you buy into the concept that there is no distinction between men and women that leads you down a path that gets you to accept homosexuality. What's the difference between a man and a man together if there is no difference between men and women?" (1999). In the case of the Vatican, the linkage between women's rights and homosexuality is made in the continual reference to a western hedonism promoting an "ideology of gender" (Pontifical Council for the Family 2000b, paragraph 8), which, through its promotion of homosexuality and the legitimation of "homosexual unions," undermines the "true" family form defined by marriage.

This, of course, begs the question: Why homosexuality? In the case of women's rights, one could understand CR UN and Vatican mobilization as a response to specific gains made by feminist activists at Cairo and

Beijing. In the case of lesbians and gays, however, any gains made at the international level have been few and far between. True, feminist groups have attempted to introduce language recognizing women's rights to control their own sexuality, and at Beijing specifically introduced language prohibiting discrimination on the basis of sexual orientation. Largely, however, there has been a failure to win substantial concrete protections for lesbians and gays at the international level. So, why the growing preoccupation with "homosexuality"?

One reason may be the relationship between CR domestic and international politics. As we discussed above, there are parallels between CR UN opposition to women's rights and CR domestic campaigns against the rights of women, lesbians, and gays. As Herman (1997) has shown, lesbian and gay rights have been a central concern for the CR, whose "antigay" agenda is a priority in their domestic politics. As many of the Protestant CR UN groups have an active, antigay domestic politics (such as Focus on the Family and Concerned Women for America), it is likely that their domestic priorities and experiences inform their international politics. Having schooled themselves in a specific antigay politics, it may be the case that when members of the CR UN turn their gaze to international human rights, they inevitably see the specter of homosexuality in the "radicalization" of women's rights. The question for the future is, will the CR UN continue to focus on "homosexuality" as the enemy of the "natural family" movement? Will homosexuality, in other words, become the "new" CR UN enemy?

Conclusion

The events of September 11, 2001, are widely known: four passenger planes were hijacked within the United States, the pilots overpowered, and the jets flown into the World Trade Center in New York and the Pentagon in Washington (a fourth crashed in a field), to devastating effect. The two towers of the World Trade Center collapsed, and nearly three thousand people are estimated to have lost their lives in the crashes and resulting destruction. The hijackers, all allegedly men of Middle Eastern origin, appear to have been acting in the name of Islam, and with the expectation of divine reward for their deeds in the afterlife.

In many respects, "September 11" is a truly postmodern event. It exposes the paper-thin artifice of national boundaries and state sovereignty, challenges categories of identity in a fluid and migratory world, and calls into question the sources of danger in a changing global order. Despite its vast military power and extensive border patrols, the United States was unable to prevent this attack on its own people within the borders of its own state. The presumed source of the attack, a network of men apparently devoted to the beliefs and politics of one man, Osama bin Laden, has proven to be a difficult enemy to characterize or, indeed, to effect retaliation upon.[1] While bin Laden himself was based in

Afghanistan, he is originally from Saudi Arabia, securing his power in the 1980s—with the help of the United States—in the war to oust the Soviet Union from Afghanistan. His followers are drawn from Muslim communities throughout the globe, reflecting various ethnicities and nationalities. Thus, "the enemy" in this case is diffuse, without a coherent national, cultural, ethnic, or political identity. Its only unifying trait is that it presents itself, or justifies its actions, in the name of a particular, conservative/fundamentalist Islam.

The events of September 11 highlight, albeit in a stark and extreme way, one of the central themes of this book: the connection between global change and religious identity. We are certainly not suggesting by this that there is any relationship between the global politics of the Christian Right and the events of September 11, except insofar as both can be read, at least in part, against the backdrop of globalization and its consequent impact on religious identity and politics. The events of September 11 expose the inherent weakness of state borders, the permeability of boundaries, and changing concepts of identity. It is precisely these developments that have motivated, and are of concern for, the CR organizations active at the UN. In this study, we have generally grouped these changes under the broader rubric of globalization, to capture not only the cultural shifts accompanying "globality" (Robertson 1992b, 132), but also the changes that have enabled the mediation of the social impact of global change. By this, we are referring, of course, to the emergence of new political spaces—in our study, UN-hosted conferences—that have enabled the growth of an international, activist nongovernmental sector.

We have examined CR activism at the international level within the context of this emerging international or, perhaps more accurately, "global" political space. As such, this study of CR politics at the UN is both the detailed account of one social movement (the CR UN), and a larger exploration of the nature of political engagement in this global political space: how issues are framed and contested, how the nature of this space shapes movement agendas, how one movement has come to view this new political terrain and its project there. In this final chapter, we highlight two distinct threads of our analysis to sketch out some of the implications of our study for understanding the nature of global political space as a terrain of struggle and the complex relationship between globalization and religion.

"Global" Political Space

A central premise of this book is that new political spaces have opened up internationally and these spaces have become arenas for contesting global change. This statement is, at first glance, self-evident and uncontroversial. As we have shown throughout this study, the United Nations has become instrumental in providing spaces, including UN-hosted conferences, for political engagement by nonstate actors. This much is obvious. However, our reference to "political space" suggests more than the mere adjustment of international structures to accommodate the views of some nonstate actors. The existence of arenas or spaces within which international policy agendas might be negotiated takes place in the context of larger, global changes in which the role of nation-states—as well as intergovernmental organizations—is being reconstituted. Intimately connected to this process are changes in political culture, in the way issues are defined in terms of global rather than just local significance. Against this backdrop, a statement about the existence of global political space within which social change is mediated is far from straightforward and entails a consideration of what we mean by "political" in a global world. What is this "space" and what makes it "global"? What does it mean to say that this space is a terrain of struggle? What implications does this have for how we conceive and make sense of global social movements?

For the CR UN, one of the key arenas for its activism is the UN-hosted conference. The UN conference is a meeting of state representatives for the purpose of negotiating a nonbinding statement on policy and planned action in a given area, from population policy, human rights, and the environment to social development and HIV/AIDS. As meetings of state representatives, these conferences are "international" events, operating within a traditional state-centered conception of international law and policy in which the main actor remains the nation-state. However, as we have discussed, these conferences allow the participation of nongovernmental organizations, which, in turn, have seized upon the conference system as an arena within which to argue for alternative policy options. And indeed, NGOs have been relatively successful in broadening the scope of the international policy agenda to include, for example, women's rights perspectives. The result is that the UN conference has become something other then a simple meeting of state representatives. It has become a forum at which various international, including nonstate, actors have access to the process of law and policy formation. It has become a place at which social movements, such as the Christian Right, have developed an international politics. Indeed, UN conferences are largely credited with the surge in activist networks, dramatically changing the character of international negotiations and the breadth of international policy agendas.

The UN conference is thus something of a *global* political space, both delimited by, but pushing beyond, the nation-state. It is an example of an arena within which issues and actors are both "transborder and transboundary," and which, in its broad reach, erodes "the distinctions between domestic and foreign affairs, internal political issues and external questions, the sovereign concerns of the nation-state and international considerations" (Held et al. 1999, 445). In this way, the UN conference contributes to a changing global order in which the role of the nation-state is renegotiated. This is not to suggest, however, that the UN conference is a radical transformation of political space and the end of the nation-state as we know it (Walker 1994, 678). Our claim is a more simple one: the emergence of spaces such as the UN conference is an example of what Held et al. refer to as the "continuation [of politics] by new means" (1999, 444).

This claim to "newness" needs some explanation. We accept that social movements have a history of international engagement (Colàs 2002, 58; Pieterse 2001, 25–26), and it would be wrong to suggest that the existence of an internationally oriented social movement in itself represents a new development. What is new, however, is the proliferation of transnational spaces for political engagement, and the related surge in the number and impact of social movements and nongovernmental organizations. Together with a changing global consciousness, this represents a new dimension in social activism of which the rise of an international CR politics is a component.

The Place of the Domestic in Global Politics

Our study of the CR UN demonstrates a movement that has seized upon the international realm as additional to, or building upon, its domestic political engagement. There is no suggestion that the CR UN or, indeed, other social movements sees the international realm as operating in isolation from domestic politics. The CR's international politics is

motivated by a combined and sometimes conflicting agenda of protecting the United States from an encroaching international realm at the
same time as working to transform this realm into a bastion of "natural
family" values (see chapter 6). For the CR UN there is an all-too-fluid
relationship between global change and U.S. domestic law and politics.

It would be a mistake, however, to characterize the CR's international
politics as simply an "add on" to their domestic politics. Throughout
this volume we have traced the points of convergence and disjunction
between the domestic and international CR. While it is clear the two
are related, the CR UN's international mission is taking it into new and
unexplored territory. But there is a larger lesson to be learned here about
the growing significance of the "international" to social movement activism. Among some scholars (Keck and Sikkink 1998a, b; Tarrow 1998),
there has been the suggestion that the rise of an international dimension
to social movement politics can be understood largely in relation to domestic political gains and losses. Margaret Keck and Kathryn Sikkink, for
example, look at transnational activism as resulting from a "boomerang
effect," where failure to secure domestic political objectives results in an
NGO accessing the international realm "to bring pressure on their states
from outside" (1998b, 222; see also 1998a, 12). Sidney Tarrow takes this
analysis further to argue that the most important part of "transnational
activism" is its effect on domestic politics. Scholars, he concludes, will
"learn more by seeing transnational networks as external actors providing resources and opportunities for domestic movements" than by "focusing on the abstraction of a global civil society" (1998, 192).

Our study of the CR UN suggests that this relationship between domestic politics and transnational activism is overdrawn in two respects.
First, the CR UN identifies feminist *success* at the international level,
rather than Christian Right *failure* at the domestic level, as one of the key
instigators for their international engagement (chapter 4). This is not to
suggest that the possible effect of feminist success on U.S. policy is not
an important concern for the CR UN. Clearly it is, but it is not the only
or indeed the primary motivator for this movement. Feminist activism
and an invigorated international civil society represent for the CR UN
a new, global front in the war on the family. In this respect, a CR global
politics needs to be seen within the particular context of global political
space that is not simply domestic politics writ large.

Second, and related to this, the international realm, and the impact of legal and policy developments agreed there, are not significant solely in terms of their possible impact on domestic policy. International decisions made about issues such as population policy, the environment, or HIV/AIDS have the potential to impact on the programs, funding, and direction of a host of international agencies and institutions. For the CR UN, it is the existence of this global aspect of law and policy that poses the biggest threat to the "natural family," and, paradoxically, offers the potential for a new world order based on the "natural family." To dismiss transnational activism as relevant only in terms of domestic politics overlooks the extent to which international law and policy are important realms in their own right. The "international" is more than just the space "outside" of the domestic. It has taken on a significance as, among other things, a site of struggle over the shape and meaning of social relations in the context of global change.

In recognizing that global or international political spaces have become terrains of struggle, we do not want to overstate the power of the international realm to transform social relations. While nonstate actors have been instrumental in expanding the international agenda to include a diverse range of social policy issues, this alone does not equate to social change. Access to international arenas remains relatively closed (see below) and the social agenda, such as it is, narrowly circumscribed. In addition, it remains to be seen how increased social activism will translate into more long-term changes in law and policy at both domestic and international levels. Much of the activism referred to in this text, for example, occurs in the context of UN conferences. The agreements reached here are not formal treaties, state consent is often offered with extensive reservations, methods of monitoring or enforcing policy decisions are weak or nonexistent, and funding commitments made at the conferences are often not met. Much research remains to be done on how policy directives at international meetings translate into changes in program delivery or the application of domestic laws. Despite this, social movements, such as the CR UN, and indeed, state representatives, look to the UN conference as a space for contesting change. Belying its "soft" law quality, the UN conferences are long, often controversial events where the individual wording of lengthy documents is heavily scrutinized and hotly contested. The UN conference has become, in effect, a key event at which social policy options are debated and refined.

For many actors, the UN conference is an important political space for this reason and notwithstanding any direct impact the resulting agreements may have on domestic policy.

Global Spaces and Social Movements

Global social movements—either those global in membership or global in perspective—are at the heart of this changing political culture. The diverse and active social movements at the international level are crucial to the invigoration of this realm, using it as a mechanism to influence the shape and direction of international policy and to network and build alliances among various organizations and interests. This is no less true for the CR UN who, despite a deep-seated distrust of the international realm, sees within it the possibility of forging a global, orthodox, "natural family" alliance. Thus, the emergence of political spaces, like the UN-hosted conference, is both a product of a global consciousness and an arena for the expansion of that consciousness.

But we want to sound a few notes of caution about the perhaps premature celebration of this new political space and the social movements active within it. While recognizing the importance of emerging political spaces, such as the UN conference, and the dynamism of an international civil society, our study suggests the need to complicate an image of unfettered global political activism. We make three arguments in this regard: first, that global political spaces are neither neutral nor static; second, that social movement activism is part of, and complicates our understanding of, globalization; and third, that the existence of a dynamic civil society is neither necessarily democratic nor progressive.

As we discussed above, emerging political spaces like UN conferences are important not just as arenas for social activism, but as places through which activist identities are formed. But this political space is not a blank slate on which a social movement, such as the CR UN, can simply write a new politics (Cohen and Rai 2001, 14–15). The space itself constrains and constructs activist agendas (Cohen and Rai 2001, 15). Importantly, neither the space itself nor the movements active within it are stable (Walker 1994, 674). Just as the UN conference emerged as an unlikely and unanticipated space of social activism, so too will other spaces emerge—meetings of the World Trade Organization, for example—and more, yet, will decline. Similarly, social movement agendas and priorities will shift both through the process of engaging with different spaces, and as the spaces themselves undergo change. This is also true for the CR UN.

As we have shown throughout this book, the CR UN developed its international activism and policy agenda largely in response to the perceived gains made by feminists and other activists at UN conferences on population, human rights, and women. In this way, the nature of the available space for activism, in this case UN conferences, shaped the form of CR UN activism. Paradoxically, the CR UN, through its involvement in events such as UN conferences, has become a participant in the very international civil society it opposes. Through this participation, the CR UN contributes to the process of negotiating social change: the globalization of social relations. Even while bringing an "alternative" viewpoint, the CR UN becomes part of the very structure through which change is enabled and made valid. Indeed, the participation of the CR UN is likely to lend further credibility to a now more diverse international civil society and its (albeit disputed) claim to democratize the international realm. As a global actor, the CR UN is "not just being globalized," it is also "globalizing" (Pieterse 2001, 26–27).

This, of course, poses a challenge to a CR UN politics opposed to the development of international civil society and the participation of nongovernmental organizations in international policy development. One of the most immediate difficulties for the CR UN may be justifying this international participation, in an alliance with orthodox Islamic actors, to a domestic constituency antagonistic to things international and Islamic "fundamentalism" in particular, and who are likely to be even more hostile post–September 11.

Second, the CR UN's international activism highlights the complex relationship between global change and political activism. While social movements such as the CR UN may oppose global change, their international activism is both oppositional *and* productive. Far from demonstrating what Richard Falk refers to as the isolationism of "ultranationalist backlash politics" (1997), the CR UN's activism is a future-oriented engagement: a "natural family" politics promoting the nuclear, heterosexual family as the basic unit of society. Its mission is to introduce a "pro-family," Christianized vision of social order into international politics for the purpose of engaging with, and influencing, global change.

CR UN activism is thus a form of resistance to globalization, but is more than this. The CR UN has embraced aspects of global change—the emergence of various global political spaces and an invigorated international civil society—as offering the possibility for social change. As such, this study suggests the need to be cautious about equating resistance with opposition to globalization. The CR UN may be resistant to aspects of what it would term "the globalization of social relations," but there is no indication that the CR UN is necessarily opposed to all aspects of globalization. Indeed, the explicit internationalization of social movements such as the Christian Right underlies the importance of what Gibson-Graham refers to as "thinking globalization as many" (1996, 146). That is, the need to recognize that the myriad of developments encapsulated under the banner "globalization" is not restricted to the realm of the economic. A recurring theme of this study is the importance of other spaces and dimensions of social discourse to a changing global consciousness, with conseqent impact on how social relations are achieved and negotiated.

Third, there is a tendency in globalization and social movements scholarship to treat social movements as having a democratizing—and progressive—impact on the international realm. Global social movements may represent a diversification of international law and policy, but this is not the same as democratization, and we urge caution in the undue celebration of global social movements as somehow bringing a pluralistic balance to the state-centric world of international politics. While we certainly agree that the international realm represents a dynamic and important forum for understanding the process of global social change, we reject the idea that an emerging international civil society is inherently democratic and progressive.

Indeed, our research demonstrates the international participation of one social movement, the CR, which stands utterly opposed to the values and principles of the so-called progressive movements. The CR's entry onto the United Nations stage is partly an attempt to steer the UN toward a different course, one compatible with CR theology and politics. There is nothing inherently "progressive" or even "of value" (to the world community) in this exercise (nor in that of any other social movement); one's evaluation of the CR UN's campaign depends on one's affinity with the underlying CR agenda.

As a "democratic" space, the international realm is even more suspect. International arenas, including UN-hosted conferences, are privileged spaces, accessible only to the limited few with the language and financial resources to attend and participate effectively. The inclusion of new identities, such as the CR, is certainly important but is not the same as democratization. International political spaces are thus not special or distinctive; globalization processes have simply helped to open up (to opposing social movement elites) a new site of struggle.

Women's Rights and Global Politics

As we discussed in chapters 4 and 5, the CR UN project arose in the context of two conferences primarily focused on women's rights at which feminists were influential: the 1994 Cairo Conference on Population and Development and the 1995 Beijing Conference on Women. The CR UN identifies feminist successes at these conferences as sounding a "wake-up call" for "natural family" advocates (Roylance 1995, ix). In many respects, CR UN politics is explicitly antifeminist. Feminists feature as a key "enemy" of the "natural family" in CR UN publicity and public statements (see chapter 3), and the range of issues on which the CR UN is active closely match those on which feminists have secured notable gains (sexual and reproductive rights, abortion, children's rights).

Despite the obvious antifeminist orientation of the CR UN, we would hesitate to call this an antifeminist movement. To do so, we argue, unduly simplifies the various theological and political strains woven together in CR UN activism (see, for example, chapters 1 and 2). The "antifeminist" label runs the risk of characterizing the CR UN as a single-focus, backlash movement, which overlooks the CR UN's own project for conservative social change (Herman 1997). The "natural family" alliance may be still fledgling, but it suggests a possible future direction for a CR UN project for international reform.

At the same time, it is important not to lose sight of the significance of feminist activism and the language of women's rights for the CR UN in particular, and global politics more generally. Feminist activism has been one of the most prominent and arguably successful aspects of an invigorated international civil society. The rise of the CR UN in response to feminist successes underscores the significance of feminist activism to the articulation of a global politics of social equality. Just as "human rights" have become "keywords" for global political practice (Appadurai 1990, 300), "women's rights" have become a paradigmatic example of the power of international activism. Together women's rights and human rights contribute to a global consciousness, providing the language and the framework for global social empowerment.

Globalization and Religion

The topic of globalization and religion is certainly not a new one (see, for example, Beckford 2000; Beyer 1994; Robertson 1989, 1992b; Vásquez and Marquardt 2000) but is likely to take on new salience in a post–September 11 world. For many theorists, globalization is most often envisioned in terms of its impact on religious self-identification in a changing global circumstance in which values and identities are increasingly "relativized" (see Robertson 1989, 1992b; Beckford 2000). A global order in which definitions of self, community, and nation are subject to renegotiation may pose particular difficulties for religious entities invested in clear boundaries. Some scholars argue that we can expect to see the impact of globalization in a rise in religious fundamentalism (Robertson 1989, 17), as different entities seek to "defend their boundaries and assert their integrity" (Beckford 2000, 180). This need not take the form of an explicit engagement with global forces, and, in some cases, may be evident in the rejection of "the very idea of globality" (Robertson 1989, 18). Scholars such as Beyer and Castells argue that the political activism of the domestic CR is itself an example of a conservative religious movement attempting to limit the impact of the "global system by asserting the exclusive validity of a particular group culture" (Beyer 1994, 114; see also Castells 1998).

We agree with this approach, which sees the relationship between globalization and religion as complex, and in which religion both shapes and is shaped by global change. But our analysis of the CR UN suggests that, in other respects, these scholars may have underestimated the ability of the Christian Right to adapt its politics to a changing world order.

Place, Space, and Beyond

In the 1990s, several scholars suggested that the CR was turning away from national forums and toward local organizing (see, for example, Rozell and Wilcox 1996). While the CR has undoubtedly focused much activity on local developments, our research suggests that an increasingly important site of CR politics is supranational, at the level of the United Nations and UN-sponsored forums. This is no small development. As we have shown, the international realm is viewed with suspicion and open hostility by many in the movement. A global Christian politics marks a clear shift in CR approaches to the international realm and an important expansion of the spaces of CR politics.

The emergence of a CR movement at the UN has defied the predictions not only of some scholars of U.S. domestic politics but also those of globalization. As we discussed above, the "globalization and religion" literature tends to categorize the American Christian Right as responding to globalization largely by resisting "globality," by focusing inward and drawing the curtains against the forces "out there." Again, this conclusion is not inaccurate, and there are certainly aspects of this isolationist approach in CR politics. However, the CR UN demonstrates that in at least some circles, there is support for an expanded CR political engagement, and one that embraces, albeit tentatively, global arenas as places for the promotion of a Christian worldview.

More importantly, this expanded political engagement also suggests a movement that is seeking a more "mainstream" political profile. This is evident in, among other things, the proliferation of sophisticated expert discourse on the "natural family." In the United States, CR activists such as David Blankenhorn, Bryce Christensen, Wade Horn, and Allan Carlson have all produced a secularized, professional discourse on "the family" that has achieved a wide impact and is rarely associated with their conservative Christian politics. Several of these individuals are key participants in the CR UN. This raises the question of the extent to which the CR's secular rhetoric is a sign of its increasing ideological assimilation within mainstream politics (Moen 1995), or, is it, instead, an example of CR "stealth tactics," a strategic acknowledgment that irate religious rhetoric does not play well in American (or international) public discourse (Diamond 1998)? Our research suggests that both these views have merit. There is no doubt that the CR is well aware of the need to "de-theologize" their public interventions—that "expert science" plays better than ideological dogma in public forums (this is a "truth" to which many social movements eventually conform). At the same time, however, we argue that there have been some real shifts in CR thinking around "the global." There may now be an increasing divergence between the domestic CR and some sectors of the CR UN around several issues, including the role of the United Nations and the relationship between the United States and the developing world. Whether the CR is "assimilationist" or "stealthy" is thus not an either/or proposition. Like most social movements engaging in mainstream politics, it is both.

Enemies, Friends, and Alliances

In 1993, Frank Lechner wrote that a future agenda for "fundamentalism" researchers could include an exploration of "whom and what [fundamentalists] demonize" (1993, 34). In relation to CR constructions of foreign enemies in the 1990s, two influential views in the social science literature predominated. One, espoused by Paul Gifford and colleagues and echoed in the work of Roland Robertson (1992a, 406), argued that the end of the cold war would inexorably lead to the identification of "Islam" as the new demon, occupying the place formerly held by "communism": "Muslim countries have now assumed the mantle of evil from the departed Soviet Union" (Brouwer, Gifford, and Rose 1996, 19; see also Gifford and Gifford 1991). For Robertson, "in the face of the relativizing dangers of globalization," the objection will switch from "secular humanism" to "the contaminating effects of exposure to alien doctrines and philosophies, such as those of Islam" (1992a, 406). Peter Beyer, on the other hand, suggested that globalization processes would prevent the CR from being able to identify any demons at all; the world as a "single place" meant that there was no "outside" zone, and therefore no outsiders, to function as "enemy others" (1990, 374; 1994, 132–33).

Our study suggests that both these assertions are subject to challenge. First, it is simply incorrect to state that the cold war is over for the American Christian Right. Anticommunism continues to thrive within CR organizations, and there is no sense in which the CR "really believes" communism has been vanquished. This is evident at the level of the CR UN in terms of its vehement opposition to increased "friendliness" between the United States and China: China is communist, communism equals atheism, atheism is a satanic force. It is also evident in terms of the CR's underlying association of "globalists" with "Marxists" and "socialists."

Second, our research indicates that Islam has *not* become the "new enemy other" for the CR. On the contrary, the CR UN has forged ahead to make alliances with conservative Islamic states and sees no contradiction in doing so. CR publications and political activists spend no more time demonizing Islam than they ever did; in other words, Islam is a perennial CR enemy, and there is little evidence that this particular foe has been parachuted into first place. It may be the case that there is an interesting divergence between how the *political* CR constructs foreign enemies versus how the *missionary* CR does so. The latter organizations may well take a more "crusading," anti-Islamic stance in their work; however, our project concerns the former and it is important not to confuse the two.

The events of September 11 might have been expected to invigorate an anti-Islam position in CR UN organizations, but there is little evidence that this has occurred. In fact, quite the contrary. Since September 11, activist publications—newsletters, bulletins, and updates—discussing the September attacks have emphasized religious "tolerance" and "pluralism." Most draw a distinction between "good" (those critical of Osama bin Laden) and "bad" Muslims (supporters of bin Laden), with the prevailing message[2] that Christians should not condemn all Muslims for the actions of "a few radicals" (Cowan 2001b; Hartwig 2001; Chun 2001). This restrained reaction is noteworthy, suggesting that the CR UN is resisting a knee-jerk, anti-Islam position, perhaps to safeguard their fledgling alliances with conservative Islamic states.

Finally, the question of "friends" is of equal interest to that of "demons." Our research suggests that Robert Wuthnow's (1988) observation that American religion has "restructured" along conservative, rather than strictly theological grounds, is both accurate, and, at the same time, limited, at least as far as the CR and the CR UN in particular are concerned. To the extent that American conservative Protestants and Catholics are increasingly working together in the CR UN and attempting to build an alliance along conservative religious lines, Wuthnow's thesis seems borne out. However, to the extent that the CR UN is still very much, and shows every sign of remaining, a profoundly *Christian* movement, there is little indication that conservatism per se is working to minimize the divide between faiths. Indeed, there is no indication that the alliance sought by the CR UN is possible, and if it is, whether this immediate political solution would alter the fundamentally Christian underpinnings of this movement.

In February 2001, delegates representing the George W. Bush presidency made their first appearance at the United Nations, to the wild applause of CR UN activists (C-Fam 2001a). Taking a strong, conservative position on children's rights and population policy funding, the Bush administration has signaled a policy direction that is much more consistent with the positions of the CR UN outlined throughout this text. Using the language of "parental rights" and "the family," the Bush administration has done much to endear itself to the Christian Right (C-Fam 2001b, 2001a). Importantly, this administration has openly aligned itself with the Christian Right, appointing notable CR activists to influential government posts and including CR representatives on official U.S. delegations at the UN. For example, Wade Horn, one of the Christian Right speakers at the World Congress of Families II, was appointed the assistant secretary for children and families at the Department of Health and Human Services, and Janice Shaw Crouse, senior fellow to the Beverly LaHaye Institute (Concerned Women for America), was included on the official U.S. delegation to the 2002 Child Summit.

In its pro-family positions, the Bush administration is also taking the lead in building alliances with conservative governments that share its position on issues such as children's rights and homosexuality. For example, at the 2002 United Nations Special Session on Children, the U.S. led a coalition of Catholic and Muslim countries that included Sudan, Iran, and Pakistan, to oppose draft language recognizing "various forms of the family" and sexual and reproductive health services for adolescents (Archibald 2002; C-Fam 2002).

The combined events of 9/11 and the conservative Bush administration raise questions and possible difficulties for the future of the CR UN and its "natural family" alliance. While CR elites may have resisted engaging in Islam-bashing following the events of 9/11, it is unclear if CR grassroots may be as forgiving. More troubling, will grassroots members who were resistant to alliances before 9/11 wish to remain members of a "natural family" network that includes Muslims?

At the same time, an active Bush administration may pose uncertainties for the CR UN and its self-appointed role as facilitating an orthodox "natural family" alliance. Will the Bush administration displace the CR UN as "leading" the push for an alliance? Will the promotion of CR groups within the Bush administration, through the inclusion of CR representatives on U.S. delegations, bolster or fragment the CR UN? How much further this Republican administration implements, courts, and allies itself with the CR and its "natural family" agenda remains to be seen, as does the impact this will have on the global politics of the CR UN.

Notes

Introduction

1. See www.worldcongress.org.

2. One example is the site operated by the Institute for First Amendment Studies, www.ifas.org.

3. There is a very brief discussion of the role of the Vatican, but Keck and Sikkink tend to dismiss its influence.

4. But see Luke and Ó Tuathail's (1998) brief discussion of "Buchananism."

5. For example, the term "fundamentalist" is used to refer both to those religious observers who choose to separate themselves from society in inward-looking communities and to those who use all the societal resources at their disposal to change or indeed overthrow dominant configurations of power. See also Keddie's discussion of terminology (1998).

6. We are not concerned in this project with conservative Christian movements elsewhere in the world, though we do consider one Canadian organization (Real Women) as well as a few Canadian CR authors (e.g., Gairdner, Morton).

7. Some argue that Mormonism is a "new world religion" (see discussion in Mauss 1994, chapter 12; Shipps 1985). This is not a debate to which we can contribute; for our purposes, we consider the conservative Mormon groups active at the UN as part of the CR as a whole.

8. By "extremist," we would agree with Aho's definition: "Thus, extremism includes: (1) efforts to deny civil rights to certain people, including their right

to express unpopular views, their right to due process at law, to own property, etc.; (2) thwarting attempts by others to organize in opposition to us, to run for office, or vote; (3) not playing according to legal constitutional rules of political fairness: using personal smears like "Communist Jew-fag" and "nigger lover" in place of rational discussion; and above all, settling differences by vandalizing or destroying the property or life of one's opponents. The test is not the end as such, but the means employed to achieve it" (1996, 190).

9. See, for example, Falk 1995; Lipschultz 1996; and Waterman 2000 (138). For a critical discussion of "international civil society," see Clark, Friedman, and Hochstetler 1998 (2–6); Colàs 2002; Eschle 2001; Keck and Sikkink 1998a (32–34); and Walker 1994 (690–91). Like these authors, we are skeptical about the existence of an international "civil society." However, we accept that the rise of social movements at the international realm and their formalized participation as NGOs have resulted in a form of "civil society" affecting, and a significant part of, international law and policy making. We cautiously use the term "international civil society" to refer to that phenomenon.

10. For a discussion of the ECOSOC process, see Aston 2001 and Otto 1996a.

11. See C-Fam.org. For a more detailed discussion of C-Fam, see Kissling and O'Brien 2001.

12. Beverly LaHaye, together with her partner, Tim LaHaye, has a long history of CR activism. The LaHayes' book, *A Nation without a Conscience* (LaHaye and LaHaye 1994) gives a good sense of the authors' religious and political values. Tim LaHaye has, in more recent years, become one of the leading writers in the CR's "prophecy fiction" genre (see chapter 1).

13. Dobson is a psychologist, author, and radio host, among other things.

14. For a description of the Howard Center, see www.profam.org/thc.

15. For information on the Religion and Society Studies Center, see www.profam.org/thc/thc_rssc.htm.

16. For information on the Swan Library, see www.profam.org/thc/thc_slfoc.htm.

17. See www.rockfordinstitute.org/About.htm. Michael Sells (1999) has argued that the RI is part of a wider, nativist network with links to more overtly racist organizations.

18. See www.pop.org.

19. Although the correct term for the Vatican in its UN capacity is the "Holy See," we use the term "Vatican" for reasons of clarity and continuity. Publications by the Vatican are listed under "Holy See" in the references list.

20. For more information on the "See Change" campaign, see www.cath4choice.org.

21. See, for example, Balmforth 2000.

22. See www.realwomenca.com/html.

1. Divinity, Data, Destruction

1. Genesis 1:26–28 is about man subduing the earth; Genesis 9:1 is an injunction to Noah to be fruitful and multiply; Deuteronomy 6:6–7 is about how to keep the commandments, 11:18–21 is the same, and 21:17 is about how to divide up property "when a man has two wives"; Proverbs 22:6 is "start a boy on the right road, and even in old age he will not leave it," 23:13 is about disciplining children; Timothy 1 is about care for "relatives" and the "aged"; Ephesians is an injunction to children to obey their parents.

2. This is reinforced in the Catholic Catechism (764).

3. The sentence that follows, however, appears to accord potential validity to other family forms: "It shall be considered the normal reference point by which the different forms of family relationships are to be evaluated" (2202). See chapter 6 for a discussion of recent Vatican pronouncements on "different families."

4. We are not suggesting that the CR is a counter*movement* per se; see chapter 7.

5. The basic contours of CR familial ideology have been extensively discussed by a range of scholars (see, for example, Klatch 1987; Kintz 1997; Lienesch 1993, chapter 2).

6. Fox-Genovese did not actually appear at the conference, but her speech was published and made available on the conference Web site; see Fox-Genovese 1999 and www.worldcongress.org/gen99_speakers/gen99_foxgenovese.htm.

7. Interestingly, the development of this genre has provoked a backlash among some conservative Christians (e.g., Hunt 1998, 35).

8. These include *Demography; Journal of the American Academy of Childhood and Adolescent Psychiatry; Journal of Family Issues; Child Development; Journal of Marriage and the Family;* and *Sociological Inquiry.*

9. *New Research* is an insert/supplement to *Family in America.* For these topics, see, respectively, Howard Center 2000c, b, h, f, g, d, e, a, and i. See also, generally, Daniels 1998.

10. Other important biblical texts include Ezekiel 37–39; Daniel 7 and 12; and Mark 13. See Boyer 1992 (chapter 1).

11. These include Chandler 1984, Henry 1971, Lienesch 1993, Pieterse 1992, and Wilson 1977. See also Norman Cohn's (1970) classic work on medieval millenarianism.

12. Though see Hagee (1996, 118), who describes the Antichrist as "the devil incarnate," the "son of Satan."

13. Catholicism's Antichrist is somewhat different; see, for example, McGinn 1994 (226–30).

14. This resonates with older "Jewish conspiracy" theories of the nineteenth century, partly based on the forged document *Protocols of the Elders of Zion.*

15. For a fascinating account of how premillennialists interpret the Holocaust in terms of their eschatology, see Ariel 1991.

16. See also Rushdoony 1978 and DeMar 1995. For discussion, see Barron and Shupe 1992; Boston 1993, chapter 9; Skillen 1990, chapter 8; Clarkson 1994; Diamond 1995 (246–49).

2. Constructing the Global

1. The passage in quotation marks is cited from *USA Today,* 29 June 1994, 15A.

2. In Protestant prophecy, a ten-nation confederacy will do battle with Christ's forces at Armageddon. For further exploration of the role of Europe in these events, see Herman 2000b.

3. When Americans are identified, they are often Jewish advisors to the Clinton administration and so, in anti-Semitic terms, are not Americans at all.

4. The demonization of Canada and Canadians in PR texts deserves further exploration.

5. Lechner (1993) uses the terms "contamination" and "creolization" (borrowing from Hannerz 1991) to describe a similar process.

3. Nation, Church, Family

1. See, for example, CR journalist Dorian Ian Atherton (2000), who argues that globalists seek to replace God with a new religion of "Global Governance"— "a virtual cornucopia of failed Socialist tenets."

2. CR UN activist literature demonstrates some concern with international financial institutions, such as the World Bank, which are seen as using their power to force population policy and "antifamily" measures on dependent, third world countries. See, for example, Landolt 1999 and Ruse 2001.

3. Article 16 (3) of the Universal Declaration of Rights (U.N. Doc. A/811) provides that: "The family is the natural and fundamental group unit of society and is entitled to protection by society and the State."

4. Peter Smith, International Right to Life Federation, quoted in C-Fam 2000f. CR UN activists list different kinds of barriers to CR UN participation, from a limit on the number of right-to-life organizations allowed to attend the Cairo +5 conference and limited accreditation of the conservative religious press (Ruse 1999c) to more malicious measures such as unfair diversionary tactics by conference chairs (Roylance 1995, 112; see also Balmforth 1999).

5. Indicators suggest that the George W. Bush administration is reversing the positions taken by his predecessor, openly allying himself to Christian Right activists and interests at the UN. This includes appointing CR representatives to the official U.S. delegation to the UN as well as taking strong conservative positions on abortion, children's rights, and so on (see discussion in conclusion).

6. At UN conferences, the main negotiation sessions generally take place between state representatives, and NGOs have limited or no rights of access.

NGOs are present at the conferences but often have to confine their lobbying of state delegates to the corridors of the conference event.

7. In addition to the CR UN groups discussed here, there are a number of other CR and political right groups, such as the John Birch Society, who despise the UN and lobby for the United States to withdraw from UN membership (see chapter 4).

8. For example, CR UN actors demonstrate a growing vigilance about the use of international law by U.S. courts, which the CR sees as violating "national sovereignty." See, for example, Ruse 2001 and C-Fam 2001c.

9. The CR UN gives as an example the Clinton administration's decision to implement the Beijing agreement by establishing the Interagency Council on Women. See, for example, CWA 1997d; Jones 1995. It is likely that under the George W. Bush regime the CR UN will be less concerned about the power of the executive and more vigilant about the introduction of international law principles into judge-made law.

10. Thanks to Jutta Brunnée for making this connection for us.

11. Riles 2000, 8. Article 38 of the Statute of the International Court of Justice lists the sources of international law as (a) international conventions; (b) international custom (i.e., the recognized general practice of states); (c) the recognized general principles of law; (d) judicial decisions and academic teaching. This means that when international lawyers try to determine what constitutes "law," they consider a range of sources, including state conduct and statements at forums like UN conferences. Thus, UN conferences are not strictly determinative of international law, but they may be one of several factors contributing to the evolution of legal norms. An increasing number of international lawyers and academics argue that a rigid interpretation of international law and Article 38 may not reflect the complex way in which international norms are now evolving, and a more nuanced understanding of international law is needed to account for the impact of developments like UN conferences and the involvement of NGOs. See, for example, Brunnée and Toope 2000. For an overview of the sources of international law, see Shaw 1997, chapter 3.

12. For a critical overview of the realist critique of international law, see Brunnée and Toope 2000, 21–24.

13. For example, a recent newsletter from the Catholic Family and Human Rights Institute (15 November 2000, on file with author) lists the following UN meetings "of supreme importance to pro-lifers": Commission on the Status of Women (on reproductive health), Commission on Population and Development, Commission on Sustainable Development (a preparatory meeting for Rio +10—the ten-year meeting following up on the UN Conference on Environment and Development held in Rio de Janeiro in 1992), the Commission on Social Development (on aging), and the Child Summit: Special Session of the General Assembly.

14. See, for example, World Family Policy Center 2001. For an overview of CR UN opposition to the Convention on the Rights of the Child, see Buss 2000a.

15. The U.S. delegation to the 2002 Children's Summit included Janice Shaw Crouse, senior fellow to the Beverly LaHaye Research Institute, a CR think tank affiliated with Concerned Women for America (see chapter 1), Bill Saunders from the Family Research Council, and John Klink, former Holy See (Vatican) ambassador to the UN. See Crouse 2002; Center for Reproductive Law and Policy 2002.

4. The Death Culture Goes Global

The title of this chapter is taken from a Concerned Women for America publication by the same name, 11 May 1998, available from http://www.cwfa.org; see also Grigg 1994. The epigraphs are quotations from speeches delivered at the World Congress of Families II, 14–17 November 1999; see Ruse 1999e and Tatad 1999.

1. This is a broad generalization about the vast apparatus involved in population-related program delivery. Not all population organizations would necessarily agree with this statement. Feminist and women's organizations, in particular, might categorize their work as providing reproductive and related health services to women and men who otherwise would not have access to them.

2. This is a simplification of a complex set of positions within "the women's movement" at Cairo. For a more detailed discussion of feminist politics at Cairo, see Buss 2000b; Corrêa 1994; Sen, Germain, and Chen 1994.

3. For a more thorough discussion of the Cairo Programme of Action, see Buss 2000b.

4. See, for example, the sidebar "Horrible but True Stories" in CWA 1997e.

5. See the Population Research Institute Web site, http://www.pop.org.

6. Morrison n.d.; see also Ruse 1999e. While Ruse does not use such colorful language, he makes a similar argument that references to sexual and reproductive rights can be seen as a change in "marketing," because "population policy" has been "discredited."

7. See Center for Reproductive Law and Policy 2000. For a discussion of the Mexico City policy, see Finkle and Crane 1985 and Crane and Finkle 1989.

8. Although revoked in 2000, the provision would continue to affect U.S. funding until February 2001; see Benshoof 2000.

9. See Dejevsky 2001; Center for Reproductive Law and Policy 2001 and 2002a. The basis of the suit, according to CRLP, is that the "global gag rule" constitutes a limitation on free speech. The case was initially dismissed by the District Court for the Southern District of New York (September 2001). An appeal to the U.S. Court of Appeals for the Second Circuit was also dismissed, on September 13, 2002.

10. For example, in January 2002, the Catholic Family and Human Rights Institute issued several appeals to its American membership to phone the White House and demand "Zero for UNFPA." See, for example, Ruse 2002.

11. The CR is also critical of other UN and related bodies, from the World Health Organization to the World Bank, for their perceived involvement in population programs. See CWA 1999f; Grigg 1994; Tatad 1999.

12. These allegations were denied by the UNFPA and Alex Marshall in particular; see Marshall 1999. According to the UNFPA, the purpose of its operations in Kosovo, under the direction of the UN High Commissioner for Refugees (UNHCR), was to coordinate reproductive health services. In that capacity, the UNFPA provided a range of "critical" services, including the provision of "equipment for safe delivery, safe blood transfusion, treatment of sexually transmitted diseases, management of miscarriages, and treatment for victims of sexual violence"; see Van Kampen and Bonk 1999; UNFPA [1999].

13. The subheading for this section is taken from a similarly titled article by Ronald A. Reno, "Exploding the Myth of the Population Bomb" (1998). The reference to a population "bomb" comes from Paul Ehrlich's 1971 book, *The Population Bomb,* in which he argues that a series of environmental disasters will accompany population growth.

14. Agreed in 1992, the UN Convention on Biological Diversity entered into force in 1993 and is designed to conserve biological diversity through the "sustainable use . . . and equitable sharing of the benefits arising out of the utilization of genetic resources." Article 1, *United Nations Convention on Biological Diversity,* reprinted in *International Legal Materials* 31 (1992): 818; see also Birnie and Boyle 1995 (30).

15. See, for example, Ruse 2000c. There is a well-developed CR critique of environmentalism, and numerous CR and related organizations oppose environmental initiatives in the United States. As our focus is on international issues, we have not discussed this aspect of CR politics in detail, though it does warrant further attention.

16. Many thanks to Clyde Wilcox for drawing this point to our attention.

17. There is, within aspects of conservative Catholicism, a more nuanced view of international issues than that taken by their Protestant counterparts. Patrick Allitt, for example, argues that the 1980s saw the emergence of a "new generation of Catholic conservatives" in the United States (1993, 297; see also Haynes 1998, 36) more ambivalent about earlier conservative Catholic positions that viewed the international situation in "apocalyptic" terms as a battle for world dominance between Christianity and the evils of communism (Allitt 1993, 82). The Vatican itself, while apparently dominated by an arguably "conservative" papal regime, is similarly supportive of international aid, while opposing the "death culture" manifested by issues like women's rights.

18. See Morrison 1997a; PRI 1999b. CR UN publications and speeches

contain stories from doctors in developing countries who complain that in their countries, contraceptives are available in great supply while basic medicines such as aspirin cannot be found. See, for example, Forsyth 1999; Grigg 1994; Hsu 1997; Wilson 1999. For the most part, the CR UN tends to quote from the same doctors in multiple publications. "Kenyan pediatrician Dr. Margaret Ogola," for example, is widely quoted as evidence of western preoccupation with birth control at the expense of basic health care. See, for example, Grigg 1994 and chapter 5.

5. In Defense of the Natural Family

1. The first WCF had involved the American CR organizations as well as an eclectic band of right-wing European Christians; see www.worldcongress.org/WCF/wcf1_home.htm.

2. Iranian speakers at the WCFII appeared to adopt both the nuclear and the extended models. Compare, for example, Sahlani 1999 with Husain 1999.

3. See, for example, Hafen 1999; Horn 1999; Farris 1999. Ironically, the Child Convention has been criticized for embodying a particularly western conception of childhood and children's needs (see discussion in Buss 2000a).

4. See, for example, the newsletters of the ICANO (International Council of Awqaf and NGOs).

5. Examples include a pamphlet for the Women's Solidarity Association of Iran and the newsletter of the International Union of Muslim Women NGOs.

6. A short paragraph on "The Family and Children" again reflects this nuclear model.

7. The committee had one Jewish and one Islamic representative.

8. See their Web site: www.oic-un.org/about/over.htm.

9. This pragmatic cynicism is also evidenced more generally in the CR UN's international alliance with so-called pariah (in international human rights terms) states such as Sudan, Iran, and Pakistan.

10. Although Israel's antipathy to the United Nations could perhaps be a basis for an alliance around certain issues.

11. Examples include newsletters of the International Union of Muslim Women NGOs (on file with author).

12. See "Overview," www.oic-un.org/about/over.htm.

6. The Gender Agenda

1. At the final General Assembly session, there were over 2,000 NGO representatives. Four hundred CR UN delegates is arguably a small contingent in this context, but it represents a substantially increased presence for the CR UN. More important, the CR UN was present and active at the crucial preparatory meetings leading to the UN General Assembly Special Session and its impact was noticeable; see Butler 2000 and C-Fam 2000e.

2. The Vatican—and some CR UN organizations—would argue that they

do not oppose women's rights except insofar as those rights exceed established guarantees, as they define them, enshrined in the Universal Declaration of Human Rights.

3. For a discussion of these "traditionalist" movements within the Catholic church, see Dinges and Hitchcock 1991.

4. These conferences include, predictably, the Cairo and Beijing conferences and five-year-review processes, but more unpredictably, tangentially related events like the negotiations for the new International Criminal Court, where the Vatican strongly opposed language recognizing "forced pregnancy" as a war crime.

5. The effects of Vatican pressure were acutely felt by Catholic countries with a strong church infrastructure. For example, Marilen J. Dañguilan, who was a member of the Philippines' delegation in the early stages of the Cairo process, details how pressure from the Vatican, both at the negotiations and through the Philippines' Catholic church, was exerted on the Philippines delegation, resulting in her removal as a member of the delegation (1997).

6. In between these two conferences was the Copenhagen Conference on Social Development. For reasons of length and coherence, we do not consider that conference here, though it did provide conservative religious actors like the Vatican with an opportunity to reconsider and introduce limitations to some of the language agreed upon at Cairo. For example, gains made at Cairo recognizing the diversity of families was undermined at Copenhagen by the inclusion of "references to wives and husbands as necessary components of families" (Charlesworth 1996, 542).

7. *Beijing Declaration and Platform for Action, Fourth World Conference on Women, Beijing, China, 4–15 September 1995.* UN Doc. DPI/1766/Wom (1996) (hereinafter referred to as Beijing Declaration).

8. *Beijing Declaration, Chapter V, Adoption of the Beijing Declaration and Platform for Action,* UN Doc. DPI/1766/Wom (1996), paragraph 11 (hereinafter referred to as "Reservations and Interpretive Statements").

9. See, for example, "Reservations and Interpretive Statements," paragraph 11.

10. Paragraph 96 of the Beijing Platform for Action, for example, reads: "The human rights of women include their right to have control over and decide freely and responsibly on matters related to their sexuality, including sexual and reproductive health, free of coercion, discrimination and violence."

11. "Reservations and Interpretive Statements," paragraph 11; see also C-Fam 2000c; CWA 2000a.

12. As a result of extensive feminist lobbying, international treaties have increasingly adopted language recognizing the global oppression of women and the need to better reflect the particularity of "women's experiences" in international initiatives. For example, the Vienna Conference on Human Rights, though riven by a dispute between the economic south and north over the universality

of human rights, adopted language recognizing that the "eradication of all forms of discrimination on the grounds of sex are priority objectives" and that "gender-based violence . . . [is] incompatible with the dignity and worth of the human person" (*Vienna Declaration and Programme of Action* 1993, paragraph 18; see also Larson 1996, 710–13).

13. "Reservations and Interpretive Statements," paragraph 11.

14. The Congregation of the Doctrine of the Faith (CDF) is described by Urquhart (2000) as the "doctrinal watchdog" for the Vatican, and is infamously known for its role in the Inquisition.

15. See, for example, McFeely 1999 and back issues of the *World Family Policy Center News,* on file with author.

16. According to Sanders, the contentious organization included within ILGA was NAMBLA, the North American Man/Boy Love Association (1996, 99–100). NAMBLA's membership in ILGA had always been controversial and in 1994, ILGA "expelled three propedophile organizations and passed a general resolution: 'Groups or associations whose predominent aim is to support or promote pedophilia are incompatible with the future development of ILGA'" (Sanders 1996, 101).

17. One of the most significant international developments for lesbian and gay rights, for example, was the decision by the United Nations Human Rights Committee (known as the "Toonen decision" after the gay activists who initiated the complaint) declaring that a legal prohibition against homosexual acts in the Australian state of Tasmania contravened the International Covenant on Civil and Political Rights (Dorf and Pérez 1995, 331). In addition, other human rights organizations, such as Amnesty International and Human Rights Watch, have lesbian and gay subsections dedicated to examining and publicizing human rights abuses suffered by sexual minorities.

18. McFeely 1999. McFeely is a senior editor for *The Report,* formerly *The Alberta Report,* which, according to its Web site (http://report.ca/) is a magazine with a "lively conservative, free enterprise, populist attitude" to news, "with heavy emphasis on family and faith."

19. "Reservations and Interpretative Statements," paragraph 11. The apparent increase in the Vatican's concern with homosexuality can be seen not just in its interventions at UN events such as Beijing, but also in the actions and statements of various Vatican bodies. For example, John Paul II has been making increasingly condemnatory statements about homosexuality (Urquhart 2000), and Vatican bodies such as the Pontifical Council for the Family have been charged with examining topics related to homosexuality.

20. See, for example, paragraph 23.

Conclusion

1. At the time of writing, the American reprisal against the Taliban regime in Afghanistan, for supporting Osama bin Laden, has resulted in its overthrow

from most areas of Afghanistan. Bin Laden himself remains elusive and the American war continues with the growing threat of spreading to Iraq and Somalia in the name of eradicating "global terrorism."

2. It is still too early to draw definitive conclusions about the impact of 9/11 on CR politics, and more research is required in this area. But a review of the Concerned Women for America Web site, in the aftermath of 9/11, suggested that CWA, at least, was less vocal than others in its support for religious pluralism. For example, Chuck Colson (2001) argued that the 9/11 terrorists were not "simply anarchists" but a product of a "major power struggle within Islam." Other CWA publications emphasized the persecution of Christians by the Taliban, or suggested that only Christianity could save Afghanistan from the Taliban (Green 2001).

References

Aguirre, Maria Sophia. 1999. "Family, Economics, and the Information Society: How Are They Affecting Each Other?" Speech delivered at the World Congress of Families II, 14–17 November, Geneva, Switzerland. http://www.world.congress.org.

Aho, James A. 1990. *The Politics of Righteousness: Idaho Christian Patriotism.* Seattle: University of Washington Press.

———. 1994. *This Thing of Darkness: A Sociology of the Enemy.* Seattle: University of Washington Press.

———. 1996. "Popular Christianity and Political Extremism in the United States." In *Disruptive Religion: The Force of Faith in Social Movement Activism,* edited by C. Smith. New York: Routledge.

Alexander, Jacqui. 1990. "Mobilizing against the State and International 'Aid' Agencies: 'Third World' Women Define Reproductive Freedom." In *From Abortion to Reproductive Freedom: Transforming a Movement,* edited by M. Gerber. Boston: South End Press.

Allitt, Patrick. 1993. *Catholic Intellectuals and Conservative Politics in America, 1950–1985.* Ithaca, N.Y.: Cornell University Press.

Ammerman, Nancy Tatom. 1987. *Bible Believers: Fundamentalism in a Modern World.* New Brunswick, N.J.: Rutgers University Press.

———. 1991. "North American Protestant Fundamentalism." In *Fundamentalisms*

Observed, edited by M. E. Marty and R. S. Appleby. Chicago: University of Chicago Press.

Amnesty International United Kingdom. 1997. *Breaking the Silence: Human Rights Violations Based on Sexual Orientation.* London: Amnesty International United Kingdom.

Antiwar.com. 2000. "Beyond Left and Right: The New Face of the Antiwar Movement." Conference, March, San Mateo, California. http://www.antiwar.com/conf2.html.

Appadurai, Arjun. 1990. "Disjuncture and Difference in the Global Structural Economy." In *Global Culture: Nationalism, Globalization, and Modernity,* edited by M. Featherstone. London: Sage.

Appleby, R. Scott. 1997. "Catholics and the Christian Right: An Uneasy Alliance." In *Sojourners in the Wilderness: The Christian Right in Comparative Perspective,* edited by C. E. Smidt and J. M. Penning. Lanham: Rowman & Littlefield.

Archibald, George. 2002. "U.S. to Help UN Redefine 'Families.'" *Washington Times,* 22 April. http://www.washtimes.com.

Archibugi, Daniele, and David Held, eds. 1995. *Cosmopolitan Democracy: An Agenda for a New World Order.* Cambridge: Polity.

Ariel, Yoakov. 1991. "Jewish Suffering and Christian Salvation: The Evangelical-Fundamentalist Holocaust Memoirs." *Holocaust and Genocide Studies* 6: 63–78.

Askin, Steve. 1994. *A New Rite: Conservative Catholic Organizations and Their Allies.* Washington, D.C.: Catholics for a Free Choice.

Aston, Jurij Daniel. 2001. "The United Nations Committee on Non-governmental Organizations: Guarding the Entrance to a Politically Divided House." *European Journal of International Law* 12, no. 5: 943–62.

Atherton, Dorian Ian. 2000. "Analysis: Global Governance—A Religion of Losers." http://www.newsmax.com.

Baden, Sally, and A. M. Goetz. 1997. "Who Needs [Sex] When You Can Have [Gender]? Conflicting Discourses on Gender at Beijing." *Feminist Review* 56: 3–25.

Balch, Robert W., John Domitrovich, Barbara Lynn Mahnke, and Vanessa Morrison. 1997. "Fifteen Years of Failed Prophecy: Coping with Cognitive Dissonance in a Baha'i Sect." In *Millennium, Messiahs, and Mayhem: Contemporary Apocalyptic Movements,* edited by T. Robbins and S. J. Palmer. New York: Routledge.

Balmer, Randall. 1994. "American Fundamentalism: The Ideal of Femininity." In *Fundamentalism and Gender,* edited by J. Hawley. New York: Oxford University Press.

Balmforth, Kathryn. 1999. "Hijacking Human Rights." Speech delivered at the World Congress of Families II, 14–17 November, Geneva, Switzerland. http://www.worldcongress.org.

————. 2000. "U.S. Wages War on Family." *Washington Times,* 29 September. http://www.christianbiblestudy.org/MOS/_MOSOPS/uswwof.html.

Bandarage, Asoka. 1997. *Women, Population, and Global Crisis: A Political-Economic Analysis.* London: Zed Books.

Barkun, Michael. 1987. "The Language of Apocalypse: Premillennialists and Nuclear War." In *The God Pumpers: Religion in the Electronic Age,* edited by M. Fishwick and R. B. Browne. Bowling Green, Ohio: Bowling Green State University Popular Press.

————. 1994. *Religion and the Racist Right: The Origins of the Christian Identity Movement.* Chapel Hill: University of North Carolina Press.

Barnes, Tonya, Richard Campbell, Wendy Jackson, Violette Lacloche, Wagaki Mwangi, and Gretchen Sidhu. 2000. "Summary of the 23rd Special Session of the General Assembly (Beijing +5): 5–10 June 2000." *Earth Negotiations Bulletin,* June 13.

Barron, Bruce, and Anson Shupe. 1992. "Reasons for the Growing Popularity of Christian Reconstructionism: The Determination to Attain Dominion." In *Religion and Politics in Comparative Perspective,* edited by B. Misztal and A. Shupe. Westport, Conn.: Praeger.

Bartlett, Kenda. 1995. "Sexual Rights: A New Human Right?" In *The Traditional Family in Peril: A Collection of Articles on International Family Issues,* compiled by S. Roylance. South Jordan, Utah: United Families International.

Barton, David. 1989. *The Myth of Separation.* Aledo, Tex.: Wallbuilders.

Bauman, Zygmunt. 1998. "Postmodern Religion?" In *Religion, Modernity, and Postmodernity,* edited by P. Heelas. Oxford: Blackwell.

Beckford, James A. 1996. "Postmodernity, High Modernity, and New Modernity: Three Concepts in Search of Religion." In *Postmodernity, Sociology, and Religion,* edited by K. Flanagan and P. Jupp. London: Macmillan.

————. 2000. "Religious Movements and Globalization." In *Global Social Movements,* edited by R. Cohen and S. Rai. London: Athlone.

Bendyna, Mary, John C. Green, Mark J. Rozell, and Clyde Wilcox. 2000. "Catholics and the Christian Right." *Journal for the Scientific Study of Religion* 39: 321–32.

Benoit, Gary. 2000. "Globalism's Growing Grasp." *New American* 16, no. 5.

Benshoof, Janet. 2000. "Global Gag Rule Dropped but Victory Is Tenuous." Center for Reproductive Law and Policy, 24 October. http://www.crlp.org.

Beyer, Peter. 1990. "Privatization and the Public Influence of Religion and Global Society." In *Global Culture: Nationalism, Globalization, and Modernity,* edited by Mike Featherstone. London: Sage.

————. 1994. *Religion and Globalization.* London: Sage.

Bianchi, Andrea. 1997. "Globalization of Human Rights: The Role of Non-state Actors." In *Global Law without a State,* edited by Guenter Teubner. Aldershot: Dartmouth.

Bilmore, Isabel. 1998. "The 'Right to Health?' According to WHO." *Insight,* Family Research Council. http://www.frc.org.

Birnie, P. W., and A. E. Boyle. 1995. *Basic Documents on International Law and the Environment.* Oxford: Clarendon Press.

Blankenhorn, David. 1996. *Fatherless America: Confronting Our Most Urgent Social Problem.* New York: Harper Perennial.

———. 1999. "A Preferential Option for the Family." Speech delivered at the World Conference of Families II, 14–17 November, Geneva, Switzerland.

Boston, Robert. 1993. *Why the Religious Right Is Wrong: About Separation of Church and State.* Buffalo: Prometheus.

Boyer, Paul. 1992. *When Time Shall Be No More: Prophecy Belief in Modern American Culture.* Cambridge, Mass.: Harvard University Press.

Breese, Dave. 1998. "Cyclone of Apocalypse." In *Forewarning,* edited by W. T. James. Eugene, Oreg.: Harvest House.

Bromley, David G., and Anson Shupe, eds. 1984. *New Christian Politics.* Macon, Ga.: Mercer University Press.

Brouwer, Steve, Paul Gifford, and Susan D. Rose. 1996. *Exporting the American Gospel: Global Christian Fundamentalism.* New York: Routledge.

Brown, Harold. 1999. "Globalization and the Family." Speech delivered at the World Congress of Families II, 14–17 November, Geneva, Switzerland. http://www.worldcongress.org/gen99_Brown.htm.

Bruce, Steve. 1990. *The Rise and Fall of the Christian Right: Conservative Protestant Politics in America, 1978–1988.* Oxford: Clarendon.

Brummet, Barry. 1984. "Premillennial Apocalyptic as a Rhetorical Genre." *Central States Speech Journal* 35: 84–93.

Brunnée, Jutta, and Stephen J. Toope. 2000. "International Law and Construction: Elements of an Interactional Theory of International Law." *Columbia Journal of Transactional Law* 39: 19–74.

Buchanan, Patrick. 1997. "Should We Evict the U.N.?" *New York Post,* 27 December, p. 15.

Bull, Chris, and John Gallagher. 1996. *Perfect Enemies: The Religious Right, the Gay Movement, and the Politics of the 1990s.* New York: Crown.

Bull, Malcolm, ed. 1995. *Apocalypse Theory and the Ends of the World.* Oxford: Blackwell.

Bunch, Charlotte, and Susana Fried. 1996. "Beijing '95: Moving Women's Human Rights from Margin to Center." *Signs* 22: 200–204.

Buss, Doris. 1998. "Robes, Relics, and Rights: The Vatican and the Beijing Conference on Women." *Social and Legal Studies* 7: 339–64.

———. 2000a. "How the U.N. Stole Childhood: The Christian Right and the International Convention on the Rights of the Child." In *Feminist Perspectives on Child Care Law,* edited by J. Bridgeman and D. Monk. London: Cavendish.

———. 2000b. "Racing Populations, Sexing Environments: The Challenges of a Feminist Politics in International Law." *Legal Studies* 20: 463–84.

Butler, Jennifer. 2000. "For Faith and Family: Christian Right Advocacy at the United Nations." *Public Eye* 9: 1–17.

Calhoun-Brown, Allison. 1997. "Still Seeing in Black and White: Racial Challenges for the Christian Right." In *Sojourners in the Wilderness: The Christian Right in Comparative Perspective,* edited by C. E. Smidt and J. M. Penning. Lanham, Md.: Rowman & Littlefield.

———. 1998. "The Politics of Black Evangelicals: What Hinders Diversity in the Christian Right?" *American Politics Quarterly* 26: 81–109.

Camilleri, Joseph A. 1995. "State, Civil Society, and Economy." In *The State in Transition: Reimagining Political Space,* edited by J. A. Camilleri, A. P. Jarvis, and A. J. Paolini. Boulder, Colo.: Lynne Rienner.

Caplan, Lionel. 1987a. Introduction to *Studies in Religious Fundamentalism,* edited by Lionel Caplan. Albany, N.Y.: State University of New York Press.

Caplan, Lionel, ed. 1987b. *Studies in Religious Fundamentalism.* Albany, N.Y.: State University of New York Press.

Carlson, Allan. 1988. *Family Questions: Reflections on the American Social Crisis.* New Brunswick, N.J.: Transaction.

———. 1999a. *For the Stability, Autonomy, and Fecundity of the Natural Family: Essays toward the World Congress of Families II.* Rockford, Ill.: The Howard Center for Family, Religion, and Society.

———. 1999b. "Rebuilding a Family-Centric Culture." *The Family in America* 13, no. 12: 1–4.

———. 2000a. "The 'Family' at the United Nations: What Went Wrong?" *Family in America* 14, no. 8: 1–7.

———. 2000b. "A History of 'the Family' in the United Nations." Presentation to UN Observer Training Seminar, 2 June, New York. http://www.worldcongress.org/WCF/carlson_UN.htm.

———. 2000c. *The New Agrarian Mind: The Movement toward Decentralist Thought in Twentieth-Century America.* New Brunswick, N.J.: Transaction.

Carter, Steven L. 1993. *The Culture of Disbelief: How American Law and Politics Trivialize Religious Devotion.* New York: Basic Books.

Cassara, Ernest. 1982. "The Development of America's Sense of Mission." In *The Apocalyptic Vision: Interdisciplinary Essays on Myth and Culture,* edited by L. P. Zamora. Bowling Green, Ohio: Bowling Green University Popular Press.

Cassesse, Antonio. 1986. *International Law in a Divided World.* Oxford: Clarendon.

Castells, Manuel, 1998. *End of Millennium.* Oxford: Blackwell.

Catholic Family and Human Rights Institute (C-Fam). 1999. "Our View: In Praise of a Truly Inclusive Society." *Friday Fax.* February.

————. 2000a. "Coercion in Peruvian Family Planning Program Imperils USAID Funding." *Friday Fax* 3, no. 23. April.

————. 2000b. "Conservative NGOs Warn U.S. Congressional Staffers about Beijing +5." *Friday Fax* 3, no. 6. 24 December.

————. 2000c. "Latin American States Proposing Radical Reproductive Rights at Beijing +5." *Friday Fax* 3, no. 27. May 26.

————. 2000d. "Powerful NGOs Gather to Put Left-Wing Pressure on UN General Assembly." *Friday Fax* 3, no. 13. 18 February. http://www.c-fam.org.

————. 2000e. "Pro-Family Lobbyists Having Major Input at UN Beijing +5 Conference." *Friday Fax* 3, no. 16. 10 March.

————. 2000f. "UN Clamps Down on NGOs/Pro-life and Pro-family NGOs Cry Foul." *Friday Fax* 3, no. 20. 7 April.

————. 2000g. "UNFPA Releases Annual Ideological Look at State of the World's Population." *Friday Fax* 3, no. 44. 29 September.

————. 2000h. "UN Issues Warning on Looming International Under-population Problem." *Friday Fax* 3, no. 19. 31 March.

————. 2001a. "Bush Negotiators Cheered for Conservative Statement at UN Child Summit." *Friday Fax* 4, no. 7. 2 February.

————. 2001b. "Clinton Holdovers Misrepresent Bush Administration at UN Meetings." *Friday Fax* 4, no. 13. 9 March.

————. 2001c. "Texas Lawyers Attempt to Use UN Resolutions to Overturn US Law." *Friday Fax* 4, no. 50. 6 December.

————. 2002. "Bush Administration Stops Abortion at UN Child Summit." Press release, 13 May. On file with author.

Center for Reproductive Law and Policy. 2000. "The New Global Gag Rule: A Violation of Democratic Principles and International Human Rights." http://www.crlp.org.

————. 2001. "CRLP v. George W. Bush: CRLP Files Suit to Overturn the Global Gag Rule." *Reproductive Freedom News* 10, no. 6 (June).

————. 2002a. "Global Gag Rule Renewal Is Bush's First Assault on Women's Reproductive Rights." *Reproductive Freedom News* 11, no. 1 (January).

————. 2002b. *Reproductive Freedom News* 11, no. 5 (May). On file with authors.

Chandler, Ralph Clark. 1984. "The Wicked Shall Not Bear Rule: The Fundamentalist Heritage of the New Christian Right." In *New Christian Politics*, edited by D. Bromley and A. Shupe. Macon, Ga.: Mercer University Press.

Charlesworth, Hilary. 1995. "Human Rights as Men's Rights." In *Women's Rights, Human Rights: International Feminist Perspectives*, edited by J. Peters and A. Wolper. New York: Routledge.

————. 1996. "Women as Sherpas: Are Global Summits Useful for Women?" *Feminist Studies* 22: 537–47.

Chen, Martha Alter. 1996. "Engendering World Conferences: The International Women's Movement and the UN." In *NGOs, the UN, and Global*

Governance, edited by T. G. Weiss and L. Gordenker. Boulder, Colo.: Lynne Rienner.

Chinkin, Christine. 1989. "The Challenge of Soft Law: Development and Change in International Law." *Comparative Law Quarterly* 38: 850–66.

Chow, Esther Ngan-ling. 1996. "Making Waves, Moving Mountains: Reflections on Beijing '95 and Beyond." *Signs* 22: 185–92.

Christensen, Bryce J. 1990. *Utopia against the Family.* San Francisco: Ignatius.

———. 1991. *When Families Fail: The Social Costs.* Lanham, Md.: University Press of America.

Chun, Trudy, 2001. "Of Terrorism and Hope: Muslim People Are Not Our Enemy." 17 September. http://www.cwfa.org.

Clark, Ann Marie, Elisabeth J. Friedman, and Kathryn Hochstetler. 1998. "The Sovereign Limits of Global Civil Society: A Comparison of NGO Participation in UN World Conferences on the Environment, Human Rights, and Women." *World Politics* 51 (October): 1–35.

Clark, Dave. 2001. "Understanding Islamic Fanaticism." *Family News in Focus,* 17 October. http://www.family.org.

Clark, Ian. 1999. *Globalization and International Relations Theory.* Oxford: Oxford University Press.

Clarkson, Fred. 1994. "Christian Reconstructionism," parts 1 and 2. *Public Eye* 8, no. 1: 1–7 and no. 2: 1–6.

Clinton, Hilary Rodham. 1996. *It Takes a Village.* Touchstone.

Clough, Patricia. 1994. "The Pope Crusades against UN Birth Control." *The Independent,* 16 June, p. 10.

Coates, James. 1987. *Armed and Dangerous: The Rise of the Survivalist Right.* New York: Hill and Wang.

Cohen, Robin, and Shirin Rai. 2000. "Global Social Movements: Towards a Cosmopolitan Politics." In *Global Social Movements.* London: Athlone.

Cohen, S. A., and Cory L. Richards. 1994. "The Cairo Consensus: Population, Development, and Women." *International Family Planning Perspectives* 20: 150–55.

Cohn, Norman. 1970. *The Pursuit of the Millennium.* Oxford: Oxford University Press.

Colàs, Alejandro. 2002. *International Civil Society.* Cambridge: Polity Press.

Collier, Richard. 1999. "Men, Heterosexuality, and the Changing Family: Reconstructing Fatherhood in Law and Social Policy." In *Changing Family Values,* edited by G. Jagger and C. Wright. London: Routledge.

Colson, Chuck. 2001. "A View from the Afghan Border: Bin Laden's Actions Represent a Major Power Struggle within Islam." 5 November. http://www.cwfa.org.

Concerned Women for America (CWA). 1996a. "The United Nations World Food (and Population) Summit: Imposing a Radical Agenda." 17 December. http://www.cwfa.org.

———. 1996b. "World Food Summit." 5 December. http://www.cwfa.org.

———. 1997a. "Feminism at the Helm of U.S. Foreign Policy." 12 May. http://www.cwfa.org.

———. 1997b. "Gore Calls for Family Planning Overseas." 3 November. http://www.cwfa.org.

———. 1997c. "Habitat II: The UN's Attempt to Control Your Family." 24 September. CWA Internet Resource Library. http://www.cwfa.org.

———. 1997d. "In the Aftermath: The UN Fourth World Conference on Women." 7 August. http://www.cwfa.org.

———. 1997e. "Paul Amendment Gets Unprecedented Support in House: Paul Amendment Would Zero Population Control Funds." 29 August. http://www.cwfa.org.

———. 1997f. "The United Nations." Policy paper. http://www. cwfa.org.

———. 1998a. "The Burden of a Child: Doomsayers Assert an Overpopulation Crisis Is Looming." 9 November. http://www.cwfa.org.

———. 1998b. "CEDAW Sells Out Women and Families: Feminists Renew Drive for Federal ERA through CEDAW." 10 September. http://cwfa.org.

———. 1998c. "Celebrating Independence: How Long?" *Family Voice.* July. CWA Internet Resource Library. http://www.cwfa.org/library/nation/1998-07_fr_globalism.shtml.

———. 1998d. "Concerned Women for America Disputes Overpopulation Myth." 8 October. http://www.cwfa.org.

———. 1998e. "Greens Capture Foreign Policy." 26 May. CWA Internet Resource Library. http://www.cwfa.org.

———. 1998f. "The Paul Amendment." E-mail alert. 21 August. On file with author.

———. 1998g. "Sovereignty under Siege: U.N. Biospheres Take U.S. Land." December. http://www.cwfa.org.

———. 1998h. "The United Nations." 15 April. http://www.cwfa.org.

———. 1998i. "Women Forcibly Sterilized in Peru: U.S. Taxpayer $$$ Contribute to Population Control Campaign via USAID." 24 February. http://www.cwfa.org.

———. 1999a. "Challenge the Assertions: Get the Facts behind Overpopulation." http://www.cwfa.org.

———. 1999b. "Dividing Women from Families: The UN Agenda for Global Feminism." 17 March. CWA Internet Resource Library. http://www.cwfa.org./library

———. 1999c. "International Women's Day." 8 March. http://www.cwfa.org.

———. 1999d. "Population and Famine." March. http://www.cwfa.org.

———. 1999e. "Population Control and Human Rights." March. http://www.cwfa.org.

———. 1999f. "Population Controllers on the Move: UNFPA Funding and Quinacrine Approval Sought." 12 May. http://www.cwfa.org.

———. 1999g. "Population Controllers Target the Vulnerable: UNFPA Action in Pakistan and Kosovo." 1 June. http://www.cwfa.org.

———. 2000a. "Beijing +5: Why You Should Be Concerned." 29 February. http://www.cwfa.org.

———. 2000b. "Final Beijing +5 Centers around Abortion: Gideon's Army Prevails." 20 June. http://www.cwfa.org.

———. 2000c. "Radicals Bash Pro-family Lobbyists as 'Right-wing Anti-feminist Groups': Twenty-Third Special Session of the UN General Assembly Begins." 5 June. http://www.cwfa.org.

———. n.d. "Description of the Beverly LaHaye Institute and Short Bio of the Senior Fellow Janice Shaw Crouse." Paper on file with authors.

———. n.d. "Exposing CEDAW." http://www.cwfa.org.

Connor, Steve. 1994. "Chalker at Odds with the Vatican: Tension over Population Meeting." *The Independent,* 12 July, p. 5.

Copelon, Rhonda, and Rosalind Petchesky. 1995. "Toward an Interdependent Approach to Reproductive and Sexual Rights as Human Rights: Reflection on the ICPD and Beyond." In *From Basic Needs to Basic Rights: Women's Claim to Human Rights,* edited by M. A. Schuler. Washington: Institute for Women, Law, and Development.

Corbett, Christopher. 1997. "The U.S. and Other U.N. Serfdoms." In *Foreshocks of Antichrist,* edited by W. T. James. Eugene, Oreg.: Harvest House.

———. 1998. "Energy, Ecology, Economy: A Foreboding Forecast." In *Forewarning: Approaching the Final Battle between Heaven and Hell,* edited by W. T. James. Eugene, Oreg.: Harvest House.

Corrêa, Sonia, in collaboration with Rebecca Reichmann. 1994. *Population and Reproductive Rights: Feminist Perspectives from the South.* London: Zed Books; New Delhi: Kali for Women and in association with DAWN.

Cowan, Mark. 2001a. "Reaching Muslims." *Family News in Focus.* 17 October. http://www.family.org.

———. 2001b. "Terrorism: A Cause for Reflection." *Citizenlink,* September. http://www.family.org.

Crane, Barbara B. 1994. "International Population Institutions: Adaptation to a Changing World Order." In *Institutions for the Earth: Sources of Effective International Environmental Protection,* ed. Peter M. Haas. Cambridge, Mass.: MIT Press.

Crane, Barbara B., and Jason L. Finkle. 1989. "The United States, China, and the United Nations Population Fund: Dynamics of U.S. Policymaking." *Population and Development Review* 15: 23–59.

Crane, Barbara B., and S. L. Isaacs. 1995. "The Cairo Programme of Action: A New Framework for International Cooperation on Population and Development Issues." *Harvard International Law Journal* 36: 295–306.

Crouse, Janice Shaw. 2002. "World Summit for Children Formal Sessions Begin." 8 May. http://www.cwfa.org.

Cuneo, Michael W. 1997a. *The Smoke of Satan: Conservative and Traditionalist Dissent in Contemporary American Catholicism.* New York: Oxford University Press.

————. 1997b. "The Vengeful Virgin: Case Studies in Contemporary American Catholic Apocalypticism." In *Millennium, Messiahs, and Mayhem: Contemporary Apocalyptic Movements,* edited by T. Robbins and S. J. Palmer. New York: Routledge.

Dañguilan, Marilen. 1997. *Women in Brackets: A Chronicle of Vatican Power and Control.* Manila, Philippines: Philippine Center for Investigative Journalism.

Daniels, Cynthia R., ed. 1998. *Lost Fathers.* London: Macmillan.

Davis, David Brion. 1971. *The Fear of Conspiracy: Images of Un-American Subversion from the Revolution to the Present.* Ithaca, N.Y.: Cornell University Press.

Deacon, Bob. 1997. *Global Social Policy: International Organizations and the Future of Welfare.* London: Sage.

De Hart, Jane Sheron. 1991. "Gender on the Right: Meanings behind the Existential Scream." *Gender and History* 3: 246–67.

Dejevsky, Mary. 2001. "Bush's First Move Is to Block U.S. Money Going to Groups Involved in Abortion." *The Independent,* 23 January.

DeMar, Gary. 1995. *America's Christian History: The Untold Story.* Atlanta: American Vision.

De Vos, Pierre. 2000. "The Constitution Made Us Queer: The Sexual Orientation Clause in the South African Constitution and the Emergence of Gay and Lesbian Identity." In *Sexuality in the Legal Arena,* edited by C. Stychin and D. Herman. London: Athlone.

Diamond, Sara. 1989. *Spiritual Warfare: The Politics of the Christian Right.* Boston: South End.

————. 1995. *Roads to Dominion: Right-wing Movements and Political Power in the United States.* New York: Guilford.

————. 1998. *Not by Politics Alone: The Enduring Influence of the Christian Right.* New York: Guilford.

Dinges, William D. 1995. "'We Are What You Were': Roman Catholic Traditionalism in America." In *Being Right: Conservative Catholics in America,* edited by M. J. Weaver and R. S. Appleby. Bloomington: Indiana University Press.

Dinges, William D., and James Hitchcock. 1991. "Roman Catholic Traditionalism and Activist Conservatism in the United States." In *Fundamentalisms Observed,* edited by M. E. Marty and R. S. Appleby. Chicago: University of Chicago Press.

Dobson, James. 1995. *Focus on the Family Newsletter.* August. On file with authors.

Dobson, James, and Gary Bauer. 1990. *Children at Risk.* Dallas: Word.

Donaldson, Peter J. 1990. "On the Origins of the United States Government's International Population Policy." *Population Studies* 40: 385–99.

Dorf, Julie, and Gloria Careaga Pérez. 1995. "Discrimination and the Tolerance of Difference: International Lesbian Human Rights." In *Women's Rights Human Rights: International Feminist Perspectives*, edited by J. Peters and A. Wolper. New York: Routledge.

Druelle, Anick. 2000. "Right-wing Anti-feminist Groups at the United Nations." Unpublished paper. Translated by Sharon Gubbay Helfer. On file with authors.

Duck, Daymond. 1998. "Harbingers of Humanism's Hurricane." In *Forewarning*, edited by W. T. James. Eugene, Oreg.: Harvest House.

Durham, Martin. 2000. *The Christian Right, the Far Right, and the Boundaries of American Conservatism*. Manchester: Manchester University Press.

Dyer, Charles H. 1993. *World News and Bible Prophecy*. Wheaton, Ill.: Tyndale House.

Eagle Forum. 1997. *Global Governance: The Quiet War against American Independence*. Video hosted by Phyllis Schlafly.

Eberstadt, Nicholas. 1999. "World Population in the Twenty-First Century: Last One Out Turn Off the Lights." Speech delivered at the World Congress of Families II, 14–17 November, Geneva, Switzerland. http://www.worldcongress.org.

Ehrlich, Paul. 1971. *The Population Bomb*. London: Pan Books.

Ehrlich, Paul, and Anne Ehrlich. 1970. *Population, Resources, Environment*. San Francisco: W. H. Freeman and Co.

Elliott, Lorraine. 1998. *The Global Politics of the Environment*. Basingstoke: MacMillan.

Eschle, Catherine. 2001. "Globalizing Civil Society? Social Movements and the Challenge of Global Politics from Below." In *Globalization and Social Movements*, edited by P. Hamel, H. Lustiger-Thaler, J. N. Pieterse, and S. Roseneil. Basingstoke, Hampshire: Palgrave.

Falk, Richard. 1987. "The Global Promise of Social Movements: Explorations at the Edge of Time." *Alternatives* 12: 173–96.

———. 1995. *On Human Governance: Toward a New Global Politics*. Cambridge: Polity.

———. 1997. "The World Order between Inter-state Law and the Law of Humanity: The Role of Civil Society Institutions." In *Cosmopolitan Democracy: An Agenda for a New World Order*, edited by D. Archibugi and D. Held. Cambridge: Polity.

———. 2000. "Resisting 'Globalization-from-above' through 'Globalization-from-below.'" In *Globalization and the Politics of Resistance*, edited by B. K. Gills. Basingstoke: MacMillan.

Farris, Mike. 1999. "Parental Rights." Speech delivered at the World Congress of Families II, 14–17 November, Geneva, Switzerland. http://www.worldcongress.org.

Featherstone, Mike, ed. 1990. *Global Culture: Nationalism, Globalization, and Modernity.* London: Sage.

Fenster, Mark. 1999. *Conspiracy Theories: Secrecy and Power in American Culture.* Minneapolis: University of Minnesota Press.

Finkle, Jason L., and Barbara B. Crane. 1985. "Ideology and Politics at Mexico City: The United States at the 1984 International Conference on Population." *Population and Development Review* 11: 1–28.

Finkle, Jason L., and C. Alison McIntosh, eds. 1994. "The New Politics of Population: Conflict and Consensus in Family Planning." A supplement to *Population and Development Review* 20: 3–34.

Fisk, Robert. 1994. "Cairo Takes Its Own Precautions: Egypt Locks up Islamic Fundamentalists to Protect Delegates at UN Population Conference." *Independent on Sunday,* 4 September, p. 9.

Flanagan, Kieran, and Jupp, Peter C. 1996. *Postmodernity, Sociology, and Religion.* London: Macmillan.

Flanders, Laura. 1999. "Commentary: Giving the Vatican the Boot." *Ms. Magazine,* October/November.

Focus on the Family. 2001. "Dr. James Dobson Reflects on a Changed Nation." *Citizenlink,* 20 September. http://www.family.org.

Forsyth, Cecilia. 1999. "Foreign Affairs in Collusion with Planned Parenthood." *REALity,* January/February. http://www.realwomenca.com.

Fox-Genovese, Elizabeth. 1999. "Gender as a Natural Construct." Speech for the World Congress of Families II, 14–17 November, Geneva, Switzerland.

Francis, Charles. 1998. "The Wrongs of the United Nations' Rights of the Child." *Insight.* Family Research Council. http://www.frc.org.

Freedman, Lynn P. 1996. "The Challenge of Fundamentalisms." *Reproductive Health Matters* 8: 55–69.

Friedman, Elisabeth. 1995. "Women's Human Rights: The Emergence of a Movement." In *Women's Rights Human Rights: International Feminist Perspectives,* edited by J. Peters and A. Wolper. New York: Routledge.

Fuller, Robert. 1995. *Naming the Antichrist: The History of an American Obsession.* New York: Oxford University Press.

Furedi, Frank. 1997. *Population and Development: A Critical Introduction.* Cambridge, UK: Polity.

Gager, John G. 1983. "The Attainment of Millennial Bliss through Myth: The Book of Revelation." In *Visionaries and Their Apocalypses,* edited by P. D. Hanson. Philadelphia: Fortress.

Gairdner, William D. 1992. *The War against the Family.* Toronto: Stoddart.

———. 1999. "Democracy against the Family." Speech delivered at the World

Congress of Families II, 14–17 November, Geneva, Switzerland. http://www.worldcongress.org.

Gallup, George, Jr., and D. Michael Lindsay. 1999. *Surveying the Religious Landscape: Trends in U.S. Beliefs.* Harrisburg, Penn.: Morehouse.

Germain, Adrienne, Sia Nowrojee, and Hnin Hnin Pyne. 1994. "Setting a New Agenda: Sexual and Reproductive Health and Rights." In *Population Policies Reconsidered: Health, Empowerment, and Rights,* edited by G. Sen, A. Germain, L. C. Chen. Boston: Harvard School of Public Health.

Gibson-Graham, J. K. 1996. *The End of Capitalism (as We Knew It): A Feminist Critique of Political Economy.* Cambridge, Mass.: Blackwell.

Gifford, Paul, and Edward Gifford. 1991. *The New Crusaders: Christianity and the New Right in Southern Africa.* London: Pluto.

Glanz, Dawn. 1982. "The American West as Millennial Kingdom." In *The Apocalyptic Vision in America: Interdisciplinary Essays on Myth and Culture,* edited by L. P. Zamora. Bowling Green, Ohio: Bowling Green University Press.

Gould, Christoper. 1994. "The Catholic Right in 1994." Addendum 2 to Steve Askin, *A New Rite: Conservative Catholic Organization and Their Allies.* Washington, D.C.: Catholics for a Free Choice, 2–3.

Graham, Billy. 1983. *Approaching Hoofbeats: The Final Horsemen of the Apocalypse.* London: Hodder & Stoughton.

———. 1992. *Storm Warning.* Dallas: Word.

Grant, George, and Mark A. Horne. 1993. *Legislating Immorality: The Homosexual Movement Comes out of the Closet.* Chicago: Moody.

Green, T. L. 2001. "Afghan Women Brutalized by Taliban." 20 October. http://www.cwfa.org.

Grigg, William. 1994. "A Covenant with Death." *New American* 12, no. 21.

———. 1995. *Freedom on the Altar: The UN's Crusade against God and Family.* Appleton, Wis.: American Opinion Publishing.

Guarnizo, Luis E., and Michael Peter Smith. 1998. "The Locations of Transnationalism." In *Transnationalism from Below,* edited by M. P. Smith and L. E. Guarnizo. New Brunswick, N.J.: Transaction.

Gusdek, Elizabeth. 1998. "Parental Rights Are Fundamental Rights." *Insight.* http://www.frc.org.

Guth, James L., John C. Green, Lyman A. Kellstedt, and Corwin E. Smidt. 1995. "Faith and the Environment: Religious Beliefs and Attitudes on Environmental Policy." *American Journal of Political Science* 39: 364–82.

Hafen, Bruce. 1999. "Motherhood and the Moral Influence of Women." Speech delivered at the World Congress of Families II, 14–17 November, Geneva, Switzerland. http://www.worldcongress.org.

Hagee, John. 1996. *Beginning of the End: The Assassination of Yitzhak Rabin and the Coming Antichrist.* Nashville: Nelson.

———. 1998. *Final Dawn over Jerusalem.* Nashville: Nelson.

Haley, George. 1999. "Family." Speech delivered at the World Conference of Families II, 14–17 November, Geneva, Switzerland. http://www.worldcongress.org.

Hamm, Mary Suarez. 1995. "Gender Identity: Where Nature and Nurture Meet." In *The Traditional Family in Peril: A Collection of Articles on International Family Issues,* compiled by S. Roylance. South Jordan, Utah: United Families International.

Hannerz, U. 1991. "Scenarios for Peripheral Cultures." In *Culture, Globalization, and the World-system,* edited by A. D. King. Binghamton: State University of New York.

Hannigan, John A. 1991. "Social Movement Theory and the Sociology of Religion: Toward a New Synthesis." *Sociological Analysis* 52: 311–31.

Hannum, Hurst. 1992. *Guide to International Human Rights Practice,* 2d ed. Philadelphia: University of Philadelphia Press.

Hanson, Eric. 1987. *The Catholic Church in World Politics.* Princeton, N.J.: Princeton University Press.

Harding, Susan. 1991. "Representing Fundamentalism: The Problem of the Repugnant Cultural Other." *Social Research* 58: 373–93.

Hardisty, Jean. 1999. *Mobilizing Resentment: Conservative Resurgence from the John Birch Society to the Promise Keepers.* Boston: Beacon.

Harrison, Paul. 1992. *The Third Revolution: Population, Environment, and a Sustainable World.* London: Penguin Books.

Hartmann, Betsy. 1987. *Reproductive Rights and Wrongs: The Global Politics of Population Control and Contraceptive Choice.* New York: Harper & Row.

Hartwig, Mark. 2001. "Osama Examined." *Citizenlink,* 17 September. http://www.family.org.

Hashemi, Fatemeh. 1999. "In the Name of God, the Compassionate, the Merciful." Speech delivered to the World Congress of Families II, 14–17 November, Geneva, Switzerland. http://www.worldcongress.org.

Hawley, John S., and Wayne Proudfoot. 1994. Introduction to *Fundamentalism and Gender,* edited by J. Hawley. New York: Oxford University Press.

Haynes, Jeff. 1998. *Religion in Global Politics.* London: Longman.

Held, David. 1995. *Democracy and the Global Order: From the Modern State to Cosmopolitan Governance.* Cambridge: Polity.

Held, David, and Anthony McGrew. 1998. "The End of the Old Order? Globalization and the Prospects for World Order." *Review of International Studies* 24: 219–43.

Held, David, Anthony McGrew, David Goldblatt, and Jonathan Perraton. 1999. *Global Transformations: Politics, Economics, and Culture.* Cambridge: Polity.

Henry, Carl F., ed. 1971. *Prophecy in the Making.* Carol Stream, Ill.: Creation House.

Herman, Didi. 1997. *The Antigay Agenda: Orthodox Vision and the Christian Right.* Chicago: University of Chicago Press.

———. 2000a. "The Gay Agenda Is the Devil's Agenda: The Christian Right's Vision and the Role of the State." In *The Politics of Gay Rights,* edited by C. Rimmerman, K. Wald, and C. Wilcox. Chicago: University of Chicago Press.

———. 2000b. "'The New Roman Empire': European Envisionings and American Premillennialists." *Journal of American Studies* 34: 23–40.

———. 2001. "Globalism's Siren Song: The United Nations in Christian Right Thought and Prophecy." *Sociological Review* 49: 56–77.

Higer, Amy, J. 1999. "International Women's Activism and the 1994 Cairo Population Conference." In *Gender Politics in Global Governance,* edited by M. K. Meyer and E. Prügl. Lanham, Mass.: Rowman & Littlefield.

Hirsen, James L. 1999. *The Coming Collision: Global Law vs. U.S. Liberties.* Lafayette, La.: Huntington House.

Hitchcock, James. 1991. "Catholic Activist Conservationism in the United States." In *Fundamentalisms Observed,* ed. M. E. Marty and R. S. Appleby. Chicago: University of Chicago Press.

Hofstadter, Richard. 1966. *The Paranoid Style in American Politics and Other Essays.* London: Jonathan Cape.

Holton, Robert. 2000. "Globalization's Cultural Consequences." *Annals of the American Academy of Political and Social Science* 570: 140–53.

Holy See. 1993. *Vienna Declaration and Programme of Action.*

———. 1994a. "Statement at the International Conference on Population and Development." September. On file with authors.

———. 1994b. "Statement of the Head of Delegation at the Beginning of the III Session of the Preparatory Committee for the International Conference on Population and Development." 5 April. On file with authors.

———. 1995. "Report of the Holy See in Preperation [sic] for the Fourth World Conference on Women." On file with authors.

———. 1998. "Intervention of the Holy See at the Commission on the Status of Women." 4 March. On file with authors.

———. 1999a. "Intervention of the Delegate for the Holy See at the International Forum on Population and Development." 10 February. On file with authors.

———. 1999b. "Intervention of the Holy See at the Commission on the Status of Women." 4 March. On file with authors.

———. 2000a. "Intervention by the Holy See Delegation at the Twenty-Third Special Session of the General Assembly of the United Nations: 'Women 2000: Gender Equality, Development, and Peace for the Twenty-First Century.'" 9 October. On file with authors.

———. 2000b. "Intervention of Cardinal Angelo Sodano at the Millennium Summit of the United Nations." 8 September. On file with authors.

———. 2000c. "Statement of H. E. Mons. Renato Raffaele Martino to the

LV Ordinary Session of the General Assembly of the United Nations." 28 September. On file with authors.

hooks, bell. 1984. *Feminist Theory: From Margin to Center.* Boston: South End Press.

Hoover, Stewart M. 1998. *Religion in the News: Faith and Journalism in American Public Discourse.* Thousand Oaks, Calif.: Sage.

Hopson, Ronald E., and Donald R. Smith. 1999. "Changing Fortunes: An Analysis of Christian Right Ascendance within American Public Discourse." *Journal for the Scientific Study of Religion* 38: 1–13.

Horn, Wade. 1999. "The Family, Civil Society, and the State." Speech delivered at the World Congress of Families II, 14–17 November, Geneva, Switzerland. http://www.worldcongress.org.

Horowitz, Irving Louis. 1983. "Struggling for the Soul of Social Science." *Society,* July/August, 4–15.

Howard Center. 1999. "Handicapped Blacks." *New Research* 3 in *The Family in America* 13, no. 11.

———. 2000a. "Armed and Fatherless." *New Research* 1–2 in *The Family in America* 14, no. 1.

———. 2000b. "The Doctor's In; the Patient's Out." *New Research* 2 in *The Family in America* 14, no. 5.

———. 2000c. "Explaining the Epidemic." *New Research* 2 in *The Family in America* 14, no. 10.

———. 2000d. "Fatherless Fornicators." *New Research* 2 in *The Family in America* 14, no. 6.

———. 2000e. "Growing up Too Fast." *New Research* 1 in *The Family in America* 14, no. 2.

———. 2000f. "Missing More Than Money." *New Research* 2 in *The Family in America* 14, no. 4.

———. 2000g. "Murder vs. Matrimony." *New Research* 2 in *The Family in America* 14, no. 7.

———. 2000h. "Stepdads + Working Moms = Child Sexual Abuse." *New Research* 2–3 in *The Family in America* 14, no. 5.

———. 2000i. "Sudden Death." *New Research* 3 in *The Family in America* 14, no. 9.

Howard, John. 1999. Letter to the editor. *National Review,* 31 July.

———. 2001. "Putting Our Own House in Order." Howard Center, 27 September. http://profam.org.jah._poohio.htm.

Hsu, Gracie S. 1995a. "Gender Benders in Beijing." *Perspective,* 24 August.

———. 1995b. "Reinventing Family Values in Beijing." *Perspective,* 21 August. On file with authors.

———. 1997. "Population Imperialism: The Growing Backlash against U.S. Policy." *Family Policy* 10, no. 4.

Human Life International. 2000. "Women's Conference Features Face-Off between Vatican, Pro-Abortion Groups." *PR Newswire,* 5 June. On file with authors.

Hunt, Dave. 1994. *A Woman Rides the Beast: The Roman Catholic Church in the Last Days.* Eugene, Oreg.: Harvest House.

————. 1998. "Flashes of Falling Away." In *Forewarning,* edited by W. T. James. Eugene, Oreg.: Harvest House.

Hurlburt, Catherina. 2001. "UN Convention on the Rights of the Child. A Treaty to Undermine the Family." September. http://www.cwfa.org.

Husain, Syed Shahid. 1999. "Family Policies That Work." Speech delivered at the World Conference of Families II, 14–17 November, Geneva, Switzerland. http://www.worldcongress.org.

Hutchings, Noah W. 1998. "The Deadly Chinese Typhoon." In *Forewarning,* edited by W. T. James. Eugene, Oreg.: Harvest House.

Independent. 1994a. "Islamists Try to Block UN Conference." 26 August, 11.

————. 1994b. "A Rather Unholy Religious Pact." 11 August, 17.

Ingersoll, Julie J. 1995. "Which Tradition, Which Values? 'Traditional Family Values,' in American Protestant Fundamentalism." *Contention* 4: 91–104.

Ingraham, Jane H. 1994. "UN Takeover of the Child." *New American* 10, no. 16.

Introvigne, Massimo. 1997. "Latter-Day Revisited: Contemporary Mormon Millenarianism." In *Millennium, Messiahs, and Mayhem: Contemporary Apocalyptic Movements,* edited by T. Robbins and S. J. Palmer. New York: Routledge.

James, Edgar C. 1991. *Armageddon and the New World Order.* Chicago: Moody.

James, William T. 1997a. "Globalism's Siren Song." In *Foreshocks of Antichrist,* edited by W. T. James. Eugene, Oreg.: Harvest House.

James, William T., ed. 1997b. *Foreshocks of Antichrist.* Eugene, Oreg.: Harvest House.

————. 1998. *Forewarning.* Eugene, Oreg.: Harvest House.

Jarvis, Anthony P., and Albert J. Paolini. 1995. "Locating the State." In *The State in Transition: Reimagining Political Space,* edited by J. A. Camilleri, A. P. Jarvis, and A. J Paolini. Boulder, Colo.: Lynne Rienner.

Jeffrey, Grant R. 1991. *Messiah: War in the Middle East and the Road to Armageddon.* New York: Bantam.

————. 1995. *Final Warning: Economic Collapse and the Coming World Government.* Toronto: Frontier Research.

Joachim, Jutta. 1999. "Shaping the Human Rights Agenda: The Case of Violence against Women." In *Gender Politics in Global Governance,* edited by M. K. Meyer and E. Prügl. Lanham, Mass.: Rowman & Littlefield.

John Paul II. 1994. "Address to Dr. Nafis Sadik, Secretary General of the 1994 International Conference on Population and Development and Executive Director of the United Nations Population Fund." 18 March. On file with author.

————. 1995a. "Address to Mrs. Gertrude Mongella, Secretary General of the Fourth World Conference on Women." 26 May. On file with authors.

————. 1995b. "Letter to Women." 29 June. On file with authors.

————. 1996. "Address to the United Nations General Assembly." July 8. On file with author.

————. 1998. "Address of His Holiness Pope John Paul II to the International Conference on 'Women's Health Issues.'" 20 February. http://www.vatican.va.

————. 1999. "Speech to the Participants at the Meeting for the John Paul II Institute on Marriage and Family." 27 August. On file with authors.

————. 2000. "Holy Father's Address to the Secretary General and the Administrative Committee on Coordination of the United Nations." 7 April, paragraph 4. On file with authors.

Johnson, George. 1983. *Architects of Fear: Conspiracy Theories and Paranoia in American Politics.* Los Angeles: Jeremy P. Tarcher.

Johnston, Alastair Iain. 2000. "Treating International Institutions as Social Environments." *International Studies Quarterly* 45, no. 4 (December): 587–615.

Jones, Gracia N. 1995. "U.N. Agencies and Conferences: With Reports Pertaining to Women and Children." In *The Traditional Family in Peril: A Collection of Articles on International Family Issues,* compiled by S. Roylance. South Jordan, Utah: United Families International.

Jones, Lawrence. 1992. "Apocalyptic Responses to the War with Iraq." In *Christianity and Hegemony,* edited by J. P. N. Pieterse. New York: St. Martin's.

Joseph, Rita. 1999. "Deconstructing the Family." Speech delivered at the World Conference of Families II, 14–17 November, Geneva, Switzerland. http://www.worldcongress.org.

Kaplan, Robert D. 1994. "The Coming Anarchy: How Scarcity, Crime, Overpopulation, Tribalism, and Disease Are Rapidly Destroying the Social Fabric of Our Planet." *Atlantic Monthly* 273: 44–76.

Kaufman, Matt. 1998a. "The Depopulation Bomb." *Citizen Magazine,* May. http://www.fotf.org.

————. 1998b. "Feminists Thwarted at U.N.—No Thanks to U.S." *Citizen Magazine,* May. http://www.fotf.org.

Keck, Margaret E., and Kathryn Sikkink. 1998a. *Activists beyond Borders: Advocacy Networks in International Politics.* Ithaca: Cornell University Press.

————. 1998b. "Advocacy Networks in a Movement Society." In *The Social Movement Society: Contentious Politics for a New Century,* ed. David Meyer and Sidney Tarrow. Lanham: Rowland and Littlefield.

Keddie, Nikki R. 1998. "The New Religious Politics: Where, When, and Why Do 'Fundamentalisms' Appear?" *Comparative Studies in Society and History* 40: 696–723.

Keely, Charles B. 1994. "Limits to Papal Power: Vatican Inaction after *Humanae Vitae.*" *Population and Development Review* 20: 220–40.

Kettle, Martin. 2000. "Apocalyptic Fundamentalists Set to Shove Harry Potter Aside." *Guardian,* 9 June.

Kintz, Linda. 1997. *Between Jesus and the Market: The Emotions That Matter in Right-Wing America.* Durham, N.C.: Duke University Press.

Kissling, Frances. 1999. President of Catholics for a Free Choice. Interview by author, 4 October.

Kissling, Frances, and Jon O'Brien. 2001. *Bad Faith at the UN: Drawing Back the Curtain on the Catholic Family and Human Rights Institute.* Washington, D.C.: Catholics for a Free Choice.

Kjos, Berit. 1997. "Classroom Earth: Educating for One World Order." In *Foreshocks of Antichrist,* edited by W. T. James. Eugene, Oreg.: Harvest House.

Klatch, Rebecca E. 1987. *Women of the New Right.* Philadelphia: Temple.

Koch, Klaus. 1983. "What Is Apocalyptic? An Attempt at a Preliminary Definition." In *Visionaries and Their Apocalypses,* edited by P. D. Hanson. Philadelphia: Fortress.

Kunz, J. 1952. "The Status of the Holy See in International Law." *American Journal of International Law* 46: 308–14.

LaHaye, Tim. 1978. *What Everyone Should Know about Homosexuality.* Wheaton, Ill.: Tyndale House.

———. 1998. "America's Perilous Times Have Come." In *Forewarning,* edited by W. T. James. Eugene, Oreg.: Harvest House.

LaHaye, Tim, and Jerry Jenkins. 1995. *Left Behind.* Wheaton, Ill.: Tyndale House

———. 1997. *The Rise of Antichrist Nicolae.* Wheaton, Ill.: Tyndale House.

———. 2000a. *The Indwelling.* Wheaton, Ill.: Tyndale House.

———. 2000b. *The Mark: The Beast Rules the World.* Wheaton, Ill.: Tyndale House.

———. 2001. *Desecration: The Antichrist Takes the Throne.* Wheaton, Ill.: Tyndale House.

LaHaye, Tim, and Beverly LaHaye. 1994. *A Nation without a Conscience.* Wheaton, Ill: Tyndale House.

Lamy, Philip. 1997. "Secularizing the Millennium: Survivalists, Militias, and the New World Order." In *Millennium, Messiahs, and Mayhem: Contemporary Apocalyptic Movements,* edited by T. Robbins and S. J. Palmer. New York: Routledge.

Landolt, C. Gwendolyn. 1999. "The Family at the United Nations: Where Do We Go from Here?" Speech delivered at the World Congress of Families II, 14–17 November, Geneva, Switzerland. http://www.worldcongress.org.

Larson, Elizabeth. 1996. "United Nations Fourth World Conference on Women: Action for Equality, Development, and Peace (Beijing, China: September 1995)." *Emory International Law Review* 10: 695–739.

Lawrence, Bruce B. 1989. *Defenders of God: The Fundamentalist Revolt against the Modern Age.* San Francisco: Harper & Row.

———. 1998. "From Fundamentalism to Fundamentalisms: A Religious Ideology in Multiple Terms." In *Religion, Modernity, and Postmodernity*, edited by P. Heelas. Oxford: Blackwell.

Lechner, Frank J. 1993. "Global Fundamentalism." In *A Future for Religion? New Paradigms for Social Analysis*, edited by W. H. Swatos, Jr. Newbury Park, Calif.: Sage.

Levitt, Zola. 1997. "Israel: Earth's Lightning Rod." In *Foreshocks of Antichrist*, edited by W. T. James. Eugene, Oreg.: Harvest House.

Liebman, Robert C., and Robert Wuthnow. 1983. *The New Christian Right: Mobilization and Legitimation*. Hawthorne, N.Y.: Aldine.

Lienesch, Michael. 1993. *Redeeming America: Piety and Politics in the New Christian Right*. Chapel Hill: University of North Carolina Press.

Lindsey, Hal. 1970. *The Late Great Planet Earth*. Grand Rapids, Mich.: Zondervan.

———. 1994. *Planet Earth—2000 A.D.* Palos Verdes, Calif.: Western Front.

———. 1998. *Planet Earth: The Final Chapter*. Beverly Hills, Calif.: Western Front.

Linklater, Andrew. 1998. *The Transformation of Political Community: Ethical Foundations of the Post-Westphalian Era*. Cambridge: Polity.

Lippy, Charles H. 1982. "Waiting for the End: The Social Context of American Apocalyptic Religion." In *The Apocalyptic Vision in America: Interdisciplinary Essays on Myth and Culture*, edited by L. P. Zamora. Bowling Green, Ohio: Bowling Green University Press.

Lipschutz, Ronnie D., with Judith Mayer. 1996. *Global Civil Society and Global Environmental Governance: The Politics of Nature from Place to Planet*. Albany, N.Y.: State University of New York Press.

Luke, Timothy W., and Gearóid Ó Tuathail. 1998. "Global Flowmations, Local Fundamentalisms, and Fast Geopolitics: 'America' in an Accelerating World Order." In *An Unruly World? Globalization, Governance, and Geography*, edited by A. Herod, G. Ó Tuathail, S. M. Roberts. London: Routledge.

Macdonald, M. Anastasia. 1999. Catholics for a Free Choice. Interview by author, 4 October.

MacLeod, Laurel. 1997. "Sovereignty under Siege: The United Nations' Plan for Your Home." *Family Voice*, April. http://www.cwfa.org.

MacLeod, Laurel, and Catherina Hurlburt. 2000. "Exposing CEDAW: The United Nations Convention on the Elimination of All Forms of Discrimination Against Women." 5 September. http://www.cwfa.org.

Mann, Kirk, and Sasha Roseneil. 1999. "Poor Choice? Gender, Agency, and the Underclass Debate." In *Changing Family Values*, edited by G. Jagger and C. Wright. London: Routledge.

Marrs, Texe. 1987. *Dark Secrets of the New Age*. Westchester, Ill.: Crossway.

———. 1993. *Big Sister Is Watching You: Hilary Clinton and the White House*

Feminists Who Now Control America—and Tell the President What to Do.
Austin, Texas: Living Truth.

Marshall, Alex. 1999. "Fogging up the Abortion Debate." Letter to the editor,
New York Post, 26 August, 34.

Marshall, Paul, with Lela Gilbert. 1997. *Their Blood Cries Out: The Worldwide
Tragedy of Modern Christians Who Are Dying for Their Faith.* Dallas: Word.

Martin, William. 1999. "The Christian Right and American Foreign Policy."
Foreign Policy 114: 66–80.

Martineau, Raymonde. 1999. "The Contribution of NGOs to UN Activities."
Speech delivered at the World Congress of Families II, 14–17 November,
Geneva, Switzerland. Notes on file with authors.

Martinez, Kathy Hall. 1999. Center for Reproductive Law and Policy. Interview by author, 7 October.

Marty, Martin E., and R. Scott Appleby. 1993a. Introduction to *Fundamentalisms and the State: Remaking Polities, Economies, and Militance,* edited by
M. E. Marty and R. S. Appleby. Chicago: University of Chicago Press.

Marty, Martin E., and R. Scott Appleby, eds. 1991. *Fundamentalisms Observed*
(The Fundamentalism Project, vol. 1). Chicago: University of Chicago
Press.

———. 1993b. *Fundamentalisms and Society* (The Fundamentalism Project,
vol. 2). Chicago: University of Chicago Press.

———. 1993c. *Fundamentalisms and the State* (The Fundamentalism Project,
vol. 3). Chicago: University of Chicago Press.

———. 1994. *Accounting for Fundamentalisms* (The Fundamentalism Project,
vol. 4). Chicago: University of Chicago Press.

———. 1995. *Fundamentalisms Comprehended* (The Fundamentalism Project,
vol. 5). Chicago: University of Chicago Press.

Mauss, Armand L. 1994. *The Angel and the Beehive: The Mormon Struggle with
Assimilation.* Urbana: University of Illinois Press.

Mauss, Armand L., and Philip L. Barlow. 1991. "Church, Sect, and Scripture:
The Protestant Bible and Mormon Sectarian Retrenchment." *Sociological
Analysis* 52: 397–414.

Maxwell, David. 1998. "'Delivered from the Spirit of Poverty?': Pentecostalism,
Prosperity, and Modernity in Zimbabwe." *Journal of Religion in Africa* 28:
350–73.

McDermott, Anthony. 2000. *The New Politics of Financing the UN.* Basingstoke: MacMillan.

McFeely, Tom. 1999. "Homosexuality Is *Not* a 'Universal Human Right.'"
Insight. http://www.frc.org.

McGinn, Bernard. 1994. *Antichrist: Two Thousand Years of the Human Fascina-
tion with Evil.* San Francisco: HarperCollins.

McIntosh, C. Alison, and Jason L. Finkle. 1994. "The Politics of Family

Planning and Issues for the Future." A supplement to *The New Politics of Population* 20: 265–75.

———. 1995. "The Cairo Conference on Population and Development: A New Paradigm?" *Population and Development Review* 21: 223–60.

McLaughlin, Abraham, and Gail Russell Chaddock. 2002. "Christian Right Steps in on Mideast." *Christian Science Monitor,* April 16.

McManus, John F. 1999. "'Population Control' Eyewitness: Interview with Steven W. Mosher," *New American* 15, no. 8

Meier, Paul. 1993. *The Third Millennium.* Nashville: Thomas Nelson.

Meier, Paul, and Robert Wise. 1996. *The Fourth Millennium.* Nashville: Thomas Nelson.

Mertus, Julie. 2000. "Considering Nonstate Actors in the New Millennium: Toward Expanded Participation in Norm Generation and Norm Application." *New York University Review of International Law and Politics* 32: 537–66.

Meyer, David S., and Suzanne Staggenborg. 1996. "Movements, Counter-movements, and the Structure of Political Opportunity." *American Journal of Sociology* 10: 1628–60.

Meyer, Thomas. 2001. *Identity Mania: Fundamentalism and the Politicization of Cultural Differences.* Translated by M. Reddy and L. Hinchman. London: Zed Books.

Miller, Alice M. 1999. "Women's Human Rights: Nongovernmental Organizations and the United Nations Treaty Bodies." In *Gender Politics in Global Governance,* edited by M. K. Meyer and E. Prügl. Lanham, Mass.: Rowman & Littlefield.

Miller, Patricia. 1999. Catholics for a Free Choice. Interview by author, 4 October.

Misztal, Bronislaw, and Anson Shupe. 1992. "Making Sense of the Global Revival of Fundamentalism." In *Religion and Politics in Comparative Perspective: Revival of Religious Fundamentalism in East and West,* edited by B. Misztal and A. Shupe. Westport, Conn.: Praeger.

Misztal, Bronislaw, and Anson Shupe, eds. 1992b. *Religion and Politics in Comparative Perspective: Revival of Religious Fundamentalism in East and West.* Westport, Conn.: Praeger.

Moen, Matthew C. 1992. *The Transformation of the Christian Right.* Tuscaloosa: University of Alabama Press.

———. 1995. "Political and Theological Adjustment in the U.S. Christian Right." *Contention* 4: 75–90.

Mohanty, Chandra Talpade. 1991. "Of Struggle: Third World Women and the Politics of Feminism." Introduction to *Third World Women and the Politics of Feminism,*" edited by C. T. Mohanty, A. Russo, and L. Torres. Bloomington: Indiana University Press.

Moloney, Sheila. 1999. Eagle Forum. Interview by author, 5 October.

Morfaw, Maria. 1999. "Modernity, Globalization, and Progress." Speech delivered at the World Congress of Families II, 14–17 November, Geneva, Switzerland. http://www.worldcongress.org.

Morgan, Robin. 1996. "Dispatch from Beijing." *Ms. Magazine* 6: 12–21.

Morgan, Wayne. 2000. "Queering International Human Rights Law." In *Sexuality in the Legal Arena,* edited by C. Stychin and D. Herman. London: Athlone.

Morrison, David. n.d. "Family Planning: Population Control in Drag." *Population Research Institute.* http://www.pop.org.

———. 1997a. "Pop Control While People Die: As 'Family Planning' Devours Aid Budgets and [sic] Old Killer Stalks the Poor." *Population Research Institute Review,* November/December. http://www.pop.org.

———. 1997b. "Weaving a Wider Net: United Nations Moves to Consolidate Antinatalist Gains." *Population Research Institute,* January/February. http://www.pop.org.

———. 1998. "Population Control Efforts: A Gross Abuse of Human Rights." *Insight.* http://www.frc.org.

Morton, Ted. 1999. "A Preferential Option for the Family." Speech delivered at the World Congress of Families II, 14–17 November, Geneva, Switzerland. http://www.worldcongress.org.

Mouly, Ruth W. 1985. *The Religious Right and Israel: The Politics of Armageddon.* Chicago: Midwest Research.

Moynihan, Robert. 1995. "The Battle in Peking." *Inside the Vatican* 3, no. 8/9.

Navarro-Valls, Joaquin. 1995a. Press briefing, 25 August. Reproduced in *L'Osservatore Romano* 36, no. 6: 2, 4.

———. 1995b. "To Promote Women's Equal Dignity." *L'Osservatore Romano* 36, no. 6: 2, 4.

O'Brien, Robert, Anne Marie Goetz, Jan Aart Scholte, and Marc Williams. 2000. *Contesting Global Governance: Multilateral Economic Institutions and Global Social Movements.* Cambridge: Cambridge University Press.

Ogola, Margaret. 1995. "The Dignity of the African Woman." Speech delivered at the UN Conference on Women, Beijing. http://www.cco.caltech.edu/~newman/women-cp/kenyatext.

———. 1999. "Sex and the Family." Speech delivered at the World Conference of Families II, 14–17 November, Geneva, Switzerland. http://www.worldcongress.org.

O'Leary, Dale. 1998. "Human Rights and the Gender Perspective." *Insight.* Family Research Council. http://www.frc.org.

O'Leary, Stephen. 1994. *Arguing the Apocalypse: A Theory of Millennial Rhetoric.* Oxford: Oxford University Press.

Otto, Dianne. 1996a. "Holding up Half the Sky, But for Whose Benefit? A Critical Analysis of the Fourth World Conference on Women." *Australian Feminist Law Journal* 6: 7–28.

———. 1996b. "Nongovernmental Organizations in the United Nations System: The Emerging Role of International Civil Society." *Human Rights Quarterly* 18: 107–41.

———. 1999. "A Post-Beijing Reflection on the Limitations and Potential for Human Rights Discourse for Women." In *Women and International Human Rights Law,* vol. 1, edited by K. D. Askin and D. M. Koenig. Ardsley, N.Y.: Transnational Publishers.

Palmer, Susan. 1997a. *AIDS as an Apocalyptic Metaphor in North America.* Toronto: University of Toronto Press.

———. 1997b. "Woman as World Saviour: The Feminization of the Millennium in New Religious Movements" In *Millennium, Messiahs, and Mayhem: Contemporary Apocalyptic Movements,* edited by T. Robbins and S. J. Palmer. New York: Routledge.

Petchesky, Rosalind P. 1998. Introduction to *Negotiating Reproductive Rights: Women's Perspectives across Countries and Cultures,* edited by R. Petchesky and K. Judd. London: Zed Books.

Peters, Julie, and Andrea Wolper. 1995. *Women's Rights Human Rights: International Feminist Perspectives.* New York: Routledge.

Phillips, Oliver. 2000. "Constituting the Global Gay: Issues of Individual Subjectivity and Sexuality in Southern Africa." In *Sexuality in the Legal Arena,* edited by C. Stychin and D. Herman. London: Athlone.

Pieterse, Jan P. Nederveen. 1992. "The History of a Metaphor: Christian Zionism and the Politics of Apocalypse." In *Christianity and Hegemony,* edited by J. P. N. Pieterse. New York: St. Martin's.

———. 2001. "Globalization and Collective Action." In *Globalization and Social Movements,* edited by Pierre Hamel, Henri Lustiger-Thaler, Jan Nederveen Pieterse, and Sasha Roseneil. New York: Palgrave.

Pontifical Council for the Family. 2000a. "Declaration of the Pontifical Council for the Family Regarding the Resolution of the European Parliament dated March 16, 2000, Making De Facto Union, Including Same Sex Unions, Equal to the Family." 17 March. On file with authors.

———. 2000b. "Family Marriage, and 'De Facto' Unions." Report, 26 July. On file with authors.

Popenoe, David. 1988. *Disturbing the Nest: Family Change and Decline in Modern Societies.* New York: Aldine de Gruyer.

———. 1996. *Life without Father: Compelling New Evidence That Fatherhood and Marriage Are Indispensable for the Good of Children and Society.* New York: Free Press.

Population Research Institute. 1999a. "Milosevic and UNFPA 'Team up' to Target Kosovars: 'Stealth' Ethnic Cleansing to Continue with Help of UNFPA and U.S. Tax Dollars." *Population Research Institute Weekly News Briefing* 1, no. 9 (13 July). http://www.pop.org.

———. 1999b. "Money for Nothing: Why the United States Should Not Resume UNFPA Funding." *Population Research Institute Special Publications,* 25 February. http://www.pop.org.

———. 1999c. "Population Control and the New Global Racism." *PRI Weekly News Briefing Archives* 1, no. 21 (19 October). http://www.pop.org.

———. 1999d. "UN Agenda Targets Refugees: UN High Commissioner Takes up Population Control." *Population Research Institute Review,* November/December. http://www.pop.org.

———. 1999e. "UN Skirmishes in War on Family: The Hague Forum Marred by Questionable Procedures and Controversial Results." *Population Research Institute Review* 9 (April/May). http://www.pop.org.

———. 2000. "Women's Conference Features Face-off between Vatican, Pro-abortion Groups." *PR Newswire,* 5 June. On file with authors.

Price, J. Randall. 1998. "False Peace: The Pseudo-storm Shelter." In *Forewarning,* edited by W. T. James. Eugene, Oreg.: Harvest House.

Real Women of Canada. 1998. "World Families at Risk." *REALity,* September/October. http://www.realwomenca.com.

———. 1999a. "Taming the Serpent of the UN." *REALity,* March/April. http://www.realwomenca.com.

———. 1999b. "Troubling Concerns about International Charities." *REALity,* September/October. http://www.realwomenca.com.

———. 1999c. "UN Population Fund Acquires More Influence." *REALity,* November/December. http://www.realwomenca.com.

———. 1999d. "UN Trampling on Religious Rights." *REALity,* November/December. http://www.realwomenca.com.

Redman, Barbara J. 1993. "Strange Bedfellows: Lubavitcher Hasidism and Conservative Christians." *Journal of Church and State* 34: 521–48.

Reese, Thomas J. 1996. *Inside the Vatican: The Politics and Organization of the Catholic Church.* Cambridge, Mass.: Harvard University Press.

Reid, Denesha. 1999. Concerned Women for America. Interview by author, 4 October.

Reno, Ronald, A. 1998. "Exploding the Myth of the Population Bomb." *Citizen Link,* 1 October. http://www.fotf.org.

Reuther, Rosemary Radford. 2001. *Christianity and the Making of the Modern Family.* London: SCM.

Riesebrodt, Martin. 1993. *Pious Passion: The Emergence of Modern Fundamentalism in the United States and Iran,* translated by Don Reneau. Berkeley: University of California Press.

Riles, Annelise E. 2000. *The Network Inside Out.* Ann Arbor: University of Michigan Press.

Robbins, Thomas, and Susan J. Palmer, eds. 1997. *Millennium, Messiahs, and Mayhem: Contemporary Apocalyptic Movements.* New York: Routledge.

Roberts, Dorothy. 1998. "The Absent Black Father." In *Lost Fathers,* edited by C. R. Daniels. London: Macmillan.

Robertson, Pat. 1982. *The Secret Kingdom.* Nashville: Thomas Nelson.

———. 1990. *The New Millennium.* Dallas: Word.

———. 1991. *The New World Order.* Dallas: Word.

———. 1995. *The End of the Age.* Dallas: Word.

Robertson, Roland. 1989. "Globalization, Politics, and Religion." In *The Changing Face of Religion,* edited by J. Beckford and T. Luckmann. London: Sage.

———. 1991a. "The Globalization Paradigm." In *Religion and the Social Order,* edited by D. G. Bromley. Greenwich, Conn.: JAI Press.

———. 1991b. "Social Theory, Cultural Relativity, and the Problem of Locality." In *Culture, Globalization, and the World-system,* edited by A. D. King. Houndmills: MacMillan.

———. 1992a. "Globality, Global Culture, and Images of World Order." In *Social Change and Modernity,* edited by H. H. Kamp and N. J. Smelser. Berkeley: University of California.

———. 1992b. *Globalization: Social Theory and Global Culture.* London: Sage.

Robertson, Roland, and J. Chirico. 1985. "Humanity, Globalization, and Worldwide Religious Resurgence." *Sociological Analysis* 46: 219–42.

Roylance, Susan. 1995. "Evaluation of Fourth World Conference on Women." In *The Traditional Family in Peril: A Collection of Articles on International Family Issues,* compiled by S. Roylance. South Jordan, Utah: United Families International.

Rozell, Mark J., and Clyde Wilcox. 1996. "Second Coming: The Strategies of the New Christian Right." *Political Science Quarterly* 111: 271–94.

Rudolph, Susanne Hoeber, and James Piscatori. 1997. *Transnational Religion and Fading States.* Boulder, Colo.: Westview.

Ruse, Austin. 1998a. "Feminists at UN: Seek Redefinition of Universal Human Rights." 13 November. http://www.newsmax.com.

———. 1998b. "Cairo +5 PrepCom Stalls in New York." *Population Research Institute Review* 9, no. 3 (April/May). http://www.pop.org.

———. 1998c. "UN Skirmishes in War on Family: The Hague Forum Marred by Questionable Procedures and Controversial Results." *Population Research Institute Review* 9, no. 2 (February/March). http://www.pop.org.

———. 1999a. "Don't Buy the Spin Control from the UN Butchers." Letter to the editor, *New York Post,* 30 August, 36.

———. 1999b. "Kosovar Refugee Women 'Just Say No' but Milosevic Invites UNFPA to Target Kosovars upon Their Return Home." *Population Research Institute Review* 9, no. 4 (June/July). http://www.pop.org.

———. 1999c. President, Catholic Family and Human Rights Institute. Interview by author, 7 October.

———. 1999d. "Radical NGOs Meet in Seoul." Newsletter, 21 October. On file with authors.

————. 1999e. "Toward a Permanent United Nations Pro-family Bloc." Paper delivered at the World Congress of Families II, 14–17 November, Geneva, Switzerland. http://www.worldcongress.org.

————. 2000a. Newsletter, 9 June. On file with authors.

————. 2000b. Newsletter, 21 September. On file with authors.

————. 2000c. "Shoving Match, Leftist Schemes Mark UN 'Peace Summit.'" *Newsmax,* 31 August. http://www.NewsMax.com.

————. 2001. "U.S. Lawyers Use UN Resolutions to Overturn US Law." Electronic newsletter, 6 December. On file with authors.

————. 2002. Newsletter, 14 January.

Rushdoony, Rousas John. 1978. *Thy Kingdom Come.* Fairfax, Va: Thoburn.

————. 1991. *The Roots of Reconstruction.* Vallecito, Calif.: Ross House.

Sadat, Jehan. 1999. "Preservation of Family Is Promotion of Peace." Speech delivered at the World Congress of Families II, 14–17 November, Geneva, Switzerland. On file with authors.

Sahlani, Mohammad Jarad. 1999. "The Spirit of Family Rights." Speech delivered at the World Conference of Families II, 14–17 November, Geneva, Switzerland. http://www.worldcongress.org.

Sanders, Douglas. 1996. "Getting Lesbian and Gay Issues on the International Human Rights Agenda." *Human Rights Quarterly* 18: 7–106.

Schlumpf, Heidi. 1996. "How Catholic Is the Catholic Alliance?" *Christianity Today,* 20 May, 76.

Schmierer, Donald. 1999. "The Family as the Protector of Children." Speech delivered at the World Congress of Families II, 14–17 November, Geneva, Switzerland. http://www.worldcongress.org.

Scholte, Jan Aart. 1993. *International Relations of Social Change.* Buckingham, UK: Open University.

Sells, Michael. 1999. "The GOP Right, the Belgrade Lobby, and the New-Confederacy: Multiple Conversions." 14 June. http://www.glypx.com/Balkan Witness/sells2.htm.

Sen, Gita. 1995. "The World Programme of Action: A New Paradigm for Population." *Environment* 37: 10–15, 34–37.

Sen, Gita, Adrienne Germain, and Lincoln C. Chen, eds. 1994. *Population Policy Reconsidered: Health, Empowerment, and Rights.* Boston: Harvard School of Public Health.

Shaw, Malcolm N. 1997. *International Law.* 4th ed. Cambridge: Cambridge University Press.

Shepard, S. 2001. "Sen. Clinton Promotes 'Women's Rights' for Afghanistan." 17 December. *Family News in Focus.* http://www.family.org.

Shipps, Jan. 1985. *Mormonism: The Story of a New Religious Tradition.* Urbana: University of Illinois Press.

Shupe, Anson. 1997. "Christian Reconstructionism and the Angry Rhetoric of

Neo-Postmillennialism." In *Millennium, Messiahs, and Mayhem: Contemporary Apocalyptic Movements,* edited by T. Robbins and S. J. Palmer. New York: Routledge.

Simpson, John H. 1992. "Fundamentalism in America Revisited: The Fading of Modernity as a Source of Symbolic Capital." In *Religion and Politics in Comparative Perspective: Revival of Religious Fundamentalism in East and West,* edited by B. Misztal and A. Shupe. Westport, Conn.: Praeger.

Skillen, James W. 1990. *The Scattered Voice: Christians at Odds in the Public Square.* Grand Rapids, Mich.: Zondervan.

Smidt, Corwin E., and James M. Penning, eds. 1997. *Sojourners in the Wilderness: The Christian Right in Comparative Perspective.* Lanham: Rowman & Littlefield.

Smith, Christian, ed. 1996. *Disruptive Religion: The Force of Faith in Social Movement Activism.* New York: Routledge.

Smith, Jackie. 1997. "Characteristics of the Modern Transnational Social Movement Sector." In *Transnational Social Movements and Global Politics: Solidarity beyond the State,* edited by J. Smith, C. Chatfield, and R. Pagnucco. Syracuse, N.Y.: Syracuse University Press.

Spiro, Peter J. 2000. "Globalization, International Law, and the Academy." *New York University Review of International Law and Politics* 32: 567–90.

Spruill, Jennifer. 2000. "Post-with/out a Past? Sexual Orientation and the Post-Colonial 'Moment' in South Africa." In *Sexuality in the Legal Arena,* edited by C. Stychin and D. Herman. London: Athlone.

Stacey, Judith. 1996. *In the Name of the Family: Rethinking Family Values in the Postmodern Age.* Boston: Beacon.

———. 1999. "Virtual Social Science and the Politics of Family Values in the United States." In *Changing Family Values,* edited by G. Jagger and C. Wright. London: Routledge.

Stein, Dorothy. 1996. "Reproductive Politics and the Cairo Conference." *Contention* 5: 37–58.

Stephens, Philip. 2000. "A Return to Fundamentalism." *Financial Times,* 8 September, 19.

Stevenson, Nick. 1997. "Globalization, National Cultures, and Cultural Citizenship." *Sociological Quarterly* 38: 41–66.

Stienstra, Deborah. 1995. "Organizing for Change: International Women's Movements and World Politics." In *Women in World Politics: An Introduction,* edited by F. D. Amico and P. R. Bechman. Westport, Conn: Bergin & Garvey.

———. 2000. "Dancing Resistance from Rio to Beijing: Transnational Women's Organizing and United Nations Conferences, 1992–6." In *Gender and Global Restructuring: Sightings, Sites, and Resistances,* edited by M. H. Marchand and A. S. Runyan. London: Routledge.

Stychin, Carl F. 1998. *A Nation by Rights.* Philadelphia: Temple University Press.

Tarrow, Sidney. 1998. *Power in Movement: Social Movements and Contentious Politics*. 2d ed. Cambridge: Cambridge University Press.

Taskhiri, Mohammed Ali. 1999. "Evaluating the Cairo Conference and Its Attitude towards the Family Question." Speech delivered at the World Conference of Families II, 14–17 November, Geneva, Switzerland. http://www.worldcongress.org.

Tatad, Francisco. 1999. "The Family and Population Control." Speech delivered at the World Congress of Families II, 14–17 November, Geneva, Switzerland. http://www.worldcongress.org.

Thiele, Leslie Paul. 1993. "Making Democracy Safe for the World: Social Movements and Global Politics." *Alternatives* 18: 273–305.

Thomas, George M. 1991. "A World Polity Interpretation of U.S. Religious Trends Since World War II." In *World Order and Religion*, edited by W. C. Roof. Albany, N.Y: State University of New York Press.

Thompson, Damien. 1996. *The End of Time: Faith and Fear in the Shadow of the Millennium*. London: Sinclair-Stevenson.

Tinker, Irene. 1999. "Nongovernmental Organizations: An Alternative Power Base for Women?" In *Gender Politics in Global Governance*, edited by M. K. Meyer and E. Prügl. Lanham, Mass.: Rowman & Littlefield.

Turner, Bryan S. 1991. *Religion and Social Theory*. 2d ed. London: Sage.

Ugochukwu, Carol. 1999. "Women, African Culture, and the Challenge of the Future." Paper delivered at the Celebration of Families Conference, March, Salt Lake City, Utah. http://www.wowinfo.org.

United Nations Population Fund (UNFPA). [1999]. "Kosovo: U.S.-Based Group Seeks to Defame UNFPA." News release, 29 July. On file with authors.

Urquhart, Gordon. 1995. *The Pope's Armada*. London: Bantam Press.

———. 1997. "Opus Dei: The Pope's Right Arm in Europe." *Conservative Catholic Influence in Europe: An Investigative Series*. Catholics for a Free Choice.

———. 2000. "Homophobia: Winning and Losing." *The Guardian*, February 16, 7.

Van Impe, Jack. 1996. *2001: On the Edge of Eternity*. Dallas: Word.

Van Kampen, Joke, and Kathy Bonk. 1999. "Inaccurate Media Coverage of Kosovo Relief Services." Memo. On file with authors.

Vásquez, Manuel A., and Marie F. Marquardt. 2000. "Globalizing the Rainbow Madonna: Old Time Religion in the Present Age." *Theory, Culture and Society* 17: 119–43.

Wagner, Teresa R. n.d. "United Nations Project." http://www.frc.org.

Wald, Kenneth D. 1994. "The Religious Dimension to American Anti-communism." *Journal of Church and State* 36: 483–506.

Wald, Kenneth D., and Lee Sigelman. 1997. "Romancing the Jews: The Christian Right in Search of Strange Bedfellows." In *Sojourners in the Wilderness:*

The Christian Right in Comparative Perspective, edited by C. E. Smidt and J. M. Penning. Lanham: Rowman & Littlefield.

Walker, R. B. J. 1994. "Social Movements/World Politics." *Millennium* 23, no. 3: 669–700.

Waterman, Peter. 2000. "Social Movements, Local Places, and Globalized Spaces: Implications for 'Globalization from Below.'" In *Globalization and the Politics of Resistance,* edited by B. K. Gills. Basingstoke: MacMillan.

Waters, Malcolm. 1995. *Globalization.* London: Routledge.

Weaver, Mary Jo. 1995. "Who Are Conservative Catholics?" Introduction to *Being Right: Conservative Catholics in America,* edited by M. J. Weaver and R. S. Appleby. Bloomington: Indiana University Press.

Weaver, Mary Jo, and R. Scott Appleby, eds. 1995. *Being Right: Conservative Catholics in America.* Bloomington: Indiana University Press.

Weigel, George. 1995. "The Neoconservative Difference." In *Being Right: Conservative Catholics in America,* edited by M. J. Weaver and R. S. Appleby. Bloomington: Indiana University Press.

West, Lois. 1999. "The United Nations Women's Conferences and Feminist Politics." In *Gender Politics in Global Governance,* edited by M. K. Meyer and E. Prügl. Lanham, Mass.: Rowman & Littlefield.

White, O. Kendall. 1986. "A Review and Commentary on the Prospects of a Mormon New Christian Right Coalition." *Review of Religious Research* 28: 180–88.

Whitehead, John W. 1994. *Religious Apartheid: The Separation of Religion from American Public Life.* Chicago: Moody.

Wilcox, Clyde. 1992. *God's Warriors: The Christian Right in Twentieth-Century America.* Baltimore: The John Hopkins University Press.

Wilcox, Clyde, and Mark J. Rozell. 1996. "Second Coming? The New Tactics of the Christian Right." *Political Science Quarterly* 111: 271–94.

Wilcox, Clyde, and Leopoldo Gomez. 1989–90. "The Christian Right and the Pro-life Movement: An Analysis of the Sources of Political Support." *Review of Religious Research* 31: 380.

Wilcox, Clyde, Mark J. Rozell, and Roland Gunn. 1996. "Religious Coalitions in the New Christian Right." *Social Science Quarterly* 77: 543–58.

Wilkins, Richard. 1999. "Recognizing Our Shared Commitment to the Natural Family." Speech delivered at the World Congress of Families II, 14–17 November, Geneva, Switzerland. http://www.worldcongress.org.

Williams, Rhys H., and Jeffrey Blackburn. 1996. "Many Are Called but Few Obey: Ideological Commitment and Activism in Operation Rescue." In *Disruptive Religion: The Force of Faith in Social Movement Activism,* edited by C. Smith. New York: Routledge.

Wilson, Dwight. 1977. *Armageddon Now! The Premillennial Response to Russia and Israel Since 1917.* Grand Rapids, Mich.: Baker House.

Wilson, Mercedes Arzu. 1999. "A Time for Truth: Confronting the UN's Contraceptive Mentality." Speech delivered at the World Congress of Families II, 14–17 November, Geneva, Switzerland. http://www.worldcongress.org.

World Commission on Environment and Development. 1987. *Our Common Future.* New York: Oxford University Press.

World Congress of Families II. 1999. "'Background' Statement." Program for the World Congress of Families II, 14–17 November, Geneva, Switzerland. On file with authors.

World Family Policy Center. 2001. "Call to De-ratify Child Convention." Newsletter, July 5. On file with authors.

———. n.d. "World Family Policy Center," pamphlet on file with authors.

Wright, Wendy. 1999. Concerned Women for America. Interview by author, 4 October.

Wuthnow, Robert. 1988. *The Restructuring of American Religion.* Princeton: Princeton University Press.

Xanthopoulou, Paula. 1995. "Christian Coalition Launches 'Fully-owned Subsidiary for Catholics,'" *C. C. Watch,* October.

Zald, Mayer N, and Bert Useem. 1987. "Movement and Countermovement Interaction: Mobilization, Tactics, and State Involvement." In *Social Movements in an Organizational Society,* edited by J. D. McCarthy. New Brunswick, N.J.: Transnational.

Zimdars-Swartz, Sandra L. 1995. "The Marian Revival in American Catholicism." In *Being Right: Conservative Catholics in America,* edited by M. J. Weaver and R. S. Appleby. Bloomington: Indiana University Press.

Index